ESTEEM BUILDERS
COMPLETE PROGRAM

STAFF ESTEEM BUILDERS

- Building Staff Self-Esteem

- Implementing Successful Team Building

Dr. Michele Borba

JALMAR PRESS

> *A comprehensive K-8 program for educators, students, and parents to improve achievement, behavior, and school climate.*

The African proverb, "It takes a whole village to raise a child," is the perfect statement for the setting of my new program — *The Esteem Builders' Complete Program*. Yes, it takes all of us to create this "cycle of success "!

As an educator and parent, I know that there needs to be a program in the schools that reaches out to everyone. Thus the *Esteem Builders' Complete Program* was born. It now consists of **8 components** and over **1,200 activities** all cross-correlated to each grade level and subject area. It took 10 years of research and field testing esteem-building strategies before I was able to have all this information validated.

Another feature of this program is that it is **based on the Five Building Blocks of Self-Esteem: security, selfhood, affiliation, mission and competence.** Research has validated that self-esteem is a KEY factor in improving student behavior and academic achievement. Educators recognize the urgency of these findings and are asking themselves,

> "How do we enhance the self-esteem of students?"

Well, the *Esteem Builders' Complete Program* provides the answer to this question. Now that you have read why we need the program, please turn to the next page and read the description of each component and then see the model flowchart which shows how each component fits into the school and home.

It's an honor to be a member of this profession with you. Together we can make a difference! Let's start, we haven't a moment to lose!

Michele Borba

Michele Borba

The components for this complete program consist of the following materials.

- **Teacher's Guide: ESTEEM BUILDERS: A K-8 Self-Esteem Curriculum for Improving Student Achievement, Behavior, and School Climate**
  The program began in 1989 with the publication of *Esteem Builders*. Educators report that this manual has become the self-esteem curriculum of choice for hundreds of districts and thousands of schools in North America. It is being used in pre-schools through middle schools, in public and private settings, in multicultural as well as in special education, and with gifted as well as "at-risk" students. It contains over 250 theory-based and field-tested esteem-building activities **cross-correlated to all subject areas and grade levels.** Hence, with *Esteem Builders* it is possible to include self-esteem activities in the current curriculum.

- **OVERVIEW OF THE ESTEEM BUILDERS' COMPLETE PROGRAM**
  This book has been prepared to make your job easier. This book contains a comprehensive description of the major elements and their roles in the *Esteem Builders' Complete Program*, as well as Esteem Builder Teams and how they function. The book is designed to assist you in the esteem-building implementation process. Within this book, you'll find invaluable charts, guidelines, and indexes to cross-reference scores of activities and techniques. Unique features of *An Overview of the Esteem Builders' Complete Program* include:

  - **A listing of all icons and abbreviations** used in the program.
  - A **summary of all major program components** of the *Esteem Builders' Complete Program*.
  - A description of the **Esteem Builder Team** including: membership, getting started, functions.
  - A complete **table of contents of all staff development** trainings in esteem enhancement.
  - A listing of all **informal assessments** such as checklists, guideline questions and surveys for your staff, administrators and parents to assess your esteem-building climate, a student-self-esteem assessment chart for each feeling, and a checklist of educator behaviors that promote each feeling, as well as suggested sources for the best formal self-esteem assessments to measure student self-esteem.
  - An **extensive index cross-referencing** over 1,000 esteem-building activities by esteem component as well as targeted audience.
  - Assessment tools for evaluating student, administrator, and staff growth in the five building blocks of self-esteem.
  - A comprehensive **description of the major elements and their roles** in the *Esteem Builders' Complete Program* including: the trainer and staff development in esteem enhancement, staff esteem, home esteem building, student esteem building, school-wide esteem enhancement, staff team building, and the esteem builder teams.
  - The **definitions of all major terms** found within the program.

- **ESTEEM BUILDERS RESOURCES**
  - A **bibliography of self-esteem resources** for students, parents, and staff.
  - An extensive list of **current self-esteem research** and statistics validating the need for self-esteem enhancement.
  - A comprehensive **list of agencies, organizations, and resources** available to the school site to aid in the esteem-building process. A summary of each listing, as well as an address, is also included.
  - A **description of school structures** actively being implemented at various sites to enhance self-esteem.

- **TRAINER'S MANUAL**
  The key to establishing an ongoing and enthusiastic self-esteem program is having a trainer within the district or school. Using *Esteem Builders* as the text, the *Trainer's Manual* details the esteem-building premises in "ready-to-present" units. The manual provides the trainer with materials and 18 hours of scripts for training the staff in esteem-building development. Everything is provided for the trainer to ensure a successful program—all that is needed is the audience.

- **Audiocassette Program: THE FIVE BUILDING BLOCKS OF SELF-ESTEEM**
  Consists of six tapes each 30+ minutes. Dr. Borba begins with her live keynote address *"You Are the*

Door-Opener to a Child's Self-Esteem: Five Critical Keys." She then continues to lead the trainer and educator into an understanding of the five building blocks of self-esteem. A specially designed workbook that builds and reinforces the material is included. The tapes are delightfully narrated with special music created for your easy listening!

- ## STAFF ESTEEM BUILDERS
  Research substantiates that the most neglected area of educational reform is improving the esteem and relationships of the very individuals who can be the most powerful sources of students' lives—the staff. This is the administrator's bible for enhancing staff esteem. Dozens of theory-based activities are presented to build staff self-esteem, affiliation, and cohesiveness. Surveys are available to assess current staff strengths and weaknesses. A complete guide as well as scores of activities are provided for team building, staff, and shared decision-making. In addition, a complete guide to successful team building is provided along with scores of activities and administrator ideas to improve the process. Finally, "the how-to's" toward improving staff relationships, collegiateness, communication, and shared decision-making are offered.

- ## HOME ESTEEM BUILDERS
  Educators are provided with a variety of activities designed to strengthen the partnership between home and school, and to help parents in their home esteem-building endeavors. Included in this manual are 40 home esteem-building activities, 13 parent newsletters, a complete script for a parent in-service, and plans for school-wide events for parents. In addition, the manual contains dozens of techniques to enhance communication between the home and school, and handouts with esteem-building tips for educators to provide parents with during conferences.

- ## ESTEEM BUILDER POSTERS
  Eight posters featuring important esteem-building principles can be hung in the classroom, faculty room, training session room, or home to serve as visual reminders to everyone involved in the esteem-building process.

    1. *Teachers Make Differences!*

    2. *Five Building Blocks*

    3. *Esteem Builders' Implementation Model*

    4. *Brainstorming Rules*

    5. *Goal-Setting Steps*

    6. *Sparkle Statements*

    7. *Esteem Builder Thoughts*

    8. *Conflict Solving*

ESTEEM BUILDERS' IMPLEMENTATION MODEL ©

Self-Esteem Selected as Key Priority

Self-Esteem Orientation
Administrators / District Office / Board Members
Audiocassettes

Total Staff Overview
Self-Esteem, Rationale, Identification, Techniques
Audiocassettes / 8 Posters

Teacher Component
"Esteem Builders"

- Concept Circles
  Cooperative Learning
- Whole language / Literature
- Behavior Enhancement
  Sparky Puppet
  8 Posters / Activity cards

Trainer of Trainers
"Trainer's Manual"

- Presentation Skills
  Audiocassettes
- Behavior Enhancement
- Demonstration Lessons

Administration
"Staff Esteem Builders"

- Individual Staff Self-Esteem
- School-Wide Practices
  Enhancing
  Positive School Climate
- Staff Team Building

Esteem Builder Teams
"An Overview of the EBCP"

- Staff Self-Esteem
- School-Wide Implementation
- Program Assessment Materials

Resources for Everyone
"Resources for EBCP"

- Statistics / Rationale
  Research Summaries
- Comprehensive
  Bibliography / References
- Support Staff Activities for
  Students

Parent Training
"Home Esteem Builders"

- Home Activities
- Parent Groups
- Parent Communication

The **Esteem Builders' Complete Program** is founded on **researched and field-tested** esteem-building strategies. It is designed to include all aspects of the school, home, and community, with special attention to the "at-risk" student. It is based on the recognition that everyone who touches the life of a child must be involved in the enhancement process.

What Educators Say About Dr. Borba

"Dr. Borba's ideas provided our instructional and support staff with a true desire to change our perspectives on educating youth for the twenty-first century."

—Lorraine Brown, Coordinator, Multicultural Education
Sacramento, California

"The thoughtful way in which Esteem Builders approaches the learning process and classroom management is extremely relevant to educators wanting to introduce their students to a global perspective. Dr. Borba's books have helped teachers in Britain to do work with young children that helps them develop the healthy self-concepts that are essential to holding positive attitudes of people different from themselves."

—Miriam Steiner, National Coordinator Global Education
Manchester, England

"I wish it were possible to have Dr. Borba with our board full-time. After hearing Michele, we changed our school motto to read: 'The Key is We.' The Esteem Builders program is not an add-on; it blends in so well with our existing program and has given us proven results."

—Tom Green, Principal
Cornwall, Ontario, Canada

"Administrators at our school have noted changes in class climate, in particular classrooms in which [Esteem Builders] program use has been regular. Improved staff attitude toward children has been noted. Staff morale has risen through regular staff self-esteem activities."

—Chris Schmitt-Chan, Communication Handicaps Specialist
Stockton, California

"As part of the implementation of Borba's Esteem Builders program, each school has begun a 'what we are proud of, what else could we do' process. At area principal meetings, each school gives a brief report on the progress of their Success Hunts. This sharing of information has had terrific results in our county. Staff morale has definitely improved."

—Dave Schlei, Consultant, Physical Education & Health
Kitchener, Ontario, Canada

"School climate, staff morale, and parent interest and awareness have all been positively affected by using many of the Esteem Builder Activities suggested by Michele Borba."

—Barb Tarbet, Principal
Aspen, Colorado

"Michele Borba is a dynamite presenter! She is in tune with needs of her audience—students, teachers, parents and administrators...she listens and offers suggestions that fit and make sense. Michele's last visit with our staff focused on their needs as we relocated a majority of our elementary staff. Michele provided ideas that the participants knew were key to rebuilding staff cohesion. First hand... teachers were expressing the first blocks of self-esteem—security and the need to feel valued."

—Annie Podesto, Staff Development Specialist
Stockton Unified School District

STAFF ESTEEM BUILDERS
• Building Staff Self-Esteem
• Implementing Successful Team Building

Copyright © 1993 by Michele Borba, Ed.D.

Published by Jalmar Press

STAFF ESTEEM BUILDERS

• Building Staff Self-Esteem
• Implementing Successful Team Building

Author: Michele Borba
Editor: Marie Conte
Project Director: Jeanne Iler
Production Consultants: Mario A. Artavia II, Jeanne Iler, Matthew Lopez
Illustrator: Bob Burchett
Cover Illustration: Luis R. Caughman
Cover Design: Mario A. Artavia II
Typography and Production: Michael Gonzales, Matthew Lopez, Julia Tempel

Manufactured in the United States of America
First edition printing: 10 9 8 7 6 5 4 3 2
ISBN: 1-880396-04-1

STAFF ESTEEM BUILDERS

- Building Staff Self-Esteem
- Implementing Successful Team Building

Dr. Michele Borba

JALMAR PRESS
ROLLING HILLS ESTATES
CALIFORNIA

Dedication

This book is affectionately dedicated to the administrator in my life, my husband, Craig. For over two decades he has been my personal Esteem Builder and best friend. His creative gifts and global style have been invaluable to me in my work. I thank him for always filling my days with encouragement, support, and love, and for keeping my perspective on tomorrow bright.

Table of Contents

Chapter 8: Team Building: Increasing Staff Collegiality

Preface

Twenty years ago I walked into a special education classroom filled with incredible primary-age children and began my first teaching job. I remember my eagerness and passion in that first job. I was going to literally change the world of teaching. It took me only a few weeks to recognize that the countless hours of teacher training I had spent in college with my supervisor and in student teaching had not adequately taught me how to deal effectively with those students. Yes, I had been superbly trained in theory and learning style by some cream-of-the-crop professors, but it wasn't enough. I needed to know how to touch those students effectively; I needed to know how to help them recognize who they were. What I didn't know was how to help those children see themselves as capable learners. Reaching my students in this way became my new passion and goal.

When I look back on those early days of teaching, I recall one feeling above all the others—frustration—and a question stayed in my mind that I couldn't seem to find the answer to: "So how do I go about helping my students feel better about themselves?" I admit there was a smattering of "affective education" books on how to enhance self-esteem. None had what I was looking for—a sequential framework for building self-esteem which would tell me, as a teacher, where I needed to begin and how I could use the techniques in a classroom setting. During the next few years, I spent countless hours in the libraries at Stanford University and San Jose State University. I devoured any material even remotely related to the topic of self-esteem. Gradually, what I began to notice was that the elements a number of major theorists in self-esteem, resilience, and motivation considered critical to the development of positive and healthy self-perceptions were similar. Each theorist generally used different terms for the component, but the similarities of the components were too apparent to overlook. For instance, the component of Selfhood was defined usually as "a sense of self-knowledge and identity," but theorists called it by various names, such as "uniqueness, significance, identity, self-concept, body image, and worthiness."

I began to group the terms into categories, taking only the elements a number of researchers recognized as the core components of self-esteem. The next task was to analyze the elements to determine if there was a developmental sequence in their acquisition. A few years later, I developed a model for esteem building around five core feelings required for positive self-esteem: Security, Selfhood, Affiliation, Mission, and Competence. Determining the elements that make up self-esteem and the sequence in which they generally are acquired was the most difficult part of the task. The second step—creating activities that would build student self-esteem in each of the five component areas—was the fun part. Developing activities to enhance a specific concept has always been one of my favorite parts of teaching. I love watching the students' reactions as they put my activity "to task" and seeing if it works. The students have always been my greatest critics as well as my strongest supporters.

Now the years of trial and error began. This time, though, I had a lot of help along the way. Schools began to call me to in-service their teachers in the principles and techniques of self-esteem. Following the presentations, the same phenomenon would take place: a group of teachers at the site would come up, introduce themselves, and tell me they wanted to help me develop effective self-esteem activities for students. The phenomenon grew—county by county and state by state—so that at the close of an in-service, a group of teachers at each school would form a self-esteem committee to implement the principles I was addressing. Phone calls and letters poured in. Teachers tried the activities and saw the successes. They asked for a curriculum with all the activities sequenced by the feeling components so they could use the materials not only in their individual rooms but school-wide. After three years of writing, *Esteem Builders* was published.

In twenty years, our educational community has come a long way in regards to the concept of self-esteem. Research has swelled in the past ten years with studies correlating the impact self-esteem has on student achievement and behavior. Five years ago the National Council of Self-Esteem was formed by Robert Reasoner, a former school superintendent and visionary who recognized educators needed not only support but training in esteem-building principles. Assemblyman John Vasconcellos was successful in creating a statewide task force in California to study the correlation of low self-esteem to the epidemic of school dropouts, teenage pregnancy, domestic violence, drug and alcohol addiction, child abuse, and other behaviors destructive to one's self and others. Major national television producers such as Arnold Shapiro and programs such as ABC's "The Home Show" asked me to appear on the show or to consult with their producers in developing scripts on the crucial role self-esteem plays in the mental health and well-being of today's youth. I knew self-esteem had finally become a viable and credible concept to the American way of life when I received a call from none other than Ronald McDonald. He explained that the educational division of McDonald's had identified self-esteem as an important concept in education and that they were in the process of creating skits on self-esteem to bring into the schools, using Ronald McDonald as the presenter. *Esteem Builders* was one of the main publications they were using to develop the skits. I exulted. We've made it! Self-esteem is credible! I thought of how far the concept of self-esteem had come. The evidence proved that self-esteem does impact student achievement and behavior. The media was finally accepting the concept as credible. The elements impacting student self-esteem had been identified, and dozens of activities to implement those principles in the classroom and school had been developed. What could possibly be missing? Very quickly, I learned that all in the field of self-esteem programs was not well. Again, the teachers in the field set me straight.

I first received the message that all was not well when I changed the ending to my presentation. It was a simple change. I wanted teachers to recognize how powerful they are in students' lives and that they can make such differences, so I began collecting wonderful quotes about teachers from famous individuals, such as Gandhi, Goethe, Ralph Waldo Emerson, George Lucas, and Dan Rather, who all stated so eloquently how teachers had played significant roles in their lives. I wrote each quote on an overhead transparency and projected the quotes one by one while playing an inspirational song such as "The Wind Beneath My Wings." To my surprise, the impact was tremendous. No matter where I went across North America, the reaction was the same. Scores of teachers (most with tears in their eyes) would come up to me afterward and, with great emotion in their voices, thank me for the presentation, in particular for reminding them of their significance. I'll never forget one teacher in particular who told me that in twenty-five years of teaching no one had ever told him about the impact he could have on the lives of his students. And I still have the notes that participants passed to me, all thanking me for reinforcing their belief in the reason they chose their profession.

This proved to be my awakening. Powerful programs have been created for the enhancement of student self-esteem, but the most important element in that enhancement process—the individuals responsible for building student self-esteem, the teachers—were being overlooked. Never has there been a time in education when teachers are more needed. Never has there been a time when teachers can make significant life-touching changes for students. Yet, never has there been a time when teacher self-esteem is so low. The media and political leaders have chosen to blame most of the major social ills of our country on the teaching profession. No one seems to have come to grips with the fact that in the last twenty years the students themselves have changed, largely due to the lack of support systems that used to enhance student self-esteem. An analysis of how the family unit, the media, class sizes, family mobility, church attendance, and the neighborhood block have changed in the past decade helps to explain the impact such structures have on the self-esteem of youth. Many of today's students walk into classrooms minus critical support systems that could be enhancing their feelings of self-worth. The result is more pressure on teachers. It's as simple as that. The school, in many cases, has become the support network as well as the "family figure" for a large number of students.

The field of self-esteem has come a long way. The gates are opening. The opportunity for educators to make a major impact on students' lives is there. What administrators must realize, though, is that the most effective self-esteem programs are comprehensive. They do not address only the needs of students. They must simultaneously address the needs of the staff. The five components of self-esteem are universal feelings. They transcend intelligence, race, gender, and age. They are crucial not only to students but also to teachers who are the *esteem builders*. Thus, twenty years later, I recognize that this book is probably where I should have begun the process. The place to start is by building and nurturing the esteem of the individuals who can make the greatest difference in the future generations of all youth, and these individuals are the teachers. This book was specially written with the enhancement of educators' self-esteem in mind. Educators need to realize that their impact is tremendous and far-reaching, as Henry Adams said: "A teacher touches eternity... he will never know where his influence stops!"

All the best to the individuals committed to the noblest profession there is: the educators!

Michele Borba
Palm Springs, California
June 1993

Introduction

The Miracle of Collaborative Efforts

The achievements of an organization are the result of the combined efforts of each individual.
—VINCE LOMBARDI

THE MIRACLE OF BEE COLLABORATION

It is often through the miracles of science that the most powerful principles of social dynamics are gained. In this case, the social interaction of bees best describes the essence of team cohesiveness. After extensively observing the behavior of bees, scientists discovered that they are able to survive the winter solely through collaboration. In the coldest months, bees form themselves into a tight ball and keep up a steady "dance" or movement. Periodically, the bees then change places. The bees that have been on the outside of the ball move to the center and those at the center move to the outside. Through this process of collaboration, they are able to survive the winter. If at any time a small group of bees had insisted on staying in their positions, keeping others locked in theirs, all the bees would have died.

The collaborative spirit of the bees is, in reality, the same premise by which the most productive staffs are organized. The strongest groups rely on themselves to survive and get the work done. Too often schools look to "outside sources" and "quick remedies" to patch up their problems. The following scenario is typical at all too many school sites: each year the staff sits down and recognizes that student behavior has not improved, test scores and academic achievement continue to be low, and staff morale is still at a low ebb. Each year the staff chooses a new approach. One year it is the technological approach, and hundreds of thousands of dollars are spent on computers to no avail. The next year it's a different approach, for instance, large-scale in-servicing and restructuring in cooperative or whole language learning. Still no positive results are evident. In the process of changing from method to method and buying product after product, disillusionment amongst the staff begins to grow. The overriding feeling that prevails is: "We can't make a difference. Nothing seems to work." Such disillusionment regarding "my lack of power to help my students" can create deep scars among

> The most productive staffs are organized and get the work done.

individual staff members. Like an infection, the frustrations and feelings of powerlessness continue to spread until everyone else on the staff "catches it."

The greatest way to create change and enhance the learning environment is to begin the change from within.

What went wrong? Certainly, the staff intended to create a more effective learning environment. Certainly, the staff had a strong desire to learn new programs and implement new ideas. The error was in thinking that the change should come from the "outside." What research on school effectiveness and productivity clearly shows is that the greatest way to create change and enhance the learning environment is to begin the change from within. The bees certainly recognized this premise; it's up to human beings to apply the same principles to themselves. The individuals at the school site (the teacher, principal, cafeteria worker, custodian, secretary, bus driver, etc.) are without a doubt the single most important determiners of students' educational success. These are the people who directly impact children on a personal level. They are the ones who cause children to ponder over a provocative question; they are the ones who turn tears into smiles; they are the ones who recognize children's strengths and help students believe in themselves. The ancient Greek philosopher Socrates would have recognized that textbooks, computers, and overhead transparencies were not what created effective teachers. *The most powerful teaching tool lies within teachers themselves*. Research tells us that the turning point for most students is one adult who cares. This is what *Staff Esteem Builders* is all about: building schools from within by empowering the individuals who touch students' lives. After all, a school's greatest teaching resource is its staff. Let's begin by enhancing these people from within so that, like the bees, staff members learn to rely on one another and collaboratively put into use proven methodology that will ensure positive changes for their students. It is only when staff members turn to one another to solve their problems and develop outstanding curriculum that a learning environment can be created that provides students as well as staff with the opportunity to achieve their true potential.

STAFF ESTEEM BUILDER ACTIVITIES

Security Builders	Selfhood Builders	Affiliation Builders	Mission Builders	Competence Builders
SEB 1 Teacher Esteem Survey	SEB 25 Positive Working Environment	SEB 65 Group Belonging	SEB 97 Personal Clarification Activity	SEB 127 High and Achievable Expectations
SEB 2 Self-Esteem Staff Survey	SEB 26 Unique Staff Qualities	SEB 66 School and Professional Pride	SEB 98 School Mission and Major Focus	SEB 128 Strength Aid
SEB 3 Staff Checklist	SEB 27 Acknowledge Positive Behavior	SEB 67 Team Building and Peer Support	SEB 99 Decision-Making Policies	SEB 129 Individual Competencies and Strengths
SEB 4 Components Reflections	SEB 28 Unsung Heroes	SEB 68 Sunshine Committee	SEB 100 Staff Problem Solving	SEB 130 Effective Feedback Steps
SEB 5 Administrative Checklist	SEB 29 Acknowledge Successes	SEB 69 Welcome Committee	SEB 101 Snap Group Problem Solving	SEB 131 Specific Feedback
SEB 6 Esteem Builder Component Characteristics	SEB 30 Praise Pointers	SEB 70 Staff Retreat	SEB 102 Problem Cards	SEB 132 Written Hearts
SEB 7 Climate Survey	SEB 31 Positive Staff Behaviors	SEB 71 Athletic Leagues	SEB 103 Triad Problem Solving	SEB 133 Whip
SEB 8 Climate of Trust	SEB 32 Positive Messages	SEB 72 Secret Pals	SEB 104 SMART	SEB 134 Paired Sharing
SEB 9 Safety and Orderliness	SEB 33 Thought You Ought to Know	SEB 73 Message Center	SEB 105 Goal-Setting Procedures	SEB 135 You're Significant Buttons
SEB 10 Open-Door Communication	SEB 34 Just Wanted to Let You Know	SEB 74 Idea Exchange	SEB 106 Goal Map	SEB 136 Teachers Awards Banquet
SEB 11 Hold Calls	SEB 35 From the Principal's Desk	SEB 75 Lunch Bunch Group	SEB 107 Agenda Topics	SEB 137 Parent Letter Campaign
SEB 12 Back to School Party	SEB 36 Certificate of Appreciation	SEB 76 Classroom Visitations	SEB 108 Staff Survey	SEB 138 Personal Business Cards
SEB 13 Model Positivism	SEB 37 Balloon Pop	SEB 77 School Apparel	SEB 109 Brainstorming Rules	SEB 139 Central Off. Acknowledgment
SEB 14 Learn Names	SEB 38 Good Egg Award	SEB 78 Brainstorm Sessions	SEB 110 Brainstorming Sessions	SEB 140 Teacher Apprec. Assembly
SEB 15 Share Yourself	SEB 39 Terrific Teacher Notes	SEB 79 Meet in Classrooms	SEB 111 Problem Box	SEB 141 Essay Contest
SEB 16 Examine Communication	SEB 40 Teacher of the Week	SEB 80 Resource Poor	SEB 112 Problem Cards	SEB 142 Student Interviews
SEB 17 Announce Availability	SEB 41 Me Poster	SEB 81 Photo Board	SEB 113 Room Whip	SEB 143 Teacher Quotations
SEB 18 Rearrange Office	SEB 42 Special Events Recognitions	SEB 82 Cooperative Structures	SEB 114 Attitude Boosters	SEB 144 Appreciation Grams
SEB 19 Invite Compliments	SEB 43 Cake Bake	SEB 83 Loner Recognition	SEB 115 Goal Sharing	SEB 145 You Make the Difference Cards
SEB 20 Emphasize the Positive	SEB 44 Treats for Celebration	SEB 84 Mentors	SEB 116 Valuable Input	SEB 146 Books Celebrating Teachers
SEB 21 Behave Consistently	SEB 45 Special Lunches	SEB 85 Appreciation Cards	SEB 117 Committee Recommendations	SEB 147 Awareness of Teachers Efficacy
SEB 22 Listen	SEB 46 Personal Notes	SEB 86 Team Spirit	SEB 118 Celebration Sheets	SEB 148 Teacher's Pride
SEB 23 Esteem Builders Activities	SEB 47 Bombardment	SEB 87 Lounge Lift	SEB 119 SMART Process	SEB 149 Buttons and Badges
SEB 24 Acknowledge Positive Actions	SEB 48 Note of Appreciation	SEB 88 Preference Survey	SEB 120 Goal Folders	SEB 150 Scrapbook
	SEB 49 Ice Cream Social	SEB 89 Activities Survey	SEB 121 Involvement in School Decisions	SEB 151 Local Newspapers
	SEB 50 Appreciation Grams	SEB 90 Refreshments	SEB 122 Mission Statement	SEB 152 Celebrations
	SEB 51 Yard Duty	SEB 91 Open Dialogue	SEB 123 Risk Taking	SEB 153 Brag Board
	SEB 52 April Fool's Exchange	SEB 92 Team Builders	SEB 124 Personal Creed	SEB 154 Success Grams
	SEB 53 Hats Off Award	SEB 93 Publicity	SEB 125 Collective Creed	SEB 155 Experts
	SEB 54 Teacher for the Day	SEB 94 Grade Level Interaction	SEB 126 Esteem Builders Activities	SEB 156 Mini-Workshops
	SEB 55 Open Praise	SEB 95 Idea Exchange		SEB 157 Brag Sessions
	SEB 56 Staff Member of the Week	SEB 96 Esteem Builders Activities		SEB 158 Strengths and Weaknesses
	SEB 57 Thank You Balloon			SEB 159 Graphs
	SEB 58 Blackboard Message			SEB 160 Personal Expectations
	SEB 59 Intercom Announcement			SEB 161 Shared Resources
	SEB 60 Guess Who?			SEB 162 Progress Evaluation
	SEB 61 Carnations			SEB 163 Needed Support
	SEB 62 Special Parking			SEB 164 Self-Evaluations
	SEB 63 Esteem Builders Activities			SEB 165 Clear Expectations
	SEB 64 Personal Interest Survey			SEB 166 List of Strengths
				SEB 167 Commendations
				SEB 168 Ways to Improve
				SEB 169 Seminars
				SEB 170 Modeling
				SEB 171 Colleague Support
				SEB 172 Strength Fair
				SEB 173 Special Moments
				SEB 174 Compliments
				SEB 175 Certificates and Grams
				SEB 176 Esteem Builders Activities

Esteem Builders' Complete Program
Jalmar Press, Rolling Hills Estates, CA

STAFF TEAM BUILDING ACTIVITIES

Security Builders	Selfhood Builders	Affiliation Builders	Mission Builders	Competence Builders
BEGINNING ACTIVITIES	**BEGINNING ACTIVITIES**	**BEGINNING ACTIVITIES**	**BEGINNING ACTIVITIES**	**BEGINNING ACTIVITIES**
SEB 177 Get Acquainted Checklist	SEB 187 Mug File	SEB 201 Positive Finders	SEB 214 Dream Spheres	SEB 215 News Flash
SEB 178 Warm-Up Bingo	SEB 188 Positive Name Tags	SEB 202 Staff Message Center		SEB 216 Strength Medallions
SEB 179 Interviews	SEB 189 Smile Pin	SEB 203 Recognition Grams	**ADVANCED ACTIVITIES**	SEB 217 Make a Difference Posters
SEB 180 Knots	SEB 190 Graffiti Board	SEB 204 Common Points	SEB 262 Belief Ladder	
SEB 181 Faculty Lineups	SEB 191 Secrets	SEB 205 Playing Favorites	SEB 263 Belief Interviews	**ADVANCED ACTIVITIES**
SEB 182 Face-to-Face Interviews	SEB 192 Room Plan	SEB 206 Candy Bar Acknowledgments	SEB 264 Keeping the Vision Visual	SEB 270 Commitment Sustainers
SEB 183 Inside-Outside Circles	SEB 193 I Like Posters	SEB 207 Good Egg Awards	SEB 265 Staff Responses	SEB 271 Team Commitment
SEB 184 Voting... What's Your Opinion?	SEB 194 Name Collages	SEB 208 Staff Meeting Whips	SEB 266 Triads	SEB272 Team Celebration Posters
SEB 185 Find Your Counterparts	SEB 195 Name Tag Exchange	SEB 209 Webbing	SEB 267 Carousel	
SEB 186 Staff Welcome	SEB 196 Baby Picture Guess Who	SEB 210 Compliment Book	SEB 268 Solution/No Comment	
SEB 187 Mug File	SEB 197 Identity Shield	SEB 211 School Want Ad Poster	SEB 269 Goal Shooting	
SEB 188 Positive Name Tags	SEB 198 Partner Handprint	SEB 212 Staff Lounge Decorating		
SEB 189 Smile Pin	SEB 199 Birthday Recognition	SEB 213 Secret Pals		
SEB 190 Graffiti Board	SEB 200 Interest Search			
SEB 191 Secrets	SEB 201 Positive Finders	**ADVANCED ACTIVITIES**		
SEB 192 Room Plan	SEB 202 Staff Message Center	SEB 248 Downplaying Ind. Recognition		
	SEB 203 Recognition Grams	SEB 249 Team Acknowledgment		
ADVANCED ACTIVITIES	SEB 204 Common Points	SEB 250 Bulletin Board Acclaim		
SEB 218 Welcoming Committee	SEB 205 Playing Favorites	SEB 251 Team Support Grams		
SEB 219 Buddy System	SEB 206 Candy Bar Acknowledgments	SEB 252 Faculty Meeting Rotation		
SEB 220 Welcome Balloons/Flowers		SEB 253 Retreats		
SEB 221 Staff Card	**ADVANCED ACTIVITIES**	SEB 254 Switch Day		
SEB 222 Welcome Basket	SEB 241 Staff Self-Posters	SEB 255 Grade-Level Sharing		
SEB 223 Parking Space	SEB 242 Partner for Sale	SEB 256 Shared Treat Days		
SEB 224 First-Week School Pack	SEB 243 Hobby Day	SEB 257 Grade/Subject Gatherings		
SEB 225 Welcome Door Sign	SEB 244 Two-Minute Autobiographies	SEB 258 Belief Statements		
SEB 226 Name on the Marquee	SEB 245 Who Am I?	SEB 259 Staff Member Surveys		
SEB 227 Luncheon or Breakfast	SEB 246 Large Name Tags	SEB 260 "Hot Dot" Surveys		
SEB 228 Staff Coupons	SEB 247 Snowball	SEB 261 Staff Meeting Whips		
SEB 229 Video Orientation				
SEB 230 Slide Presentation				
SEB 231 Photo Album				
SEB 232 Scrapbook				
SEB 233 Yearbook				
SEB 234 Bus Ride				
SEB 235 School Narrated Tour				
SEB 236 School Checklist				
SEB 237 School and Staff Map				
SEB 238 Staff Directory				
SEB 239 Staff Yearbook				
SEB 240 School Culture Banners				

Esteem Builders' Complete Program
Jalmar Press, Rolling Hills Estates, CA

ESTEEM BUILDERS' ACTIVITIES FOR STAFF

Educators have successfully used many activities in ESTEEM BUILDERS on themselves in an upgraded version to enhance the five feeling of self-esteem. Not only is this technique a fun way for staff members to find out about each other, but it also helps build staff esteem. Here is a cross-reference list provided for *your* use!

Code	Activity	Esteem Builder Page
SECURITY		
S 6	TOOL DAY	54
S 9	SIGNIFICANT OTHER SHARING	55
S14	SIGNIFICANT OTHERS	56
S17	TIME FOR FRIENDS	60
S18	NAME BINGO	60
S19	NAME EXCHANGE	61
S20	PERSONALITY TRIVIA	61
S23	FIND A FRIEND	62
S2/3/4/5	SPECIAL RECOGNITION GRAMS	54
S24	SPARKLE STATEMENTS	62
S26	SUPER SPARKLE GRAM	63
S31/32	SPARKLE LINE	66
S34	A SPECIAL MESSAGE TO YOU	67
S35	ADD A COMPLIMENT	67
SELFHOOD		
SH 3	A SELF-PORTRAIT	102
SH 2	ME RIDDLE	102
SH17	WHO AM I?	108
SH18	MY IDENTITY SHIELD	109
SH20	PLAYING FAVORITES	110
SH21	WANTED POSTER	110
SH23	MY INTERESTS AND HOBBIES	110
AFFILIATION		
A 4	PAIRED NAME COLLAGE	167
A 3	GETTING TO KNOW YOU WHEEL	166
A 2	COMMON POINTS	166
A 9	MYSTERY PERSON	170
A10	FRIENDLY RIDDLES	171
A38	COMPLIMENT HANGING	186
MISSION		
M 1	WHAT I LIKE...WHAT I WANT TO CHANGE	223
M 2	PROBLEMS	224
M 5	BRAINSTORMING	225
M 6	STRATEGY SHEET OF SOLUTION CONSEQUENCES	226
M17	OVERCOMING OBSTACLES TO GOALS	233
M19	DAILY GOAL-SETTING	234
M21	RECORD OF WEEKLY GOALS	234
M29	HAPPY GRAM	236
COMPETENCE		
C 8	STRENGTH BARBELLS	277
C16	I CAN	280
C 2	MY INTEREST	275
C 1	HOBBY DAY CHECKLIST	275
C26	ACCOMPLISHMENT BANNER	284

Esteem Builders' Complete Program
Jalmar Press, Rolling Hills Estates, CA

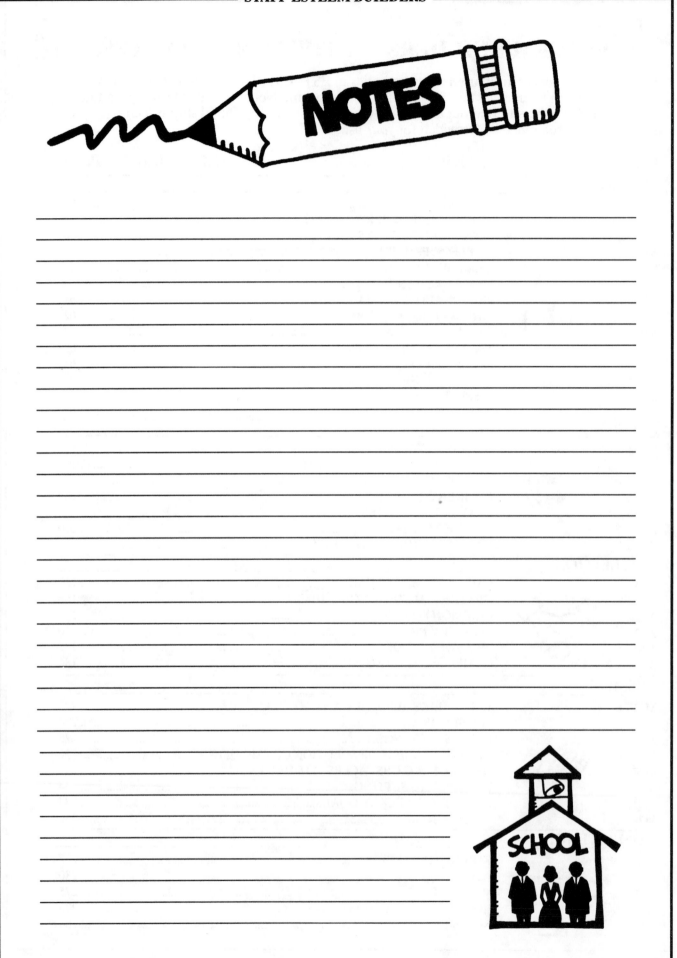

1

Staff Self-Esteem:
Steps to Esteem Building

STAFF ESTEEM BUILDERS

- The Plight of Today's Youth
- Staff Self-Esteem and Teacher Effectiveness
- Becoming an Esteem Builder
- Conditions That Enhance Staff Self-Esteem

1

Staff Self-Esteem:
Steps to Esteem Building

Neither written word nor spoken plea
Can teach young ears
What men should be,
Not all the books on all the shelves,
But what the teachers are themselves.

—ANONYMOUS

The words of this poem are old and often-used, but the message is still applicable today: teachers can and do make powerful differences in the lives of their students. One of the most important ways teachers impact their students is in the area of self-esteem. Students' self-esteem is largely determined by the external forces in their lives. Repeated patterns or experiences (positive or negative) help mold self-opinions. In many cases, teachers may be with their students longer each day than the students' parents are with them. *This time in the classroom must be recognized as a valuable opportunity for esteem building.* Whether or not an individual can enhance a student's self-esteem depends on how significant that individual is to the student. By becoming a "significant other," or esteem builder, an educator can play a critical role in self-esteem. Teachers need to recognize just how important their role is in the lives of their students.

Teachers can and do make powerful differences in the lives of their students.

In my seminars with educators across the country, one of the activities I love to have audiences do is to think about a teacher in their past who touched their lives. I ask them to quickly recall an educator who had a positive influence on their lives and then reflect on specifically what that individual did that had such an impact on them. I then ask participants to turn to another person in the audience and share who that teacher is and why they feel he or she had such a strong influence over their lives. At the end of a short discussion, participants are asked to think once more about that teacher. Each person in the audience had an average of 150 teachers in their past. Why, out of 150 teachers, I ask them, is this one particular teacher still so vivid in their minds today? Each member in the audience is to complete this open-ended sentence stem: "The single most important characteristic that made this teacher so special in my life is..."

I've asked this same question of over 150,000 educators now. Inevitably, the answers are almost always the same: "She cared about me," "I felt special," "He believed in me," "She liked me," "I felt like the teacher's pet." These are all descriptions of teachers who built their students' self-esteem. Through this simple, five-minute activity, educators are helped to recognize that they do impact student self-esteem and that even though they are no longer in this teacher's classroom, the teacher who touched their self-esteem has never left them; he or she has influenced them for a lifetime.

THE PLIGHT OF TODAY'S YOUTH

Never have teachers been more necessary in making life-changing differences for their students than they are today.

Never have teachers been more necessary in making life-changing differences in self-esteem enhancement for their students than they are today. An extensive survey, conducted by researchers affiliated with Stanford University and the National Bureau of Economic Research, declared that the status of U.S. children has declined over the last three decades on almost every score except infant mortality. American children are in trouble, warned economist Victor Fuchs and researcher Diane Reklis in an article published in the journal *Science*. "Both cultural and material changes have probably contributed to the problems." According to their research, since 1960, Fuchs and Reklis found:

- suicides and murders among teenagers have tripled;

- SAT scores dropped four percent in math and ten percent in verbal skills;

- the number of children born to unwed mothers increased five times, while the divorce rate among parents more than doubled;

- the number of children living in poverty declined slightly, but probably because the percentage of married women in the labor force with children under age six more than tripled; and

- the amount of time parents spend with their children decreased by ten hours a week. (Cited in EDCAL, "American Children Are in Trouble." Jan. 20, 1992, 4.)

What is particularly relevant about these statistics is their relationship to the issue of self-esteem. The California Task Force to Promote Self-Esteem and Personal and Social Responsibility was formed to study the effects of self-esteem and its correlation to six major social maladies (crime and violence, alcohol and drug abuse, premature pregnancy, child abuse, chronic dependence on welfare, and educational failure). After three years, the task force's final report, which Governor Deukmejian signed into law under Assembly Bill 3659, was issued containing the following statement:

"Self-esteem is the likeliest candidate for a *social vaccine,* something that empowers us to live responsibly and that inoculates us against the lure of crime, violence, substance abuse, teen pregnancy, child abuse, chronic welfare dependency, and educational failure. The lack of self-esteem is central to more personal and social ills plaguing our state and nation as we approach the end of the twentieth century." (*Toward a State of Esteem: The Final Report of the California Task Force to Promote Self-esteem and Personal and Social Responsibility,* California State Department of Education, January 1990, 4.)

STAFF SELF-ESTEEM AND TEACHING EFFECTIVENESS

It is pointless to discuss classroom activities to build student self-esteem unless we simultaneously discuss the issue of teacher self-esteem. When we consider the question of the significance teachers have on their students, we are also addressing the issue of the teachers' self-esteem. The bottom line in student self-esteem enhancement is to ensure that the teachers implementing the self-esteem strategies have high enough self-esteem to model these behaviors themselves. The most effective esteem-building schools recognize this principle and make the enhancement of teacher self-esteem a key priority in school esteem implementation. Robert Reasoner, an international expert on self-esteem, provides further rationale for the need to actively enhance staff self-esteem. Teachers low in self-esteem, Reasoner feels, are far more likely to exhibit ineffective teaching behaviors than their colleagues with higher self-esteem. Teachers lower in self-esteem tend to demonstrate the following five characteristics:

> **The enhancement of teacher self-esteem is a key priority in school esteem implementation.**

1. They tend to be more punitive with their students.

2. They are less tolerant and accepting.

3. They tend to be less patient during instruction.

4. They are less inclined to listen to students.

5. They are far less willing and open to try new solutions and classroom strategies.

Research substantiates that the level of teachers' self-esteem has a great impact on their effectiveness with students. A growing body of literature in the fields of education and psychology supports the assumption that teachers with the highest self-esteem appear to be the most successful at producing students with high self-esteem. This assumption rests on the notion that individuals who accept and like themselves have a much greater capacity to understand and accept their students. William Purkey states that "researchers have reported significant relationships between teacher self-regard and such factors as how they evaluate students, how effective they tend to be as teachers, how well students see themselves, and how well students achieve on standardized tests."[1] David Silvernail sums up this principle by stating: "Teachers who view themselves in a positive manner will project these images to their students and will provide valuable role models for them. Teachers who have realistic conceptions of themselves, who are accepting of themselves and others, and who accent their positive attributes will help students make realistic assessments and begin to view themselves in a positive light."[2] These research studies and dozens of other findings on low teacher self-esteem all point to an important premise that must be addressed in esteem building—*student self-esteem cannot be adequately enhanced unless the school is simultaneously addressing the issue of staff self-esteem.*

> **Student self-esteem cannot be adequately enhanced unless the school is simultaneously addressing the issue of staff self-esteem.**

1. Purkey, William Watson and John M. Novak. *Inviting School Success: A Self-Concept Approach to Teaching and Learning.* Belmont, CA: Wadsworth Publishing Co., 1978, 42.

2. Silvernail, David L. *Developing Positive Student Self-Concept.* Washington, DC: NEA Professional Library, 1985.

How you teach directly relates to *your* self-esteem.

Positive self-esteem is not only correlated with teaching effectiveness but with the personal character qualities that would be desired in any staff member. George Gallup Jr. of the Gallup organization was commissioned by Robert Schuller to conduct a poll on the self-esteem of the American public.[3] The poll conclusively demonstrated that people with a strong sense of self-esteem demonstrate the following qualities:

1. They have a high moral and ethical sensitivity.

2. They have a strong sense of family.

3. They are far more successful in interpersonal relationships.

4. They view success in terms of interpersonal relationships, not in crass materialistic terms.

5. They're far more productive on the job.

6. They have a far lower rate of chemical addiction.

7. They are more likely to get involved in social and political activities in their community.

8. They are far more generous to charitable institutions and give far more generously to relief causes.

BECOMING AN ESTEEM BUILDER

An esteem builder is defined as someone who:

- has the ability to change an individual's self-opinion for the better;

- has an enormous influence on a staff member's self-esteem;

- must be considered worthy, important or significant to the staff member in order to be most effective. *It is important to win a staff member's trust and respect.* Therefore, the esteem builder's attitude should invite and nurture positive self-regard in the staff.

Any individual who desires to help another improve his/her self-image should ideally possess these qualities:

- a sincere interest and concern for the staff member;

- a personal rapport such that the staff member feels significant to the esteem builder;

- a genuine recognition of the positive qualities of each individual;

- a real belief that the staff member's self-image can change and the ability to communicate that to him/her with confidence;

- a willingness to make the effort and take the time to help staff members feel better about themselves;

---

3. Schuller, Robert H. *Self-Esteem: The New Reformation*. Waco, Texas: Word Books, 1985, 17.

- the willingness to "open up" to staff members and share genuine personal qualities/experiences with them;

- the desire to build a trusting relationship and be someone who is both reliable and trustworthy;

- the willingness to review one's own self-picture periodically, being aware that the esteem builder's role model is vital to esteem building.

CONDITIONS THAT ENHANCE STAFF SELF-ESTEEM

In order for the esteem builder to most effectively enhance staff esteem, it is critical that he/she understand the conditions that increase self-esteem. The administrator, in particular, plays a key role in establishing the tone of the working environment. He/she can be vital in setting policies and procedures that lend themselves to esteem enhancement.

Staff members exhibiting high self-esteem are generally strong in five specific areas: **Security, Selfhood, Affiliation, Mission and Competence.***

> To most effectively enhance staff esteem, it is critical to understand the conditions that increase self-esteem.

- *the sense of security* or emotional safety:
  "I feel secure to trust in those I work with and risk trying new teaching strategies. I know what's expected of me."

SECURITY

- *the sense of selfhood* or identity:
  the "Who am I?" question; the freedom to forge a unique identity.

SELFHOOD

- *the sense of affiliation* or a sense of belonging and connectedness:
  "I feel I am a contributing and accepted member of this staff."

AFFILIATION

- *the sense of mission:*
  "I know what I believe in and I know where I'm headed."

MISSION

- *the sense of personal competence:*
  "I feel I am an effective professional who is capable of making differences in the lives of my students."

COMPETENCE

* The five components of self-esteem are derived from Robert Reasoner's exhaustive review of self-theory and are the basis of these five feelings.

To begin the process of consciously enhancing staff esteem, it is helpful for the esteem builder to use the following three guidelines:

1. First, the esteem builder must understand what the five building blocks of self-esteem are and how these elements ultimately impact staff motivation, productivity and self-esteem enhancement. In addition to the description of each of the five feelings in this manual, the esteem builder may also wish to refer to *Esteem Builders*, in particular pages xix, 1-10, 49-50, 99-100, 163-164, 221-222, and 273-274.

2. Second, the esteem builder should closely examine the conditions at the school to determine if they are conducive to esteem enhancement. By examining existing policies and procedures, the esteem builder will know whether current conditions enhance and value staff members or devalue and reduce feelings of self-worth. With this purpose in mind, a number of forms have been provided in this section:

Staff members should always be given the right to turn in surveys anonymously, and these surveys should never be used as a means of evaluating individual staff members. Administrators commonly choose one of the surveys for all staff members to complete near the beginning of the school year. The surveys are then filed and dated. The identical form is then given to the same staff members near the end of the year to determine what changes (if any) the staff perceives have taken place in the enhancement of staff self-esteem.

Most importantly, administrators can note major trends revealed in the completed surveys. Individual staff members may vary greatly in their perspective on the school climate, for instance, but any area that a large number of staff members believe the school is low in or does not address at all should be considered seriously. The item could then become the school site's goal for improvement. For instance, if one half of the staff perceives that their administrator "never" or only "sometimes" "follows through on his/her word and promises such that I can count on him/her," the administrator should look at ways to enhance his/her behavior in this skill. The following surveys can help administrators determine existing conditions as well as assess changes in the staff's perception of the school's esteem-building efforts:

Administrators can note major trends revealed in the completed surveys.

a. *Teacher Esteem Survey (SEB 1).*
   This survey (pages 20-21) may be used as a starting point to determine which self-esteem building blocks are already being addressed at the building site and which conditions appear to be weak. Also provided are guideline questions for administrators following each chapter discussion of the five building blocks.

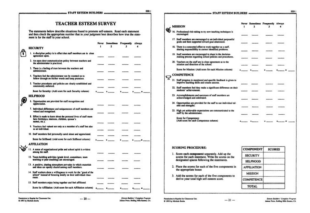

b. *Self-Esteem Staff Survey (SEB 2).*
   This form (page 22), designed by a self-esteem committee at the Rocky Mountain School in Westminster, Colorado, can be used to find out how staff members perceive the overall school climate. The form is short, yet its results can provide a clear statement of the staff's perception of school self-esteem. The survey can be filled out in a short period of time, perhaps at a faculty meeting.

c. *Staff Checklist on Administrator Behaviors That Promote Staff Self-Esteem (SEB 3)*
This survey (pages 23-24) is a more in-depth evaluation of how staff members perceive the administrator's esteem-building behaviors. Questions on the checklist are categorized according to the five components of self-esteem. The administrator can use the completed survey to determine his/her esteem-building strengths as well as weaknesses.

d. *Component Reflections (SEB 4).*

This form (page 25) serves as a visual index of the survey results. At the completion of the "Staff Checklist on Administrator Behaviors That Promote Staff Self-Esteem," staff members are asked to total the scores from each of the five components of self-esteem. For example, once each of the five statements regarding the feeling of Security are totaled, this score is then plotted as close as possible to the corresponding number on the "Component Reflection" grid. The procedure continues until all five feelings have been plotted. The grid is often an excellent tool for discussion. Staff members can turn to one another and compare grids. The administrator may also wish to collect the grids to review indepth at a later time. Staff members should be reminded that they do not have to sign their grid but may remain anonymous.

The grid is often an excellent tool for discussion.

e. *Checklist of Administrator Behaviors That Promote Staff Self-Esteem (SEB 5).*
Ideally, this form (pages 26-27) is used in conjunction with the "Staff Checklist on Administrator Behaviors That Promote Staff Self-Esteem." While staff members evaluate their perceptions of the administrator's esteem-building behaviors, the administrator completes the corresponding "Checklist of Administrator Behaviors" form. The administrator can then determine how closely his/her perceptions match the perceptions of the staff. Scores in each of the five components may be recorded in the box at the end of the survey. Simply add the scores across for each of the five components of high self-esteem to determine the overall component score.

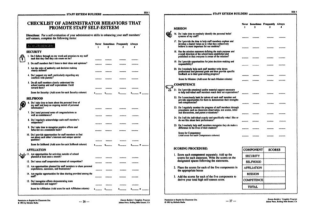

f. *Esteem Builder Component Characteristics Form (SEB 6).*
This form (page 29) helps administrators identify staff members exhibiting behaviors which indicate possible weaknesses in one or more of the five self-esteem components. This form, when completed, will be invaluable to the administrator. Specific strategies in each component, as described in *Staff Esteem Builders*, can be planned for specific staff members identified as low in those particular components. It is recommended that the administrator use the form as an ongoing form for identification as well as a planner for prescriptive staff self-esteem enhancing.

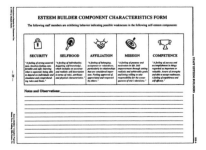

g. ***Check list of Educator Behaviors that Invite an Esteem Building Climate (SEB 7).***
An additional survey that assesses the perception of staff as well as students of the school's esteem-building climate may be found in *Esteem Builders* on pages 379 and 380.

3. Finally, the esteem builder needs to make deliberate and conscious plans to establish the conditions that build staff self-esteem. The enhancement of staff as well as student self-perceptions needs to become a major focus of the school. The thrust of esteem enhancement is demonstrated in a variety of ways: self-esteem resources and materials are purchased; research is read and discussed; a self-esteem committee is formed; in-servicing and training in esteem building is ongoing; and specific plans for esteem enhancement are developed. Once implemented, such plans should be consistently reviewed and analyzed as to their effectiveness.

The enhancement of staff as well as student self-perceptions needs to become a major focus of the school.

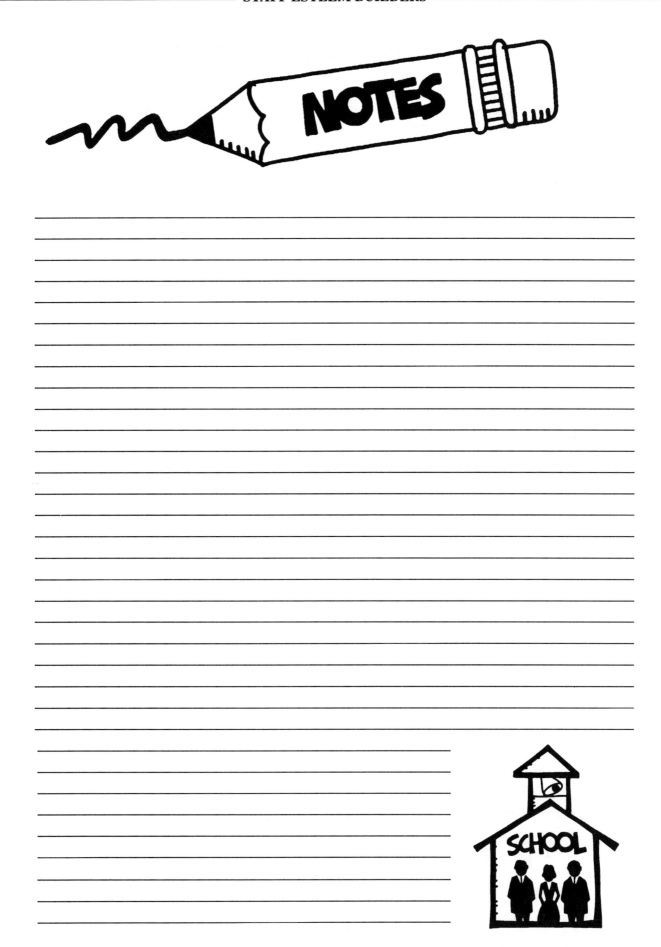

TEACHER ESTEEM SURVEY

The statements below describe situations found to promote self-esteem. Read each statement and then check the appropriate number that in your judgment best describes how true the statement is for the staff in your school.

	Never 1	Sometimes 2	Frequently 3	Always 4

SECURITY

1. A discipline policy is in effect that staff members are in close agreement upon. _____ _____ _____ _____

2. An open-door communication policy between teachers and the administrator is practiced. _____ _____ _____ _____

3. There is a feeling of trust between the teachers and administrator. _____ _____ _____ _____

4. Teachers feel the administrator can be counted on to follow through on his/her words and keep promises. _____ _____ _____ _____

5. Teacher procedures and policies are clearly established and consistently enforced. _____ _____ _____ _____

Score for Security: (Add score for each Security column) +_____ +_____ +_____ +_____ = _____

SELFHOOD

6. Opportunities are provided for staff recognition and appreciation. _____ _____ _____ _____

7. Individual differences and uniquenesses of staff members are valued and recognized. _____ _____ _____ _____

8. Effort is made to learn about the personal lives of staff members (birthdays, interests, children, spouse's names, etc.). _____ _____ _____ _____

9. Teachers feel valued not only as a member of a staff but also as an individual. _____ _____ _____ _____

10. Staff members feel personally cared about and appreciated. _____ _____ _____ _____

Score for Selfhood: (Add score for each Selfhood column) +_____ +_____ +_____ +_____ = _____

AFFILIATION

11. A sense of organizational pride and school spirit is evident among the staff. _____ _____ _____ _____

12. Team-building activities (grade level, committees, team teaching or peer coaching) are encouraged. _____ _____ _____ _____

13. A positive, sharing atmosphere pervades in which materials and ideas are openly shared among staff members. _____ _____ _____ _____

14. Staff workers show a willingness to work for the "good of the school" instead of focusing totally on their individual classroom. _____ _____ _____ _____

15. Staff members enjoy being together and feel affiliated. _____ _____ _____ _____

Score for Affiliation: (Add score for each Affiliation column) +_____ +_____ +_____ +_____ = _____

Esteem Builders' Complete Program
Jalmar Press, Rolling Hills Estates, CA

	Never 1	Sometimes 2	Frequently 3	Always 4

MISSION

16. Professional risk-taking to try new teaching techniques is encouraged.

17. Staff members are encouraged to set individual purposeful goals and then supported toward goal attainment.

18. There is a concerted effort to work together as a staff, sharing responsibility to correct identified problems.

19. Staff members are encouraged to share in the decision-making process regarding school policies and procedures.

20. Teachers on the staff are in close agreement as to the mission and direction of the school.

Score for Mission: (Add score for each Mission column)   +____ +____ +____ +____ = ____

COMPETENCE

21. Staff progress is monitored and specific feedback is given to improve teaching skills and ensure success.

22. Staff members feel they make a significant difference on their students' achievements.

23. Accomplishments and successes of staff members are acknowledged and celebrated.

24. Opportunities are provided for the staff to use individual talents and strengths.

25. High yet achievable expectations are communicated to the staff by the administrator.

Score for Competence:
(Add score for each Competence column)   +____ +____ +____ +____ = ____

SCORING PROCEDURE:

1. Score each **component** separately. Add up the scores for each statement. Write the scores on the designated spaces following the statements.

2. Place the scores for each of the five components in the appropriate boxes

3. Add the scores for each of the five components to derive your total high self-esteem score.

COMPONENT	SCORES
SECURITY	
SELFHOOD	
AFFILIATION	
MISSION	
COMPETENCE	
TOTAL	

Esteem Builders' Complete Program
Jalmar Press, Rolling Hills Estates, CA

SELF-ESTEEM STAFF SURVEY

Directions: Please complete the survey and return to your Esteem Builder Team Leader or principal by the end of the week. Your comments will help us in assessing school self-esteem.

Circle the letter which most clearly expresses your feelings about the following statements.
A=Strongly Agree   B=Agree   C=Neutral   D=Disagree   E=Strongly Disagree

1. Our school is a place that enhances my self-esteem.   A B C D E

2. At our school, student self-esteem is enhanced by the staff and programs.   A B C D E

3. At our school I am valued, recognized and trusted as a talented, contributing staff member.   A B C D E

4. Activities and curriculum which enhance self-esteem are a daily part of my lesson plans and interactions with students.   A B C D E

5. I am willing to spend time and effort to enhance and improve my co-workers' self-esteem.   A B C D E

6. I have a strong desire and lots of energy to work on enhancing students' self-esteem.   A B C D E

7. Personal high self-esteem and its modeling by staff greatly enhances students' self-esteem.   A B C D E

8. Adjustments and modifications of curriculum to promote success and enhance self-esteem are essential.   A B C D E

9. High student self-esteem positively correlates with and significantly impacts students' academic achievements.   A B C D E

10. Self-esteem involves the whole classroom environment and it is continually integrated in my daily thoughts and planning.   A B C D E

If you have any comments, please include them below.

_____
_____
_____
_____
_____
_____

Survey designed by Michael Focatura, from Rocky Mountain Elementary School, Westminster, Colorado

Esteem Builders' Complete Program
Jalmar Press, Rolling Hills Estates, CA

STAFF CHECKLIST ON ADMINISTRATOR BEHAVIORS
THAT PROMOTE STAFF SELF-ESTEEM

Directions: Please complete the following checklist on how you perceive my administrative behaviors. It will help me to focus on how I can best enhance staff self-esteem.

As a staff member, my administrator:	Never 1	Sometimes 2	Frequently 3	Always 4

SECURITY

1. Follows through on his/her word and promises so that I can count on him/her. _____ _____ _____ _____

2. Listens to my ideas and opinions. _____ _____ _____ _____

3. Has clearly defined the roles of authority and decision making at our school. _____ _____ _____ _____

4. Supports me particularly regarding any conflicts with parents. _____ _____ _____ _____

5. Helps me clearly understand the school routine, rules and expectations he/she holds toward me. _____ _____ _____ _____

SELFHOOD

6. Takes time to learn about my personal life and interests. _____ _____ _____ _____

7. Sends me personal notes of congratulations as well as condolences. _____ _____ _____ _____

8. Regularly acknowledges my uniqueness. _____ _____ _____ _____

9. Takes time to recognize my positive efforts and behavior on a consistent basis. _____ _____ _____ _____

10. Provides opportunities for our staff to find out about each other's interests and special qualities. _____ _____ _____ _____

AFFILIATION

11. Encourages opportunities for activities outside of school at least once a month. _____ _____ _____ _____

12. Plans opportunities for staff members to share personal experiences, successes, and frustrations. _____ _____ _____ _____

13. Stresses staff cooperation instead of competition. _____ _____ _____ _____

14. Provides regular opportunities for sharing of ideas among the staff. _____ _____ _____ _____

15. Takes time to recognize efforts demonstrating team collaboration and support. _____ _____ _____ _____

		Never 1	Sometimes 2	Frequently 3	Always 4

MISSION

16. Takes time to identify the personal belief systems of our staff. ____ ____ ____ ____

17. Provides the time to help our staff explore and develop a shared vision as to what we collectively believe most important for our students. ____ ____ ____ ____

18. Guides our staff in creating a mission statement defining the main purpose and overall direction of the school and helps everyone become aware of the mission. ____ ____ ____ ____

19. Provides opportunities for joint decision-making and shared responsibility. ____ ____ ____ ____

20. Routinely helps me write down professional and personal goals and provides specific feedback as to my goal-setting progress. ____ ____ ____ ____

COMPETENCE

21. Provides emotional and/or material support necessary to help me reach my set expectations. ____ ____ ____ ____

22. Consciously looks for my talents and provides opportunities for me to demonstrate my strengths and competencies. ____ ____ ____ ____

23. Regularly monitors my teaching progress through procedures such as classroom observation, test scores, informal discussions, and parent evaluations. ____ ____ ____ ____

24. Tells me exactly and specifically what he/she likes or does not like about my teaching performance. ____ ____ ____ ____

25. Routinely helps me recognize I do make a difference in the lives of their students. ____ ____ ____ ____

Esteem Builders' Complete Program
Jalmar Press, Rolling Hills Estates, CA

COMPONENT REFLECTIONS

Activity 1: Plot the total scores from the completed Staff Checklist. Use the **total score** from each of the five self-esteem components to plot on the grid below.

20 = HIGHEST
 5 = LOWEST

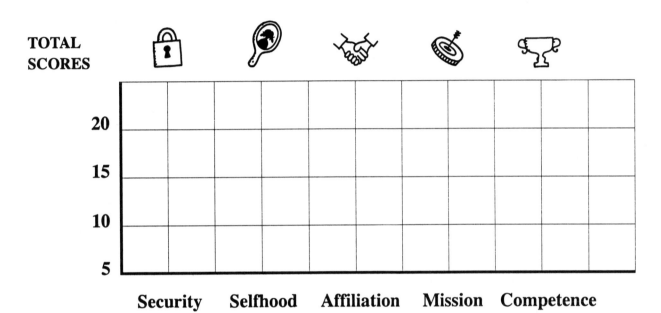

TOTAL
SCORES

20

15

10

5

Security   Selfhood   Affiliation   Mission   Competence

Now join the dots together to create a line graph!

ACTIVITY 2: Choose one of the esteem components you feel you address the least. List a few strategies or develop one specific strategy you could use to enhance the component.

_____
_____
_____
_____
_____
_____
_____
_____
_____
_____
_____
_____

Esteem Builders' Complete Program
Jalmar Press, Rolling Hills Estates, CA

CHECKLIST OF ADMINISTRATOR BEHAVIORS THAT PROMOTE STAFF SELF-ESTEEM

Directions: For a self-evaluation of your administrative skills in enhancing your staff members' self-esteem, complete the following items:

As an administrator:	Never 1	Sometimes 2	Frequently 3	Always 4

SECURITY

1. Do I follow through on my word and promises to my staff such that they feel they can count on me?

2. Do staff members feel I listen to their ideas and opinions?

3. Are the roles of authority and decision making clearly defined?

4. Do I support my staff, particularly regarding any conflicts with parents?

5. Do all staff members clearly understand the school routine and staff expectations I hold toward them?

Score for Security: (Add score for each Security column)   +____ +____ +____ +____ = ____

SELFHOOD

6. Do I take time to learn about the personal lives of my staff and keep an ongoing record of personal information?

7. Do I send personal notes of congratulations as well as condolences?

8. Do I regularly acknowledge each staff member's uniqueness?

9. Do I take time to recognize positive efforts and behavior on a consistent basis?

10. Do I provide opportunities for staff members to find out about each other's interests and unique special qualities?

Score for Selfhood: (Add score for each Selfhood column)   +____ +____ +____ +____ = ____

AFFILIATION

11. Are opportunities for activities outside of school planned at least once a month?

12. Do I stress staff cooperation instead of competition?

13. Are opportunities planned for staff members to share personal experiences, successes, and frustrations?

14. Are regular opportunities for idea sharing provided among the staff?

15. Do I recognize efforts demonstrating team collaboration and support?

Score for Affiliation: (Add score for each Affiliation column)   +____ +____ +____ +____ = ____

Esteem Builders' Complete Program
Jalmar Press, Rolling Hills Estates, CA

	Never 1	Sometimes 2	Frequently 3	Always 4

MISSION

16. Do I take time to routinely identify the personal belief systems of my staff? ____ ____ ____ ____

17. Do I provide the time to help staff members explore and develop a shared vision as to what they collectively believe is most important for our students? ____ ____ ____ ____

18. Has the mission statement defining the main purpose and overall direction of the school been established and published so that everyone is aware of the mission? ____ ____ ____ ____

19. Do I provide opportunities for joint decision-making and responsibility? ____ ____ ____ ____

20. Do I routinely help each staff member write down professional and personal goals and then provide specific feedback as to their goal-setting progress? ____ ____ ____ ____

Score for Mission: (Add score for each Mission column) ____ ____ ____ ____

COMPETENCE

21. Do I provide emotional and/or material support necessary to help individual staff members reach their set expectations? ____ ____ ____ ____

22. Do I consciously look for talents of each staff member and provide opportunities for them to demonstrate their strengths and competencies? ____ ____ ____ ____

23. Do I regularly monitor the progress of staff members through procedures such as classroom observation, test scores, informal discussions, and parent evaluations? ____ ____ ____ ____

24. Do I tell the individual exactly and specifically what I like or do not like about their performance? ____ ____ ____ ____

25. Do I routinely help staff members recognize they do make a difference in the lives of their students? ____ ____ ____ ____

Score for Competence:
(Add score for each Competence column) ____ ____ ____ ____

SCORING PROCEDURE:

1. Score each **component** separately. Add up the scores for each statement. Write the scores on the designated spaces following the statements.

2. Place the scores for each of the five components in the appropriate boxes

3. Add the scores for each of the five components to derive your total high self-esteem score.

COMPONENT	SCORES
SECURITY	
SELFHOOD	
AFFILIATION	
MISSION	
COMPETENCE	
TOTAL	

Esteem Builders' Complete Program
Jalmar Press, Rolling Hills Estates, CA

AREAS I COULD IMPROVE IN TO ENHANCE STAFF SELF-ESTEEM:

_____

_____

_____

_____

_____

_____

_____

_____

_____

_____

_____

_____

_____

_____

_____

_____

_____

_____

_____

_____

_____

_____

_____

_____

_____

_____

_____

_____

_____

_____

_____

_____

_____

_____

_____

_____

_____

_____

Esteem Builders' Complete Program
Jalmar Press, Rolling Hills Estates, CA

ESTEEM BUILDER COMPONENT CHARACTERISTICS FORM

The following staff members are exhibiting behavior indicating possible weaknesses in the following self-esteem components:

SECURITY	SELFHOOD	AFFILIATION	MISSION	COMPETENCE

"A feeling of strong assuredness. Involves feeling comfortable and safe; knowing what is expected; being able to depend on individuals and situations and comprehending rules and limits."	*"A feeling of individuality. Acquiring self-knowledge, which includes an accurate and realistic self-description in terms of roles, attributes and physical characteristics."*	*"A feeling of belonging, acceptance or relatedness, particularly in relationships that are considered important. Feeling approved of, appreciated and respected by others."*	*"A feeling of purpose and motivation in life. Self-empowerment through setting realistic and achievable goals and being willing to take responsibility for the consequences of one's decisions."*	*"A feeling of success and accomplishment in things regarded as important or valuable. Aware of strengths and able to accept weaknesses. A feeling of capableness and self-efficacy."*

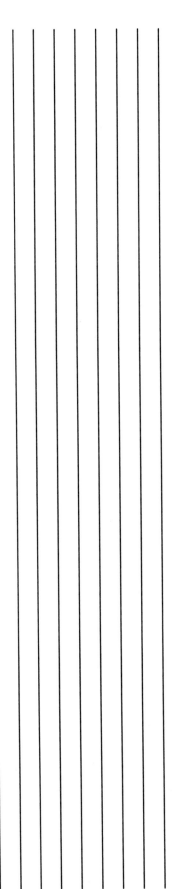

Notes and Observations:

_____

_____

_____

_____

_____

_____

_____

_____

_____

Esteem Builders' Complete Program
Jalmar Press, Rolling Hills Estates, CA

ESTEEM BUILDER COMPONENT CHARACTERISTICS

SECURITY
"A feeling of strong assuredness. Involves feeling emotionally and physically safe; knowing what is expected; being able to depend on individuals and situations; and comprehending rules and limits."

Esteem Builder Steps	Strong Component Indicators	Low Component Indicators	Staff Behavior Statements
• Build a trusting relationship. • Set reasonable limits and rules that are consistently enforced. • Create a positive and caring environment.	• Likes to participate in a collegial support group or peer observation program. • Looks forward to observations of classroom teaching. • Feels he/she can count on and trust friends. • Is excited about proposed changes. • Invites colleagues to deal openly with issues.	• Tends to avoid the administrator or other authority figure. • Distrusts others, hesitates or avoids close personal attachments. • May exhibit anxious or defensive behaviors. • Often asks for repeated explanations or clarification. • Is uncomfortable with new programs or changes. • Apprehensive about personal observations.	• *"I would like to participate in a collegial support group or peer observation program."* • *"I'm looking forward to your observation of me tomorrow."* • *"I count on and trust my friends."* • *"I'm excited about the grade level change."* • *"I am committed to the idea that my colleagues are able to come to me and deal openly and directly with issues or concerns."* • *"I'd like to serve on the new task force."*

SELFHOOD
"A feeling of individuality acquiring self-knowledge, which includes an accurate and realistic self-description in terms of roles, attributes and physical characteristics. 'The Who am I?' question."

• Reinforce more accurate self-descriptions. • Provide opportunities to discover major sources of influence on the self. • Build an awareness of unique qualities. • Enhance ability to identify and express emotions and attitudes.	• Says "thank you" to compliments. • Congratulates self on job well done. • Accepts criticism when needed to improve. • Knows who he/she is. • Acknowledges weaknesses. • Acknowledges strengths. • Stresses personal adequacies over inadequacies.	• Frequently uses negative statements regarding self and others. • Embarrasses easily, oversensitive. • Overanxious to please and "do well." • Often complains. • Is uncomfortable asking for help. • Stresses personal inadequacies over personal adequacies.	• *"Thank you for that compliment."* • *"I think I did really well with that problem."* • *"I think you have a good point. I'll try to work on improving that."* • *"I am a lot of things. I am a teacher, a coach, an artist, a reader, a skier, a dad, etc."* • *"Some qualities I need to work on are my impatience and lack of organization."* • *"I like the fact that I am responsible and dependable."*

Esteem Builders' Complete Program
Jalmar Press, Rolling Hills Estates, CA

Esteem Builder Steps	Strong Component Indicators	Low Component Indicators	Staff Behavior Statements
AFFILIATION — *"A feeling of belonging, acceptance or relatedness, particularly in relationships that are considered important. Feeling approved of, appreciated and respected by others."* • Promote inclusion and acceptance within the group. • Provide opportunities to discover interests, capabilities and backgrounds of others. • Increase awareness of and skills in friendship making. • Encourage peer approval and support.	• Develops good relationships with colleagues. • Sets aside time to be with people considered important. • Has family and friends who care about the individual. • Is sought out by others in friendships. • Enjoys working as part of a team. • Likes being with people. • Is sensitive to others.	• Withdraws or isolates self from the staff, appears lonely. • Seldom helps others or shares materials. • Is uncomfortable working in groups. • Dictates, dominates or bullies others. • Feels others don't value him/her. • Ridicules or rejects others. • Lacks a feeling of school pride or cohesiveness.	• *"It is important to me that I have good relationships with my co-workers."* • *"I make sure to set aside time to be with people who are important to me."* • *"My friends and family care about me."* • *"People seek me out in friendships."* • *"I enjoy working as part of a team."* • *"I like being with people."* • *"It is important to be sensitive to others."*
MISSION — *"A feeling of purpose and motivation in life. Self-empowerment through setting realistic and achievable goals and being willing to take responsibility for the consequences of one's decisions."* • Enhance ability to make decisions, seek alternatives and identify consequences. • Aid in charting present and past academic and behavioral performances. • Teach the steps to successful goal-setting.	• Sets goals and strives for them. • Willing to try something new. • Accepts consequences for actions. • Able to make decisions. • Feels confident in ability to work through problems.	• Lacks motivation and initiative. • Feels powerless. • Appears aimless, without direction. • Sets unrealistic goals. • Is overly dependent on authority for direction, encouragement. • Avoids taking responsibility for own actions, blames others.	• *"I've decided to pursue my Master's Degree."* • *"I've never applied for a grant before, but I'm familiar with the process and I'm going to try it."* • *"Trying new things can be risky, but I'm willing to accept the consequences of my actions."* • *"Making decisions is not difficult for me."* • *"I've had success in the past in working with this person in my building. I know what I need to do to work through this current problem."*
COMPETENCE — *"A feeling of success and accomplishment in things regarded as important or valuable. A sense of efficacy and empowerment due to a feeling of control over one's destiny. Awareness of strengths and able to accept weaknesses."* • Provide opportunities to increase awareness of individual competencies and strengths. • Teach how to record and evaluate progress. • Provide feedback on how to accept weaknesses and profit from mistakes. • Teach the importance of self-praise for accomplishments.	• Willing to take risks and try something new. • Accepts weaknesses and recognizes strengths. • Turns mistakes into learning opportunities and tries again. • Takes pride in achievements. • Works on improving areas of low capability. • Accepts feedback and works on improving.	• Is reluctant to contribute ideas or opinions, may depend on others. • Has difficulty accepting weaknesses and identifying strengths. • Is a poor loser, magnifies any loss or failure. • Discredits achievements. • Easily discouraged, has difficulty recognizing progress.	• *"Although I've never attempted this before, I'm willing to give it a try."* • *"It can be risky to confront, but sometimes we need to do it anyway."* • *"I'm good at a lot of things, although sometimes I take on too much at one time."* • *"Sometimes I blow up without thinking. I'm working on this all the time."* • *"If I make a mistake, I'll try it a different way."* • *"I think I'm a really good parent."*

Esteem Builders' Complete Program
Jalmar Press, Rolling Hills Estates, CA

BUILDING BLOCKS OF STAFF SELF-ESTEEM

RATIONALE: Staff Members with high self-esteem generally possess five critical characteristics: Security, Selfhood, Affiliation, Mission, Competence. These characteristics can be identified in any individual and built by the Esteem Builder.

BUILDING BLOCK (Acquired Feeling)	ESTEEM BUILDING STEPS (Administrator Functions)
SECURITY: A feeling of strong self-assuredness. Involves feeling emotionally and physically safe; knowing what is expected; being able to trust and to depend on individuals and situations; and comprehending rules and limits.	1. Create a climate of trust. 2. Establish a safe and orderly environment. 3. Establish an open-door communication policy.
SELFHOOD: A feeling of individuality. Acquiring self-knowledge, which includes an accurate and realistic self-description in terms of roles, attributes, and physical characteristics.	1. Display accepting and caring behaviors. 2. Recognize unique qualities and provide opportunities to display individuality. 3. Recognize the individual and make him feel appreciated.
AFFILIATION: A feeling of belonging, acceptance, or relatedness, particularly in relationships that are considered important. Feeling approved of, appreciated and respected by others.	1. Build staff cohesiveness and affiliation. 2. Foster a sense of school and professional pride. 3. Promote team building collaboration and peer support.
MISSION: A feeling of purpose and motivation in life. Self-empowerment through setting realistic and achievable goals and being willing to take responsibility for the consequences of one's decisions.	1. Develop the major focus or mission of school. 2. Provide opportunities for joint decision-making and shared responsibility. 3. Encourage personal and professional goal-setting.
COMPETENCE: A feeling of success and capableness in things regarded as personally important or valuable. Aware of strengths and able to accept weaknesses. A sense of empowerment and self-efficacy over the direction of one's life.	1. Provide opportunities to recognize and demonstrate individual competencies. 2. Set high and achievable expectations. 3. Monitor progress and provide specific feedback. 4. Help individuals recognize they do make a difference.

Esteem Builders' Complete Program
Jalmar Press, Rolling Hills Estates, CA

ADMINISTRATOR STAFF ESTEEM ASSESSMENTS

COMPONENT	ADMINISTRATOR GUIDELINE QUESTIONS	
		PAGE
Security	SEB 8 A Climate of Trust	42
	SEB 9 Safety and Orderliness	43
	SEB 10 Open Door Communication Policy	45
Selfhood	SEB 25 Positive & Accepting Work Environment	57
	SEB 26 Recognition of Unique Staff Qualities	59
	SEB 31 Recognition of Positive Staff Behaviors	63
Affiliation	SEB 65 Group Belonging	84
	SEB 66 School and Professional Pride	85
	SEB 67 Team Building and Peer Support	87
Mission	SEB 98 School Mission & Major Focus	106
	SEB 99 Decision-Making Policies	109
	SEB 105 Goal-Setting Procedures	120
Competence	SEB 127 High & Achievable Staff Expectations	145
	SEB 129 Individual Competencies & Strengths	151
	SEB 130 Effective Feedback Steps	152
	SEB 147 Awareness of Teacher Efficacy	161
The Building Blocks of Self-Esteem	SEB 1 Teacher Esteem Survey	15, 20-21
	SEB 2 Self-Esteem Staff Survey	15, 22
	SEB 3 Staff Checklist on Administrator Behaviors That Promote Staff Self-Esteem	16, 23
	SEB 4 Component Reflections	16, 25
	SEB 5 Checklist of Administrator Behaviors That Promote Staff Self-Esteem	17, 26-27
	SEB 6 Esteem Builder Component Characterisitics Form	17, 29
	SEB 7 Checklist of Educator Behaviors That Invite an Esteem-Building Climate	18
	(Actual form located in *Esteem Builders* page 379)	

Esteem Builders' Complete Program
Jalmar Press, Rolling Hills Estates, CA

_____
_____
_____
_____
_____
_____
_____
_____
_____
_____
_____
_____
_____
_____
_____
_____
_____
_____
_____
_____
_____
_____
_____
_____
_____
_____
_____

2

A Strong Foundation: Building Security

STAFF ESTEEM BUILDERS

- Create a Climate of Trust
- Establish a Safe and Orderly Environment
- Establish an Open-Door Communication Policy
- Security Esteem Builders

STAFF SECURITY
CONTENTS

Security:

A feeling of strong assuredness. Involves feeling emotionally and physically safe, knowing what is expected, being able to trust and depend on individuals and situations, and comprehending rules and limits.

LOW SECURITY INDICATORS	HIGH SECURITY INDICATORS
• tends to avoid the administrator or other authority figure	• likes to participate in a collegial support group or peer observation program
• distrusts others, hesitates or avoids close personal attachments	• looks forward to observations of classroom teaching
• may exhibit anxious or defensive behaviors	• feels he/she can count on and trust friends
• often asks for repeated explanations or clarification	• is excited about proposed changes
• is uncomfortable with new programs or changes	• invites colleagues to deal openly with issues
• apprehensive about personal observations	• enjoys serving on teams

2

A Strong Foundation:
Building Security

Not a gift of a cow, nor a gift of land, nor yet a gift of food,
is so important as the gift of safety,
which is declared to be the great gift among all gifts in this world.

—PANCHATANTRA (5th Century)

Stephen Jobs, co-founder of Apple Computers, was once asked the poignant question: "How does Apple do it?" Jobs described the reason for the enormous success of his business by saying: "We hire great people and create an environment where people can grow and make mistakes." In a simplistic answer, Jobs alludes to the central premise of esteem enhancement—create the conditions that foster staff security and people will be able to grow and succeed. His response has important implications for anyone in the business of human connectedness.

A feeling of security or trust is the foundation of self-esteem. To be effective, staff members must feel safe enough to risk. They must perceive the environment as trusting and orderly, and know what is expected. When policies, procedures, and guidelines are clearly established, individuals know what roles they play and how they should function.

The feeling of security or trust is the foundation of self-esteem.

The administrator plays a key role in the fostering of security. He/she can do this by behaving in a predictable manner and consistently supporting the established procedures. Such behaviors help convey a climate of trust to the staff. The administrator is perceived as an individual who cannot only be counted on to stick to his word but who will at the same time support individual staff members. This perception has formed largely because the administrator consciously works at creating an open-door communication policy. An emotionally safe environment gradually evolves. Here is a place where individuals can feel secure in risking, open in communication and sharing, and safe in growing.

LOW AND HIGH SECURITY INDICATORS

When a staff member feels insecure and unsafe, he/she may indicate this in a variety of behaviors, such as:

- tends to avoid the administrator or other authority figure;

- distrusts others, hesitates or avoids forming close personal attachments;

- may exhibit anxious or defensive behaviors;

- often asks for repeated explanations or clarification;

- is uncomfortable with new experiences, programs, or changes;

- apprehensive about personal observations and evaluations.

These behaviors greatly reduce the teacher's classroom effectiveness. The teacher's insecurity may very well handicap his/her students for several reasons:

Teachers who feel insecure and unsafe greatly reduce their class-room effectiveness.

1. The teacher who limits himself/herself by an unwillingness to try new instructional strategies could deprive students of effective learning techniques.

2. An individual low in security may be less tolerant and empathetic of students, especially students low in self-esteem who need the most empathy. These students may very well suffer since the teacher is not able to provide the support, patience, and tolerance they need.

3. Students low in the feeling of security often exhibit psychological symptoms of tension and stress. They have a strong need to be with another person who feels secure and can help alleviate these symptoms.

On the other hand, a staff member with a strong sense of security may be heard making the following types of statements:

I would like to participate in a collegial support group or peer observation program.

I'm looking forward to your observation of me tomorrow.

I count on and trust my friends.

I'm excited about the grade level change.

I am committed to the idea that my colleagues are able to come to me and deal openly and directly with issues or concerns.

I'd like to serve on the new task force.

List individuals exhibiting behaviors indicating possible *low security:*

_____   _____
_____   _____
_____   _____
_____   _____

List individuals exhibiting behaviors indicating possible *high security:*

_____   _____
_____   _____
_____   _____
_____   _____

ESTEEM BUILDER STEPS TO ENHANCING SECURITY

A sense of security or trust among the staff can be enhanced when the esteem builder takes the following steps:

1. **Create a climate of trust.**
2. **Establish a safe and orderly environment.**
3. **Establish an open-door communication policy.**

ESTEEM BUILDER #1

CREATE A CLIMATE OF TRUST

"I hold it more important to have the players' confidence than their affection."
—VINCE LOMBARDI

The first and perhaps most critical condition to foster among the staff is a climate of trust. The esteem builder must consistently convey the feeling: "I can be counted on" and "You can feel safe with me." Such perceptions enable staff members to feel secure because they know what to expect. Teachers must feel that they will be supported, particularly when parental complaints are involved. They must perceive that the administrator's promises will be kept. This feeling of trust between staff and administration often takes a long time to evolve; therefore, the administrator must consistently reflect upon personal practices to ensure that his/her behavior does indeed convey trust. Because secure and trusting environments are the starting place for self-growth, such a climate will have dramatic ramifications.

The most critical condition to foster among the staff is a climate of trust.

Guideline Questions: A Climate of Trust (SEB 8)

The following questions are provided as guidelines for the administrator to help determine if conditions are being fostered to create a climate of trust:

	Regularly	Seldom	Never
• Do I follow through on my word?	_____	_____	_____
• Does my staff feel they can count on me?	_____	_____	_____
• Do I consistently attempt to convey trust to my staff?	_____	_____	_____
• Do I keep my promises?	_____	_____	_____
• Do I support my staff, particularly regarding any conflicts with parents?	_____	_____	_____
• Do I honor confidentiality with my staff?	_____	_____	_____

If I were a member of my staff, how would I perceive how trustworthy I am?

Reflection:
The administrator should now take a moment to review his or her own personal style of building trust with the staff. Ask yourself: "If I were a member of my staff, how would I perceive how trustworthy I am?" Now jot down a few thoughts about your own style of trustworthiness as an administrator.

_____
_____
_____
_____
_____
_____
_____

How can I convey a greater sense of trust to my staff?

Next, ask yourself: "How can I convey a greater sense of trust to my staff as a whole as well as toward individual staff members?" Write down your ideas. Finally, choose one idea to implement that will enhance your sense of trustworthiness with the staff. Write down specifically what you will do and when you will do it.

_____
_____
_____
_____
_____
_____
_____

ESTEEM BUILDER #2

ESTABLISH A SAFE AND ORDERLY ENVIRONMENT

In a secure environment, the administrator must also create a working environment that conveys a sense of safety and orderliness. In short, to feel secure, individuals must know what is expected of them. They must clearly understand the policies, procedures, and guidelines that have been established. Finally, they must sense that these practices will be consistently enforced. Predictability and consistency are hallmarks of security. Insecurity often develops when guidelines are *inconsistent,* when administrators respond to policies in an *unpredictable* manner, and when the teacher is unsure of what is expected. Anxiety and stress often are the outcome when guidelines, procedures, and policies have not been clearly established or are not consistently reinforced. Administrators foster security when they take steps to help their staff understand what the school procedures and discipline policies are, who has authority regarding certain decisions, and what specific roles staff and administrators play in creating a safe and orderly environment.

To feel secure, individuals must know what is expected of them.

Guideline Questions: Safety and Orderliness (SEB 9)

The following questions are provided as guidelines for the administrator to help determine if conditions are being fostered to create a working environment that conveys to the staff a sense of safety and orderliness.

	Regularly	Seldom	Never
• Are staff handbooks available that clearly spell out school policies and procedures?	_____	_____	_____
• Are school policies and procedures continually updated?	_____	_____	_____
• Are plans in effect to help new staff members understand these policies and procedures?	_____	_____	_____
• Is the school discipline policy spelled out in writing?	_____	_____	_____
• Are parents aware of the school discipline policy and do they understand the consequences for any infractions?	_____	_____	_____
• Do all staff members clearly understand the school routine and staff expectations, including work hours, discipline procedures, grading, curriculum planning, etc.?	_____	_____	_____
• Do all staff members understand the policy for ordering special materials and supplies?	_____	_____	_____
• Are my expectations concerning the staff clearly understood?	_____	_____	_____
• Are roles of authority and decision-making clearly defined?	_____	_____	_____

Reflection:
Read through the guideline questions for a second time. Now ask, "In what specific ways can I provide a working environment that conveys to the staff a sense of safety and orderliness?" List specific methods on the left side of the T-bar below. Recognize that if the staff's sense of security is to be enhanced, the administrator must take deliberate steps to ensure that this second esteem builder is in place. On the right side of the T-bar, list any ideas that could be implemented to increase the sense of safety and orderliness for the staff.

CURRENT WAYS	NEW WAYS

• Now put an asterisk next to the one idea you could implement. •

ESTEEM BUILDER #3

ESTABLISH AN OPEN-DOOR COMMUNICATION POLICY

The third step toward enhancing security is to establish an open-door communication policy between the administration and staff. Such a procedure fosters respect, which is essential to the enhancement of self-esteem. Staff members must perceive that their ideas and opinions are worthy of being heard. They must also sense that they will be safe in expressing their concerns, anxieties, and fears. To let staff know they are being heard, the administrator often assumes the role of "listener" and not "judge." In such an atmosphere, a dialogue is created, and staff members are given an opportunity to provide input. The administrator conveys an open-door policy through effective communication skills, but these are not easy to achieve; they must be continually practiced and reflected upon. An administrator who has developed effective listening skills helps create an ongoing, open dialogue among staff and administration, and thus enhances the feeling of security.

Effective communication skills creates an "open dialogue among staff and administrators."

Guideline Questions: Open-Door Communication Policy (SEB 10)

The following questions are provided as guidelines for the administrator to help determine if conditions are being fostered to establish an open-door communication policy between the administration and staff.

	Regularly	Seldom	Never
• Do I listen without always being judgmental?	_____	_____	_____
• Do staff members feel I listen to their ideas and opinions?	_____	_____	_____
• Do staff members share the feeling that "My door is always open?"	_____	_____	_____
• Do staff members know when I am available to talk?	_____	_____	_____
• Do I deliberately take time to be available and visible to my staff?	_____	_____	_____
• Do I respect confidentiality in our conversations?	_____	_____	_____
• Do staff members feel comfortable expressing anxieties, concerns, and fears to me?	_____	_____	_____
• Is my office arranged in a manner conducive to two-way communication?	_____	_____	_____
• Do I make conscious efforts to improve my communication skills?	_____	_____	_____
• Do I take time to listen to staff member's ideas and opinions?	_____	_____	_____

Reflection:
Take a moment to reflect on the communication policy you convey to the staff. Think about a particular staff member whose behavior might indicate low security. Sit on his/her side of the table for a moment. If an outsider asked that individual to describe your style of communication, what might that staff member say about you? Write it below.

_____

_____

_____

_____

What one thing could you do to enhance the flow of communication with this individual?

_____

_____

_____

_____

SECURITY ESTEEM BUILDERS   SEB 11-24

1. *Hold Calls (SEB 11).* When you are in a private conversation with a staff member, ask your secretary to hold your calls. This practice clearly sends the message: "You are more important."

2. *Organize a Back-to-School Party (SEB 12).* Plan a fun staff gathering prior to the beginning of school. Any informal activity (barbecue, potluck dinner, large family picnic, etc.) will be effective in setting the tone for the year.

3. *Model Positivism (SEB 13).* Start each day by being visible. Purposefully walk the halls, playground, classrooms, and bus stops before school starts. Make a special point of saying "Good morning!" to as many classrooms and individuals as possible.

4. *Learn Names (SEB 14).* As quickly as possible, learn the names of staff members and students. Provide name tags for as long as you need them.

5. *Share Yourself (SEB 15).* Make yourself (your interests, strengths, family) personal. Let staff members know about you.

6. *Examine Communication Practices (SEB 16).* Seriously examine your communication skills. Is it time to take a refresher course on communication skills or read more on the topic? Are your communication practices inviting to staff members?

7. *Announce Availability (SEB 17).* Let staff members know when you are available to them. Make it a point to provide unscheduled time during the day for any problems that may emerge.

8. *Rearrange Office (SEB 18).* Arrange your office furniture so the room is comfortable and conducive to communication. For instance, instead of talking across your desk to a staff member, place two comfortable chairs in a corner so the two of you can talk in an informal setting.

9. *Invite Compliments (SEB 19).* Tape up a long piece of butcher paper to the staff room wall. With a marking pen, write a caption that reads: "Write Something Nice to a Colleague." Staff members can jot down comments and compliments to one another on an ongoing "instant message center." Replace the page as needed.

10. *Emphasize the Positive (SEB 20).* Hang up banners, posters, and signs all over the school grounds to highlight the message that positivism is being accentuated.

11. *Behave Consistently (SEB 21).* Make sure that when you give your word you follow through. Keep your promises.

12. *Listen (SEB 22).* When engaged in a conversation with a staff member, deliberately practice the skill of listening. Don't interrupt and don't pass judgment—just listen.

13. *Use Esteem Building Activities (SEB 23).* Educators have successfully used many activities in *Esteem Builders* on themselves in an upgraded version to enhance the feeling of security. Not only are these techniques a fun way for staff members to find out about each other, but they also help build staff esteem. Activities you may wish to try are:

Code	Title	Page
S6	Tool Day	54
S9	Significant Other Sharing	55
S14	Significant Others	56
S17	Time for Friends	60
S18	Name Bingo	60
S19	Name Exchange	61
S20	Personality Trivia	61
S23	Find a Friend	62

14. *Acknowledge Positive Actions (SEB 24).* Encourage staff members to send positive greetings to one another, recognizing each other's special, positive actions. Certificates and grams in *Esteem Builders* that are appropriate for this objective include:

Code	Title	Page
S2/3/4/5	Special Recognition Grams	54
S24	Sparkle Statements	62
S26	Super Sparkle Gram	63
S31/32	Sparkle Line	66
S34	A Special Message to You	67
S35	Add a Compliment	67

A Strong Foundation: Building Security
SUMMARY

A sense of security is prerequisite to all other components of self-esteem; therefore, it is essential that the esteem builder create an environment where such a feeling is paramount. There are three steps the esteem builder can take to increase the sense of security for the staff member:

> **1.** Create a climate of trust.
> **2.** Establish a safe and orderly environment.
> **3.** Establish an open-door communication policy.

Keeper

The most important idea I want to remember about the concept of security is:

_____
_____
_____
_____
_____
_____
_____
_____
_____

One way I will apply this idea to my staff is: _____

_____
_____
_____
_____
_____
_____
_____
_____
_____
_____
_____

ACTION PLAN FOR ENHANCING A SENSE OF SECURITY

Take time to think through your action strategies. What will you personally do to enhance the sense of security for your staff? The importance of this planning cannot be overemphasized.

In an effort to enhance the feeling of security of my staff, I will implement the following ideas and actions:

To create a climate of trust among my staff, I will:

1. _____
_____

2. _____
_____

3. _____
_____

To establish a safe and orderly environment for my staff, I will:

1. _____
_____

2. _____
_____

3. _____
_____

To establish an open-door communication policy for individual staff members, I will:

1. _____
_____

2. _____
_____

3. _____
_____

Date of Commitment: _____

Follow-up Date: _____

Esteem Builders' Complete Program
Jalmar Press, Rolling Hills Estates, CA

NOTES

3

Clarifying the Inner Picture: Building Selfhood

STAFF ESTEEM BUILDERS

- Display Accepting and Caring Behaviors
- Recognize Unique Qualities and Provide Opportunities to Display Individuality
- Recognize Individuals and Make Them Feel Appreciated
- Selfhood Esteem Builders

STAFF SELFHOOD
CONTENTS

Selfhood:

A feeling of individuality and uniqueness; self-knowledge which includes an accurate and realistic self-description in terms of roles, attributes, and physical characteristics.

LOW SELFHOOD INDICATORS

- frequently uses negative statements regarding self and others
- embarrasses easily, oversensitive
- overanxious to please and "do well"
- often complains
- is uncomfortable asking for help
- stresses personal inadequacies over personal adequacies

HIGH SELFHOOD INDICATORS

- says "thank you" to compliments
- congratulates self on job well done
- accepts criticism when needed to improve
- knows who he/she is
- acknowledges weaknesses
- acknowledges strengths
- stresses personal adequacies over inadequacies

STAFF ESTEEM BUILDERS FOR SELFHOOD	PAGE

3

Clarifying the Inner Picture: Building Selfhood

What a man thinks of himself,
that it is which determines
or rather indicates his fate.
—HENRY DAVID THOREAU

Once the feeling of security is firmly established, administrators can actively work at nurturing an environment conducive to the enhancement of selfhood. Selfhood or self-concept is a feeling of individuality. Individuals who possess a high sense of selfhood have a feeling of uniqueness, worthiness or specialness; they generally have an accurate identity. In short, these staff members know who they are. They know their interests, attitudes, and strengths. They also have realistic knowledge of their weaknesses and short-comings, and can accept these weaknesses without belittling themselves. Because they are more accepting of themselves, they are usually more accepting of other staff members. Individuals who perceive themselves as worthwhile and effective educators will act in much more productive ways than teachers who have the opposite opinion of themselves. They generally act in positive ways consistent with the pictures they have acquired about themselves. They are willing to try new programs and ideas, and they are more open to suggestions and feedback.

Staff members who possess a high sense of selfhood know who they are!

LOW AND HIGH SELFHOOD INDICATORS

A staff member with a weak sense of selfhood may be identified by the following behavioral characteristics:

- frequently uses negative statements regarding self and others;

- embarrasses easily, oversensitive to criticism;

- overanxious to please and "do well";

- is uncomfortable with praise: denies, undermines, disregards or becomes embarassed when complimented;

- often complains;

- is uncomfortable asking for help;

- stresses personal inadequacies over adequacies.

On the other hand, a staff member with a strong sense of selfhood may be heard making the following types of statements:

Thank you for that compliment.

I think I did really well with that problem.

I think you have a good point. I'll try to work on improving that.

I am a lot of things. I am a teacher, a coach, an artist, a reader, a skier, a dad, etc.

Some qualities I need to work on are my impatience and lack of organization.

I like the fact that I am responsible and dependable.

List individuals exhibiting behaviors indicating possible *low selfhood.*

_____   _____
_____   _____
_____   _____
_____   _____

List individuals exhibiting behaviors indicating possible *high selfhood.*

_____   _____
_____   _____
_____   _____
_____   _____

ESTEEM BUILDER STEPS TO ENHANCING SELFHOOD

The administrator plays a central role in fostering the development of selfhood. The esteem builder who is working with staff members on selfhood should:

1. **Display accepting and caring behaviors.**
2. **Recognize unique qualities and provide opportunities to display individuality.**
3. **Recognize individuals and make them feel appreciated.**

ESTEEM BUILDER #1

DISPLAY ACCEPTING AND CARING BEHAVIORS

William James, the father of American psychology, stated years ago that 90 percent of what motivates a person is the desire to feel important and be appreciated. Enhancing this feeling is basic to the development of selfhood. All people want to feel valued not only as members of a particular group but also as individuals. Esteem builders must consciously work to create an accepting and caring attitude toward each staff member as an individual. Among the many ways to convey caring are sending a personal note, giving compliments, showing personal interest, taking time to learn about others' lives outside of work, recognizing birthdays, celebrating success and acknowledging setbacks, and listening to concerns and ideas. Such interest, though, must be genuine. Nothing turns off another person more quickly than insincerity. Making efforts to nurture an honest, accepting, caring, personal working environment can be one of the most valuable uses of your time. These efforts send the message: "You are accepted and cared about."

Esteem building must work to create an accepting and caring attitude by always being genuine.

Guideline Questions: Positive and Accepting Work Environment (SEB 25)

The following questions are provided as guidelines for the administrator to help determine if conditions are being fostered to create a positive and accepting working climate.

	Regularly	Seldom	Never
• Do I take time to learn about the personal lives of my staff?	_____	_____	_____
• Do I recognize individual staff member's birthdays?	_____	_____	_____
• Do I send personal notes of congratulations as well as condolences?	_____	_____	_____
• Do I take the time to show concern for staff members experiencing personal crises or illnesses?	_____	_____	_____
• Do I greet all staff members by name?	_____	_____	_____
• Does my behavior convey friendliness and openness?	_____	_____	_____
• Do I keep an ongoing file of personal information such as the names of staff member's spouses and children, etc.?	_____	_____	_____

Reflection:
List ways you display accepting and caring behaviors toward the staff.

_____

_____

_____

_____

Now list one or two additional ways you could show the staff you value them as *individuals* as well as employees.

_____

_____

_____

_____

_____

_____

ESTEEM BUILDER #2

RECOGNIZE UNIQUE QUALITIES AND PROVIDE OPPORTUNITIES TO DISPLAY INDIVIDUALITY

Stanley Coopersmith in his hallmark book, *The Antecedents of Self-Esteem,* describes individuals possessing a strong sense of selfhood as having the feeling of "significance."[1] Individuals with a high level of selfhood accept themselves for who they are with all their uniquenesses. Recognizing the unique qualities of individual staff members and providing opportunities for them to display their individuality at the school site sends a powerful esteem-building message. It says to the individual: "Not only do you like who you are but we do too."

A teacher is first an individual then a member of the school staff.

Keep in mind that the teacher is first an individual who happens to also be a member of a school staff. A staff roster comprised of ninety-five teachers means ninety-five individuals are bringing to that school site their own unique styles and personalities. Acknowledging and celebrating uniquenesses creates a greater feeling of acceptance among the staff, and it validates the notion that no one member is better than anyone else. Each one affirms that they do contribute to the profession and to this school site in uniquely different ways.

To sucessfully foster this perception, esteem builders must consciously be aware of the interests and qualities of each staff member that make him or her unique. Possible ways to achieve this might be to conduct interest surveys among staff members and/or keep ongoing interests cards on file for each individual. Interests and attitudes should be noted as they are discovered. For example, knowledge of each teacher's subject and grade level preferences should be continually monitored. These preferences can be capitalized upon by encouraging teachers to join committees, take part in joint projects, or try cooperative teaching assignments in areas corresponding to stated preferences. Once the staff is aware of one another's interests, information such as upcoming in-services, research or resources can be shared. Knowing what special skills, hobbies, or interests particular staff members possess encourages teachers to seek out one another for help, support, or sharing ideas. Fostering staff individuality and recognizing uniquenesses can become a powerful esteem builder.

---

1. Coopersmith, Stanley. *The Antecedents of Self-Esteem.* San Francisco, CA: W.H. Freeman, 1964

Guideline Questions: Recognition of Unique Staff Qualities (SEB 26)

The following questions are provided as guidelines for the administrator to help determine if conditions are being fostered to recognize individual staff member's unique qualities and provide opportunities to display individuality.

	Regularly	Seldom	Never
• Do I keep abreast of each staff member's interests?	____	____	____
• Do I know the subject and grade level each staff member prefers?	____	____	____
• Do I acknowledge each teacher's uniquenesses?	____	____	____
• Do I provide opportunities for teachers to display their interests and individuality either among the staff or in the classroom with students?	____	____	____
• Do I provide the opportunity for staff members to find out about each other's interests and unique qualities?	____	____	____

Reflection:

Recognizing the unique qualities of individual staff members is a critical esteem-building principle. Use a separate sheet of paper to keep an ongoing list of each staff member's uniquenesses. Next to the name of each staff member write at least one quality that describes his/her individuality. An example is given below:

Recognizing the unique qualities of individual staff members is a critical esteem-building principle.

Name	Unique Quality
Sarah	*Loves to work as a team member.*
John	*Highly artistic.*
Kevin	*Musical! Has recorded children's songs.*
Sue	*Outgoing. A natural "sunshine committee" leader.*

Name	Unique Quality

ESTEEM BUILDER #3

RECOGNIZE INDIVIDUALS AND
MAKE THEM FEEL APPRECIATED

Andrew Carnegie is an individual who few would hesitate to qualify as being successful. At one point, the entrepreneur had more than forty-three millionaires working for him. A reporter, curious as to Carnegie's hiring techniques, asked him pointedly how he was able to employ so many wealthy individuals. Carnegie explained that the men certainly were not millionaires when they were hired. They had, instead, become millionaires by working for him. To the aghast reporter, Carnegie explained his employment philosophy in the following manner:

Nothing seems to increase positive behavior faster than positive recognition.

"When you work with people it is a lot like mining for gold. When you mine for gold you must literally move tons of dirt to find a single ounce of gold. However, you do not look for the dirt. You look for the gold!" Carnegie's technique is well-worth emulating. Nothing seems to increase positive behavior faster than positive recognition. It is a powerful esteem-building technique.

Here are a few points the administrator should keep in mind as he/she "looks for the gold:"

- **Deliberately work at recognizing positive work and behavior (SEB 27).** Try keeping a list of all staff member's names in a conveniently located folder. Each time you observe a staff member demonstrating a positive behavior deserving recognition, quickly jot down the behavior next to the individual's name. When the time is right, tell the person specifically what you saw and why you liked what he or she did or said.

- **Look for the quiet, unsung heroes to recognize and publicize their efforts (SEB 28).** Too often, the same people are recognized and rewarded. Other staff members may be demonstrating behavior that should also be rewarded but they may not be verbalizing their efforts so that others are aware of what they are doing. Consciously look for individuals you may be overlooking. In particular, identify and acknowledge staff members who:

  - can always be counted on but may not publicize their efforts;
  - are rarely absent;
  - spend long, extra hours on projects or working with students;
  - consistently do high quality work;
  - frequently help others;
  - you can always count on;
  - always volunteer to help.

- **Acknowledge complete successes as well as partial successes and attempts (SEB 29).** It seems we always are quick to celebrate and honor individuals who have succeeded. We must also consciously work at recognizing partial successes, or even failed attempts. This is the time colleagues need the most encouragement and support. Consider sending a personal note or seeking them out to let them know that you appreciate their attempts and hope they will try again.

There are many ways to acknowledge staff members' positive behavior, among them:

- Announce a "thank you" to these individuals over the loudspeaker.
- Place a blurb describing their behaviors on a faculty bulletin board.
- Bring lunch or have lunch delivered to them.
- Walk into their classroom and say "thank you" to these teachers in front of their class.
- Provide them with a special parking space for the week.
- Read a story to their class.
- Extend their lunch that day.
- Publicly acknowledge the effort in the principal's bulletin board or newspaper.
- Thank them at a school assembly.
- Thank them at a board meeting.
- Send a letter to the superintendent acknowledging their efforts.
- Place a letter in their cum file acknowledging their efforts.
- Relieve them of yard duty that day.
- Deliver a single carnation to their classroom.
- Send a helium balloon with a positive message attached.
- Leave a personal note in their box.
- Leave a large, conspicuous THANK YOU on their blackboard.
- Give them unlimited front line privileges at the copier that day.
- Relieve them from their classroom so they can visit another room.
- Allow them to go to an in-service of their choice.
- Buy them a children's literature selection for their class library.
- Purchase a special coffee mug at a stationery store for them.
- Make a button describing the deed and give it to them.
- Give them funds to go to lunch with a student.
- Provide them with a gift certificate for a family dinner.

EFFECTIVE PRAISE POINTERS   SEB 30

Staff members with a feeling of low selfhood often have a difficult time accepting praise. To be more effective in praising such individuals, keep in mind the following points:

- **Deserved and Earned.** Staff members are quite perceptive and know if they really earned the praise they received. Be sure that the praise you give is deserved or your statements will seem insincere.

- **Immediate.** The best time to give praise is on the spot. This may sometimes be inconvenient, and if so, wait until the first convenient opportunity arises. If possible, praise as soon as the action is performed.

Individuals with low selfhood often have a difficult time accepting praise.

- **Behavior-Centered.** To begin, limit your praise to specific behaviors instead of positive attributes. Stick to what the individual did. Telling individuals low in selfhood that they are "nice" and "sweet" often does not fit their existing inner self-image; consequently, the praise will be met with disbelief. Relate the praise to a behavior.

- **Individual.** Individuals low in selfhood are often highly threatened by praise. They embarrass easily and may deny the praise in front of a group. Respect their dignity and praise them on an individual basis.

- **Specific.** The most effective praise is very concrete and lets the individual know exactly what was done well. When you observe an effective technique, for instance, don't say "good job;" instead, word your message specifically, like this: "Greg, you did a terrific job in the reading lesson today. You were well-prepared and had everything you needed in front of you. It made the lesson move much smoother and the students stayed with you this time."

GREG, YOU DID A TERRIFIC JOB IN THE READING LESSON TODAY. YOU WERE WELL-PREPARED AND HAD EVERYTHING YOU NEEDED IN FRONT OF YOU. IT MADE THE LESSON MOVE MUCH SMOOTHER AND THE STUDENTS STAYED WITH YOU THIS TIME.

Guideline Questions: Recognition of Positive Staff Behaviors (SEB 31)
The following questions are provided as guidelines for the administrator to help determine if conditions are being fostered that provide staff members with recognition for positive behavior and help them feel appreciated for their efforts.

	Regularly	Seldom	Never
• Do I regularly acknowledge staff members' positive efforts and behavior?	_____	_____	_____
• Do I recognize positive behavior consistently?	_____	_____	_____
• When I recognize individuals, do I tell them specifically what I liked about their behavior?	_____	_____	_____
• Do I consciously attempt to recognize all staff members?	_____	_____	_____
• Do I attempt to praise the individual as soon as convenient?	_____	_____	_____

Reflection:
Take a few moments to review the recognition techniques that are currently in use at your building site. Ask yourself: "How does my staff acquire recognition for positive efforts at the present time?" and "How consistently is recognition being awarded?" Finally, reflect: "Who are the individuals who receive the recognition?" and "Are there other individuals who appear to be forgotten?"

How does my staff acquire recognition for positive efforts at the present time?"

STAFF RECOGNITION REVIEW

How does my staff acquire recognition now?	How can I create more opportunities for staff recognition?

POSITIVE MESSAGES   SEB 32

Many top corporate leaders who are enormously powerful in the corporate world have one trait in common: they write quick daily notes to their staff. Former Ford chairman, Donald Peterson, is just one leader among many who swears by their effectiveness. Peterson was largely credited for turning the corporation around in the 1980's when he began making it a practice to jot down positive messages every day to his workers. The leader explained, "I'd just scribble them on a memo pad or the corner of a letter and pass them along. The most important ten minutes of your day are those you spend doing something to boost the people who work for you." Peterson continued, "Too often people we genuinely like have no idea how we feel about them. Too often we think, I haven't said anything critical; why do I have to say something positive? We forget human beings need positive reinforcement—in fact, we thrive on it!"

Positive messages to your staff should become a common practice.

Positive messages to your staff should become a common practice. Fred Bauer in his article, "The Power of a Note," explains there are four S's of successful note writing. Keep the four S's in mind as you incorporate the method with your staff:

> ### BAUER'S FOUR S'S OF EFFECTIVE MESSAGES
> - SINCERE
> - SHORT
> - SPECIFIC
> - SPONTANEOUS

- SINCERE. The most powerful messages are sincere and come from the heart. Anything less than sincere will be seen as "undeserved recognition" from the recipient. Never undermine their intelligence by trying to give a staff member recognition that is unearned.

- SHORT. Messages don't have to be lengthy to be effective. In this hurried world, time is of the essence. Bauer makes a rule: "If you can't speak your peace in three sentences, you're probably straining."

- SPECIFIC. Individuals benefit when your praise is specific. Be sure to tell them exactly what they did that you appreciated. Specific pointers help staff members know exactly what they can do again next time. Be specific so the behavior will be repeated.

Recognition that is immediate is always the best.

- SPONTANEOUS. Write the message on the spot as it happens. Many managers keep note pads handy in their pocket or purse. Recognition that is immediate is always the best. It's also the easiest![2]

---

2. Bauer, Fred. "The Power of a Note," *Reader's Digest*. December 1991, 72-75.

MESSAGE GRAMS   SEB 33-36

A few samples of positive messages are provided in this manual. Directions for using these message grams with the staff are described below. Consider duplicating a large quantity of the messages so they are readily available. Print shops can have the notes printed up as pads if you desire to make them even more convenient. However you choose to have them printed, use them! Norman Vincent Peale aptly described the purpose of writing inspirational notes when he wrote: "Build others up because there are too many people in the demolition business today!"[3]

Thought You Ought to Know (SEB 33). Run off a supply of notes (form on page 70) on cardstock weight paper. Whenever possible, carry some with you. Use the note cards to write quick messages to staff members who deserve special recognition. The deed should be one that you actually saw yourself. Use the four S's of effective note writing. Be *sincere, short, specific, and spontaneous* in your writing and leave the note in a visible location. "Thank you for taking the time to help Alfred on the playground today. I know it took extra time, but the smile that he had when he left you said it all!" or "I received a special phone call from Mr. Dexter today. He told me the great job you've been doing in reading lab with his son. What a difference you're making." *Suggested by Educator and Trainer, Joseph W. Hoff, New York.*

Just Wanted to Let You Know (SEB 34). Duplicate the form on page 71 on bright-colored paper. At the end of an evaluation or quick classroom walk-through, write a 4S message to the teacher. Tell him/her one thing you observed that was particularly successful and leave it on the teacher's desk. *Suggested by Dr. Steve Mahoney, Principal of Landau Elementary School, Palm Springs Unified School District.*

From the Principal's Desk (SEB 35). Keep a plentiful supply of the form on page 72 duplicated on bright-colored paper. Quickly jot down a note of appreciation to a staff member and leave it in their box.

Certificate of Appreciation (SEB 36). Duplicate the form on page 73 on parchment or colored paper. Present the form to a staff member who deserves special praise or recognition. You may wish to present the certificate to the recipient during a faculty gathering to give this person public recognition.

---

3. Bauer, Fred. "The Power of a Note," *Reader's Digest*. December 1991, 72-75.

SELFHOOD ESTEEM BUILDERS   SEB 37-64

---

1. *Balloon Pop (SEB 37)*. Hand every staff member at a gathering a blown-up balloon. (Inside each balloon, prior to blowing it up, insert a small slip of paper with the name of a different staff member.) Each person takes the balloon, pops it, and locates the name slip of a staff member. Emphasize the names should remain anonymous. Each staff member is now to watch for positive actions from that person. At the next faculty meeting, "secret spies" report their findings to the group.

2. *Good Egg Award (SEB 38)*. Purchase a large papier-mâché egg and choose one deserving staff member to become the egg's recipient ("Good Egg of the Week"). Write a message on a strip of paper describing what the recipient did to deserve the award and present it to the honoree. Each week pass it on to a new recipient.

3. *Terrific Teacher Notes (SEB 39)*. Cheryl Petermann, principal of Schallenberger School in San Jose, California, writes Terrific Teacher Notes for her staff. The bulletin, which is distributed among the staff, consists of short blurbs about activities and successes each staff member is having with his/her students.

4. *Teacher of the Week (SEB 40)*. Create a Teacher of the Week Board. Each week highlight a different staff member on a bulletin board display. The individual being recognized brings in photographs, articles, objects and short "blurbs" that describe his/her interests, hobbies, background, and family.

5. *Me Poster (SEB 41)*. Each staff member designs a Me Poster on a 24" x 28" piece of posterboard. This could also become a staff project, or students could design the poster about their teacher. The poster should include information about the person's interests, hobbies, strengths, background, and family life. Hang up finished posters to decorate the staff room.

6. *Special Events Recognition (SEB 42)*. Recognize special events in the life of each staff member (birthdays, special vacations, weddings, anniversaries).

7. *Cake Bake (SEB 43)*. Designate a staff member, parent, or cook to bake a cake for each staff member's birthday.

8. *Treats for Celebrations (SEB 44)*. Periodically place an inexpensive treat in each staff member's box with a note attached to let them know they're appreciated. These are some treat suggestions:

   - package of Lifesavers: "You've been a lifesaver."
   - Fifth Avenue candy bar: "You're the tops."
   - Three Musketeers bar: "We're all for one and one for all."
   - Payday candy bar: "You don't need to wait for payday to know you're worth your weight in gold."

- Hershey's Kiss: "Thanks!"
- Mr. Goodbar candy bar: "Thanks for the good work."
- Long-stemmed carnation: "Your sweet nature has a powerful effect."

9. *Special Lunches (SEB 45).* Randomly select a staff member and take him/her out to lunch.

10. *Personal Notes (SEB 46).* Take time to write personal notes of encouragement and appreciation. Let staff members know exactly what it is you appreciate about them.

11. *Bombardment (SEB 47).* Use the activity of "bombardment" at a faculty meeting. Staff members verbally express what they appreciate about others on the staff.

12. *Note of Appreciation (SEB 48).* Always keep with you a supply of personal notes with your name printed on them. After any walk-through, leave a brief note of appreciation to the staff member. State one thing you saw that was positive.

13. *Ice Cream Social. (SEB 49).* Hold an after-school ice cream social.

14. *Appreciation Grams (SEB 50).* Provide an ample supply of Appreciation Grams found on page 169. Stock them along with pens by staff members' boxes. Place a sign nearby that reads, "Write a Note to a Staff Member," and encourage individuals to thank, congratulate, or acknowledge one another on a regular basis.

15. *Yard Duty (SEB 51).* As a special treat to recognize a teacher, take over the teacher's yard duty.

16. *April Fool's Exchange (SEB 52).* Just for fun, on April Fool's Day, have teachers change places with each other for several hours or for the whole day. Students love it.

17. *Hats Off Award (SEB 53).* Find an old hat and designate it for the Hats Off Award. At each faculty meeting, recognize a staff member for a specific positive deed, explain the deed to all at the meeting, and hand the person the hat. They are to keep the hat until the next meeting when the award is presented to another colleague.

18. *Teacher for the Day (SEB 54).* Take over a teacher's class to provide a relief period or to give special recognition.

19. *Open Praise (SEB 55).* Thank a teacher for specific efforts in front of his or her class.

20. *Staff Member of the Week (SEB 56).* Have the Staff Member of the Week (a randomly chosen individual) share what he/she is doing in his/her classroom at a faculty meeting.

21. *Thank You Balloon (SEB 57).* Attach a balloon (with the words "thank you" written in black marking pen) to a staff member's chair.

22. *Blackboard Message (SEB 58)*. Write positive comments to a staff member on the blackboard in his/her classroom before the teacher arrives.

23. *Intercom Announcement (SEB 59)*. Announce over the intercom appreciation or recognition of a staff member for a special effort or a job well done.

24. *Guess Who? (SEB 60)*. Prior to a faculty meeting, write on a blackboard "Guess Who?" followed by the special effort or deed the individual did. At the end of the meeting, announce who the "Guess Who?" individual is.

25. *Carnations (SEB 61)*. Buy a carnation for each staff member on back to school night.

26. *Special Parking (SEB 62)*. Set aside a special parking place marked "For a Great Person," and each day select a different individual to use the space. Be sure to let the individual know why they were selected.

27. *Use Esteem Builder Activities (SEB 63)*. There are many activities designed for students that can easily (and successfully) be adapted for adults. Activities from *Esteem Builders* that staff members can do as a staff to enhance the feeling of self-hood include:

Code	Title	Page
SH2	Me Riddle	102
SH3	A Self-Portrait	102
SH17	Who Am I?	108
SH18	My Identity Shield	109
SH20	Playing Favorites	110
SH21	Wanted Poster	110
SH23	My Interests and Hobbies	110

28. *Personal Interest Survey (SEB 64)*. This form on page 74 is designed to help the administrator keep abreast on personal as well as professional information regarding each staff member. Duplicate copies for staff members and ask them to complete and return it to you. After reviewing the information on the forms, you might wish to comment on a few particular facts by sending a personal memo to each staff member. "I didn't realize how many different grade levels you've taught!" or "You'll be a great asset to our staff" or "I noticed you have an interest and expertise in astronomy. I hope we can capitalize on your skills at a faculty meeting some-time." Store the survey in each member's personnel file.

Clarifying the Inner Picture
SUMMARY

A sense of selfhood is the second feeling individuals with high self-esteem possess. Such individuals generally have a strong sense of identity and acceptance of self. The esteem builder can enhance the feeling of selfhood by consciously fostering conditions to build the following three steps:

> **High selfhood individuals** have a strong sense of identity and acceptance of self.

1. Display accepting and caring behaviors.
2. Recognize unique qualities and provide opportunities to display individuality.
3. Recognize individuals and make them feel appreciated.

Keeper

The most important idea I want to remember about the concept of selfhood is:

_____

_____

_____

_____

_____

_____

_____

_____

_____

_____

One way I will apply this idea to my staff is: _____

_____

_____

_____

_____

_____

_____

_____

_____

_____

THOUGHT YOU OUGHT TO KNOW

YOU GOT CAUGHT DOING THE **NEATEST** THING...

AND I KNOW BECAUSE I WAS THERE !

Esteem Builders' Complete Program
Jalmar Press, Rolling Hills Estates, CA

I JUST WANTED TO LET YOU KNOW THAT YOU WERE DOING A FANTASTIC JOB WHEN I WAS IN YOUR CLASS TODAY.

Esteem Builders' Complete Program
Jalmar Press, Rolling Hills Estates, CA

Esteem Builders' Complete Program
Jalmar Press, Rolling Hills Estates, CA

ESTEEM BUILDERS
COMPLETE PROGRAM

Certificate of Appreciation

Presented to

in recognition of

Date

Esteem Builders' Complete Program
Jalmar Press, Rolling Hills Estates, CA

PERSONAL INTEREST SURVEY

Name: _____

Address: _____

Phone: _____ Birthday: _____

Family Information

Marital Status: _____ Anniversary: _____

Spouse's/Significant Other's Name: _____

Occupation: _____

Children's Names and Ages: _____

_____

Pets: _____

Education

Colleges Attended: _____

_____

Majors/Degrees: _____

_____

Background

State Born in: _____

Interesting Personal Fact You Want Us to Know: _____

_____

_____

Interests and Hobbies

Favorite Color: _____

Things I Like to Collect: _____

Favorite Snack Foods: _____

Favorite Things I Like to Do: _____

_____

_____

Travel Experiences: _____

_____

Teaching Experience

Grades and Subjects Taught: _____

Favorite Grade Level: _____

Favorite Subject: _____

A Successful Lesson You Could Share with Us Is: _____

_____

In-services and Staff Development Training: _____

_____

Esteem Builders' Complete Program
Jalmar Press, Rolling Hills Estates, CA

ACTION PLAN FOR ENHANCING A SENSE OF SELFHOOD

Take time to think through your action strategies. What will you personally do to enhance the sense of identity for your staff? The importance of this planning cannot be overemphasized.

In an effort to enhance the feeling of selfhood of my staff, I will implement the following ideas and actions:

To display behaviors that are accepting and caring to my staff, I will:

1. _____
   _____

2. _____
   _____

3. _____
   _____

To recognize unique qualities and provide opportunities to display individuality among staff members, I will:

1. _____
   _____

2. _____
   _____

3. _____
   _____

To recognize individual staff members and make them feel appreciated, I will:

1. _____
   _____

2. _____
   _____

3. _____
   _____

Date of Commitment: _____

Follow-up Date: _____

Esteem Builders' Complete Program
Jalmar Press, Rolling Hills Estates, CA

NOTES

4

A Cooperative Spirit: Building Affiliation

STAFF ESTEEM BUILDERS

- Build Staff Cohesiveness and Affiliation
- Foster a Sense of School and Professional Pride
- Promote Team Building Collaboration and Peer Support
- Affiliation Esteem Builders

STAFF AFFILIATION
CONTENTS

Affiliation:

A feeling of belonging, acceptance, or relatedness, particularly in relationships that are considered important; feeling approved of, appreciated, and respected by others.

LOW AFFILIATION INDICATORS

- withdraws or isolates self from the staff, appears lonely
- seldom shares materials or helps others
- is uncomfortable working in groups
- dictates, dominates or bullies others
- feels others don't value him/her
- ridicules or rejects others
- lacks a feeling of school pride or cohesiveness

HIGH AFFILIATION INDICATORS

- develops good relationships with colleagues
- sets aside time to be with people considered important
- has family and friends who care about the individual
- is sought out by others in friendships
- enjoys working as part of a team
- likes being with people
- is sensitive to others

4

A Cooperative Spirit: Building Affiliation

*Friendship is the result of our efforts
to be interested in what's
going on in people's lives.*
—DALE CARNEGIE

A recent survey of educators in *Learning Magazine* (April 1987) cited "teacher isolation" as a major concern of those polled. A Phi Delta Kappan article voiced a similar opinion, stating that "the school reform movement will fail unless we solve the problem of teacher isolation." Peter Pillsbury, principal of Yuba Feather School in California, calls the teacher isolation issue the "castle and moat" problem. Teachers, Pillsbury feels, too often live in their own kingdom protected from intrusion by other teachers and the principal. They are practicing the castle and moat theory. The classroom, Pillsbury states, is their castle enclosed by imaginary but impenetrable walls, and surrounded by a moat with no drawbridge.

Indeed, staff isolation is a growing and perplexing school issue. It is particularly threatening to the issue of esteem enhancement. A universal need of human beings is to connect and bond with others. The third critical condition for esteem building is to create a sense of affiliation and belonging. Yet, so much of the school's framework defeats this goal. Consider a few of the following factors in schools which are defeating to human connectedness: four walls separate the teacher from the rest of the staff; staff lounges are too often crowded and uninviting; schedules are not conducive to the staff gathering at the same time; and layouts usually feature long corridors with staff members miles from one another. All too frequently, the only opportunities for staff bonding are quick thirty-second parking lot chats or ten-minute breaks in cluttered staff lounges. The sense of belonging is an essential element of high self-esteem. Teachers need to feel they belong to a community of professional individuals who care about each other.

A universal need of human beings is to connect and bond with others.

LOW AND HIGH AFFILIATION INDICATORS

Staff members who have a weak sense of affiliation may be identified by the following behavioral characteristics:

- withdraws or isolates self from the staff, may appear to be lonely;

- seldom shares materials with or helps others;

- is uncomfortable working in group activities which may result in behaviors such as: withdrawal, reticence, nervousness, isolating self from group, complaining, monopolizing or domineering;

- dictates, dominates, or bullies others;

- feels that others don't value him/her;

- ridicules or rejects others, is insensitive to their emotions and needs;

- lacks a feeling of school pride or cohesiveness;

- has few friends, tends to associate with only one or two other staff members.

On the other hand, a staff member with strong affiliation may be heard making the following types of statements:

It is important to me that I have good relationships with my co-workers.

I make sure to set aside time to be with people who are important to me.

My friends and family care about me.

People seek me out in friendships.

I enjoy working as part of a team.

I like being with people.

It is important to be sensitive to others.

List individuals exhibiting behaviors indicating possible *high affiliation:*

_____   _____
_____   _____
_____   _____
_____   _____
_____   _____

List individuals exhibiting behaviors indicating possible *low affiliation*:

_____   _____
_____   _____
_____   _____
_____   _____
_____   _____

ESTEEM BUILDER STEPS TO ENHANCING AFFILIATION

Administrators can help foster the conditions necessary for enhancing the feeling of affiliation or connectedness by addressing the following esteem-builder steps:

1. **Build staff cohesiveness and affiliation.**
2. **Foster a sense of school and professional pride.**
3. **Promote team-building collaboration and peer support.**

ESTEEM BUILDER #1

BUILD STAFF COHESIVENESS AND AFFILIATION

The first step in fostering a feeling of affiliation is for the esteem builder to promote belonging and acceptance within the group. These feelings do not emerge overnight, but instead take time to evolve. Frequent opportunities for staff members to find out about each other on a personal level are essential. There are many ways to create these moments. Outside-of-school staff gatherings such as wine and cheese parties, Friday-before-school coffee and donut gatherings, potluck dinners at a staff member's home, after-school exercise walks or after-school coffee and dessert parties are just a few ideas. Such functions help staff members feel more comfortable with each other.

The first step is to promote belonging and acceptance within the group.

Allowing teachers to observe in each other's rooms or rotating faculty meetings among individual classrooms helps staff members learn about one another's professional teaching styles. Taking time during staff meetings for teachers to share personal experiences, successes, and frustrations builds personal connectedness. Planning staff events that are purely fun, such as holiday parties and staff retreats, creates fond memories. The planning is worth the effort because over time a sense of staff cohesiveness evolves. When staff members know each other on a personal level, they are more willing to show concern and acceptance towards each other. An openness to share ideas and work together is more apparent. A human bond forms and the staff literally begins to stick together on both a professional and personal basis. Individuals show a greater willingness to work for the "good of the school as a whole" instead of focusing totally on the individual classroom. A "turned-on" team emerges.

Guideline Questions: Group Belonging (SEB 65)

The following questions are provided as guidelines for the administrator to help determine if conditions are being fostered to promote belonging and acceptance within the group.

	Regularly	Seldom	Never
• Are outside-of-school activities planned at least once a month?	_____	_____	_____
• Do staff members have the opportunity to visit one another's classrooms?	_____	_____	_____
• Are opportunities planned for staff members to share personal experiences, successes, and frustrations?	_____	_____	_____
• Are opportunities planned for staff members to share teaching ideas and strategies?	_____	_____	_____
• Is the staff lounge conducive to staff comfort and communication?	_____	_____	_____
• Is staff cooperation stressed instead of competition?	_____	_____	_____
• Do staff members feel safe to be themselves?	_____	_____	_____
• Are special efforts made to help new staff members feel a sense of belonging?	_____	_____	_____

Reflection:

Reflect upon ways the school site builds affiliation for staff members. On the left side of the T-bar below, write down the kinds of opportunities to enhance staff affiliation that already exist. List each method individually (i.e. Sunshine Committee, After-School Walk-A-Thons, Yearly Retreat, Holiday Dinner, etc.). On the right side of the paper list other methods that might be implemented at the school site to enhance the feeling of staff belonging.

STAFF AFFILIATION BUILDERS

Ways my staff can enhance their affiliation with each other now.	Ways we can create opportunities for a greater sense of staff belonging.

===== **ESTEEM BUILDER #2** =====

FOSTER A SENSE OF SCHOOL AND PROFESSIONAL PRIDE

Once a feeling of belonging and acceptance has been promoted among individual staff members, the next step is to foster a sense of school and professional pride. Such pride helps individuals feel they are part of a cohesive team, thus increasing the sense of affiliation. The image that results can best be described as the "Three Musketeer Effect" or "It's all for one and one for all." Tom Peters in his best selling book, *In Search of Excellence,* points out the critical impact group pride can have on staff effectiveness when he says, "The difference between a turned-on team is not 2%, 5%, or 10%, but 5000%!"

Pride helps individuals feel they are part of a cohesive team.

Esteem builders can contribute to the development of organizational pride by helping staff members feel good about what they do. School accomplishments can be publicized in newsletters and the community newspaper. Activities of the school as a whole, such as plays, assemblies, and special programs, can be photographed or videotaped to be shown at a later time to parents or members of the community. Special school-wide efforts by staff members should be credited and recognized with plaques, gifts, personal "thank you" notes, pins, certificates or flowers.

Finally, seek out ways to display school pride and cohesiveness. The school name, colors, mascot, and mission statement can be printed on an endless variety of apparel, such as pins, visors, shirts, hats and even socks. Each staff member can wear the item on a designated Spirit Day or to any school event. The creative ways in which staff members can build and display school pride are endless. Such efforts help create what Tom Peters referred to as a "turned-on team."

Guideline Questions: School and Professional Pride (SEB 66)

The following questions are provided as guidelines for the administrator to help determine if conditions are being fostered to build a sense of school and professional pride.

	Regularly	Seldom	Never
• Are school achievements publicized in school newsletters or community newspapers?	_____	_____	_____
• Are individuals who contribute to school-wide efforts regularly recognized?	_____	_____	_____
• Are school-wide events photographed or videotaped?	_____	_____	_____
• Are opportunities provided for parents and community members to view the videotapes or photographs of school-wide events?	_____	_____	_____
• Are days set aside for staff members to display school pride, such as by wearing school colors, pins, or other apparel?	_____	_____	_____
• Do I take the time to let the staff know of their school's accomplishments?	_____	_____	_____

Reflection:

List ways you have helped the staff foster a sense of school and professional pride.

_____

_____

_____

_____

_____

_____

_____

_____

What one main idea to enhance the staff's sense of school and professional pride would you like to try?

_____

_____

_____

_____

_____

_____

_____

_____

_____

ESTEEM BUILDER #3

PROMOTE TEAM BUILDING COLLABORATION AND PEER SUPPORT

Efforts from the previous steps to foster staff affiliation and school pride begin to pay off. The staff now works more closely together as a cooperative team. Individuals are generally more accepting and open toward one another. The feeling of staff cohesiveness has helped individuals feel less threatened by one other. A greater willingness to share materials and ideas is demonstrated. Cooperative efforts toward accomplishing school or grade-level goals are more plausible. Organizational efficiency and productivity are ripening, particularly when the esteem builder works to promote team-building concepts and peer support. All of these efforts are helping to develop a feeling of collaboration among team members.

Any team efforts demonstrating peer support, collaboration, and idea sharing should be recognized.

The next step is to promote team-building activities such as grade-level meetings, committees, team teaching, or class exchanges. For these activities to work, the administrator must be highly accessible during the beginning stages to offer support. Staff members should be encouraged to observe other's classrooms. Any team efforts demonstrating peer support, collaboration, and idea sharing should be recognized. Some staffs may be ready to take part in peer coaching. The goal of having staff members work together in a collaborative, supportive manner is closer to its target.

Guideline Questions: Team Building and Peer Support (SEB 67)

The following questions are provided as guidelines for the administrator to help determine if conditions are being fostered to promote team-building collaboration and peer support.

	Regularly	Seldom	Never
• Are opportunities provided for individual staff members to observe each other's classrooms?	_____	_____	_____
• Do teachers have the opportunity to meet with others on the same grade level?	_____	_____	_____
• Are concepts such as team teaching or cooperative teaching encouraged?	_____	_____	_____
• Are opportunities for sharing ideas provided?			
• Is a designated location provided for teachers to exchange ideas?	_____	_____	_____
• Do I recognize efforts demonstrating team collaboration and support?	_____	_____	_____

Reflection:

Think of your past efforts to promote team-building collaboration and peer support. List one or two activities which most successfully enhanced staff affiliation. When did the activity last take place? Is it time to try the activity again?

_____
_____
_____
_____
_____

AFFILIATION ESTEEM BUILDERS   SEB 68-96

1. *Sunshine Committee (SEB 68)*. Establish a Sunshine Committee of staff members who are responsible for organizing "fun" staff gatherings (brunches, after-school get-togethers, potlucks, athletic activities, etc.) and acknowledging special occasions for individuals (birthdays, weddings, sympathy) with cards.

2. *Welcome Committee (SEB 69)*. Create a Welcome Committee to recognize new staff members and make them feel comfortable and accepted.

3. *Staff Retreat (SEB 70)*. Plan a staff retreat away from the building site for staff planning and communicating.

4. *Athletic Leagues (SEB 71).* Form "leagues" (bowling, volleyball, softball, skiing, etc.) in which staff members can play together in organized athletic activities.

5. *Secret Pals (SEB 72).* Invite staff members to pull the name of another staff member to be their "secret pal." For the duration of the activity, the name puller periodically does secret deeds for the staff member. These could include: purchasing inexpensive gifts, putting flowers or apples on their desk, providing classroom ideas or writing notes of acknowledgment. The activity may last for any length of time (usually no more than one month, though). Pals try to keep their identity secret for as long as possible.

6. *Message Center (SEB 73).* Create a Message Center. Glue library book pockets onto butcher paper. Write the name of each staff member on the cover of the pocket. Encourage staff members to write notes of acknowledgment to one another.

7. *Idea Exchange (SEB 74).* Create an Idea Exchange bulletin board. Encourage teachers to pin up descriptions or samples of successful ideas that have worked for them.

8. *Lunch Bunch Group (SEB 75).* Create a Lunch Bunch Group. Periodically, lengthen the lunch recess so that staff members can go out to lunch with each other.

9. *Classroom Visitations (SEB 76).* Encourage staff members to visit one another's classrooms. Offer to cover a teacher's room so they can have this opportunity.

10. *School Apparel (SEB 77).* Enhance school pride among staff members. Encourage staff members to wear school colors on a certain day of the week. Special apparel (hats, shirts, socks, visors) with the school emblem, mascot, and colors may also be purchased for staff members to wear as a group.

11. *Brainstorming Sessions (SEB 78).* At a faculty meeting, ask staff members to brainstorm in small groups the question: "What do you need to enhance your self-esteem?" Remind groups about the rules of brainstorming (no judgments allowed, all ideas count, write everything down). At the end of five minutes, ask groups to cross out items that are "unreasonable" or that "they really have no power over" and to choose one item that they could develop a plan for. Ask each group to now develop a specific plan to enhance the staff's esteem that they could implement at the school site. The plan should be written on chart paper and shared with other groups at the end of the session.

12. *Meet in Classrooms (SEB 79).* Consider holding faculty meetings in staff member's classrooms.

13. *Resource Pool (SEB 80).* Arrange for a Grade Level Resource Pool containing supplies and extra dittos. Whenever a teacher changes grade levels, they can go to the resource pool and instantly select available materials.

14. *Photo Board (SEB 81)*. Create a staff photo board capturing pictures of staff members alone or with students. The photo board could also be adapted to become a scrapbook.

15. *Cooperative Structures (SEB 82)*. Provide opportunities for staff members to work together. Assign tasks during faculty meetings that involve cooperative learning structures.

16. *Loner Recognition (SEB 83)*. Find ways to provide positive recognition for staff members who isolate themselves from others.

17. *Mentors (SEB 84)*. Appoint a staff member for each new colleague to serve as a mentor or support person.

18. *Appreciation Cards (SEB 85)*. Have an ample supply of cards printed with statements such as: "I appreciate what you did today. You…" or "I just wanted you to know I appreciated what you did for me. You…" Encourage staff members to use them in recognizing the support of their colleagues.

19. *Team Spirit (SEB 86)*. Create opportunities during staff gatherings for members to work together to discover their commonalities. Staff members working in teams could create a name or a symbol for their group.

20. *Lounge Lift (SEB 87)*. Spruce up the faculty lounge so it is a more comfortable, inviting space.

21. *Preference Survey (SEB 88)*. Survey staff members to find out the kinds of items or changes (if any) they would like to have in their faculty lounge to create a more inviting place.

22. *Activities Survey (SEB 89)*. Survey staff members to find out the kinds of activities they would like to do with one another.

23. *Refreshments (SEB 90)*. Provide snacks and drinks at faculty meetings.

24. *Open Dialogue (SEB 91)*. Allow opportunities for staff members to share personal experiences and frustrations at faculty meetings.

25. *Team Builders (SEB 92)*. Recognize (both verbally and in writing) staff members who are team builders. Commend their actions at faculty meetings.

26. *Publicity (SEB 93)*. Publicize school-wide events in newsletters, newspapers, and videotapings.

27. *Grade Level Interaction (SEB 94)*. Provide faculty members with the opportunity to meet regularly with others teaching the same grade level. Periodically, allow faculty members to meet with other grade levels to discuss different points of view.

28. *Idea Exchange (SEB 95)*. Designate locations where teachers can exchange ideas.

29. *Esteem Builder Activities (SEB 96)*. There are many activities designed for students that can easily (and successfully) be adapted for adults. Activities from *Esteem Builders* that staff members can do together to enhance the feeling of affiliation include:

Code	Title	Page
A2	Common Points	166
A3	Getting to Know You Wheel	166
A4	Paired Name Collage	167
A9	Mystery Person	170
A10	Friendly Riddles	171
A38	Compliment Hanging	186

A Cooperative Spirit: Building Affiliation
SUMMARY

A sense of affiliation is the third feeling individuals with high self-esteem possess. Such individuals generally have a strong feeling of belonging, acceptance, or relatedness. There are three steps the esteem builder can take to increase staff affiliation:

> **1.** Build staff cohesiveness and affiliation.
> **2.** Foster a sense of school and professional pride.
> **3.** Promote team-building collaboration and peer support.

Keeper

The most important idea I want to remember about the concept of affiliation is:

_____
_____
_____
_____
_____
_____
_____
_____
_____
_____

One way I will apply this idea to my staff is: _____

_____
_____
_____
_____
_____
_____
_____
_____
_____

ACTION PLAN FOR ENHANCING A SENSE OF AFFILIATION

Take time to think through your action strategies. What will you personally do to enhance the sense of affiliation for your staff? The importance of this planning cannot be overemphasized.

In an effort to enhance the feeling of affiliation of my staff, I will implement the following ideas and actions:

To build staff cohesiveness and affiliation, I will:

1. _____
   _____

2. _____
   _____

3. _____
   _____

To foster a sense of school and professional pride among staff members, I will:

1. _____
   _____

2. _____
   _____

3. _____
   _____

To promote team building collaboration and peer support among my staff, I will:

1. _____
   _____

2. _____
   _____

3. _____
   _____

Date of Commitment: _____

Follow-up Date: _____

Esteem Builders' Complete Program
Jalmar Press, Rolling Hills Estates, CA

5

Purpose With Responsibility: Building Mission

STAFF ESTEEM BUILDERS

- Develop the Major Focus or Mission of the School
- Provide Opportunities for Joint Decision-Making and Shared Responsibility
- Encourage Personal and Professional Goal-Setting
- Mission Esteem Builders

STAFF MISSION
CONTENTS

Mission:

A feeling of purpose and motivation in life; self-empowerment through setting realistic and achievable goals and being willing to take responsibility for the consequences of one's decisions.

LOW MISSION INDICATORS	HIGH MISSION INDICATORS
• lacks motivation and initiative • feels powerless • appears aimless, without direction • sets unrealistic goals • is overly dependent on authority for direction, encouragement • avoids taking responsibility for own actions, blames others	• sets goals and strives for them • willing to try something new • accepts consequences for actions • able to make decisions • feels confident in ability to work through problems

5

Purpose with Responsibility: Building Mission

*People with goals succeed
because they know where they are going.*
—EARL NIGHTINGALE

Staff members with high self-esteem generally feel self-motivated and have a clear sense of direction. Such individuals usually succeed in life because they have in mind specific aims or intentions of what they want to achieve. In other words, they have a heightened sense of mission. They have taken the time to think about what they want to be and where they want to go. Moreover, they are able to take the necessary actions to accomplish their aim and thus become "achievers." This, in turn, enhances self-esteem. When each additional attempt is met with further success, it provides fresh ammunition to aim for other goals. These individuals' self-image as "achievers" is almost a guaranteed outcome. And so the spiral toward higher self-esteem continues. Past performances build the confidence needed to make fresh attempts and take risks. And why not? The risk is worth the gamble because higher self-esteem is the outcome.

An esteem-building school is effective because its staff members possess this feeling of mission.

An esteem-building school is effective because its staff members possess this feeling of mission. The school's strengths and weaknesses are accepted and identified. An awareness of what the school needs becomes the thrust and focus for the school year and is developed into a school-mission statement. Throughout this process, the administrator helps the staff become clear about the mission of the school and creates an atmosphere where shared decision-making is paramount. All "constituents" discuss the school's goals so that everyone has a common mission. As a result, the staff knows where they want to go and what they want to achieve.

Goals become "ours," not "yours."

Since members have shared in the process of formulating grade level and school goals, they are more committed to attaining them. Goals become "ours," not "yours." Individuals work together to achieve the group's goals, and generally, they are successful in reaching these goals because they know what is expected of them. If a problem arises, members recognize that it is a communal problem which requires cooperative decision-making. The school is committed to knowing where they are headed and working together to get there.

LOW AND HIGH MISSION INDICATORS

A staff member with a weak sense of mission can be recognized by the following behavior patterns:

- lacks motivation and initiative;

- feels powerless;

- appears aimless, without direction;

- sets unrealistic goals (goals are either too high, too low, or nonexistent);

- is overly dependent on authority figures for direction, encouragement, and decision-making;

- avoids taking responsibility for his/her own actions: blames others, denies or inveigles others to do his/her work;

- seldom involved in self or professional growth;

- rarely attempts anything new.

All these behaviors greatly diminish teacher effectiveness. On the other hand, a staff member with a strong sense of mission may be heard making the following types of statements:

I've decided to pursue my Master's Degree.

I've never applied for a grant before, but I'm familiar with the process and I'm going to try it.

Trying new things can be risky, but I'm willing to accept the consequences for my actions.

Making decisions is not difficult for me.

I've had success in the past in working with this person in my building. I know what I need to do to work through this current problem.

List individuals exhibiting behaviors indicating possible *low mission*.	
_____	_____
_____	_____
_____	_____
_____	_____
_____	_____

List individuals exhibiting behaviors indicating possible *high mission*.	
_____	_____
_____	_____
_____	_____
_____	_____
_____	_____

ESTEEM BUILDERS STEPS TO ENHANCING MISSION

Esteem builders can enhance the feeling of mission by taking the following three steps:

1. **Develop the major focus or mission of the school.**
2. **Provide opportunities for joint decision-making and shared responsibility.**
3. **Encourage personal and professional goal setting.**

ESTEEM BUILDER #1

DEVELOP THE MAJOR FOCUS OR MISSION OF THE SCHOOL

*"The best way to predict the
future is to invent it."*
—ALAN KAY

One of the common denominators in effective, esteem-enhancing environments is that they have a clear, established mission or purpose. By establishing a primary focus or collective mission for the school site, all staff members recognize what they should focus their major efforts on. The staff can make major differences for their students since their efforts are directed jointly. Collective efforts have a much stronger impact than singular work.

Collective efforts have a much stronger impact than singular work.

Research verifies the need for establishing a major focus or mission at the school site.

One of the common denominators in effective, esteem-enhancing environments is that they have a clear, established mission or purpose. By establishing a primary focus or collective mission for the school site, all staff members recognize what they should focus their major efforts on. The staff can make major differences for their students since their efforts are directed jointly. Collective efforts have a much stronger impact than singular work.

Research verifies the need for establishing a major focus or mission at the school site. Studies supporting the development of a major school mission include:

- "Effective schools require a sense of purpose and direction provided by well-developed and clearly articulated goals. To be successful in managing the goal-setting process and achieving consensus and commitment among staff, a principal first must have a comprehensive understanding of the school and all of its interacting parts and a clear vision of how the school will operate at some specific future point. This vision, based on values that are publicly articulated, leads, in turn, to clear and specific school objectives that guide day-to-day activities." (Manasse, A.L. "Effective Principals: Effective at What?" *Principal,* 1982, vol. 61, no. 4, 10-15.)

- "What is really essential is clarity and broad commitment regarding the purposes, 'mission' and goals, which should guide curriculum decisions and development." (*Excellence in Our Schools: Making It Happen.* Joint Publication of the American Association of School Administrators and the Far West Laboratory, 1984.)

- "Every excellent company we studied is clear on what it stands for and takes the process of value shaping seriously. In fact, we wonder whether it is possible to be an excellent company without clarity of values and having the right sorts of values." (Peters, Thomas and Waterman, Robert H. *In Search of Excellence: Lessons from America's Best-Run Companies.* New York: Warner Books, 1982.)

- "We believe the first ingredient in re-inventing the corporation is a powerful vision—a whole new sense of where a company is going and how to get there. The company's vision becomes a catalytic force, an organizing principle of everything that the people in the corporation do." (Naisbitt, John and Aburdene, Patricia. *Re-inventing the Corporation: Your Company for the New Information Society.* New York: Warner Books, 1985.)

The creation of a central mission or focus for an organization is essential to esteem building. Each sequential step in the process toward achieving a collective directional focus is critical. Each step clarifies the next step until the final direction is fine-tuned. Like the proverbial snowball rolling down a hill, collective efforts increase in size and rapidly gain momentum as each new enlargement builds on the one before.

DEVELOPING THE ORGANIZATION'S MISSION
1. Create personal vision.
2. Identify individual belief systems.
3. Develop shared vision.
4. Establish a mission statement.
5. Accentuate your mission.

1. Create a personal vision.

The process of developing a focused mission for an organization begins with the esteem builder creating personal vision. We all have dreams and fantasies. High achievers are those individuals who create reality out of those dreams. They begin with a firm sense of what is important to them. To be effective, the leader must know exactly what the end product looks like and what must be done to achieve it. But first he or she must clarify his or her own personal vision. Once this vision is in place, the administrator can then, and only then, help the staff stay focused on attaining the school's overall mission.

> **To be effective, the leader must know exactly what the end product looks like and what must be done to achieve it.**

PERSONAL CLARIFICATION ACTIVITY   SEB 97

Purpose: To clarify the administrator's personal vision for the school.

Materials: Sheet of paper; 3" x 5" card.

Procedure: At the top of a blank piece of paper, write one of the following questions, or another expressing a similar idea:

"What do I as an educator believe in?" or *"To create the most effective learning institution, what do I believe is most important?"*

Now take a few minutes to brainstorm. Answer the question by writing down as many ideas as you can think of that represent *your beliefs*. Remember, there are no right or wrong answers... everything counts. Write down everything that comes to mind. Continue writing until you've exhausted your thoughts.

Next, look over your ideas. Ask yourself, "Which idea(s) is the most important to me? Which do I really care about the most?" Begin crossing out ideas that are *not your most important belief statements*. This process may take a few minutes but is an essential step. Continue to cross out statements until you are left with five top choices.

Begin to rank your five top choices by numbering the remaining items from 1 to 5 (1 = what you believe in most strongly, 5 = what you believe in the least). You may find that a few of the ideas are very similar or could be ranked together. If this is the case, join these ideas to form one new idea.

Finally, write your top priority as a statement on a 3" x 5" card beginning with the words, "I believe..." Reread your belief statement. Do you feel comfortable with your final statement, or do you need to adjust the wording? Once you arrive at a finished product, keep it in a place where you can refer to again and again. Ask yourself:

Am I true to my belief statement?
Do I act in accordance with my belief statement?
Do my staff members have a firm awareness of my beliefs?

2. Identify the individual belief systems of the staff.

Leaders who motivate also have a clear understanding of what their employees care about. They take the time to identify the belief systems of the individuals they work with. This belief system is usually not readily apparent. Often the esteem builder must make a concentrated search until the beliefs crystallize. Holding informal staff gatherings where individuals can feel comfortable expressing their values and beliefs is an essential part of this process. A key question to ask to start the dialogue flowing is:

If you were a member of the perfect school, what would it look like?

You may wish to take the time to ask each individual staff member this same question. The same process you went through in developing a statement of personal belief in the previous step can be a valuable technique for individual staff members to follow also. Mission grows out of what individuals view as uniquely and especially important to them.

3. Develop a shared vision.

Creating a mission statement for the school should be a collective venture.

Before you set out on a journey, you need to know where it is you want to go. Once you have a destination in mind, a specific itinerary of how to get there can be created. This same analogy is true for charting a course toward change. If all members of the team clearly understand in which direction they're headed, they certainly will be much clearer as to where they should focus their effort, time, and energy. "Turned-on" teams are powerful when they collectively focus on the same issues. Creating a mission statement for the school should be a collective venture. Once individuals have an awareness of their personal belief systems, they can begin together to explore where they are headed.

Begin this process by analyzing what's worked in the past, what hasn't and why. Analyzing concrete information is helpful in this process. An examination of particular academic areas that have previously been focused upon is also important. A few areas to analyze are:

- Explore the organization's past objectives and goals.

- Survey the staff and community as to where they feel the primary focus of the organization has been in the past. Very often the staff has quite a different opinion from the community as to this focus. It is important to recognize this difference in opinion.

- Analyze past test scores. Where have significant achievement gains been made? What areas in general are low?

- Analyze the types of in-servicing given in the past. Which topics or areas of professional development have been addressed already?

- Reread past principal newsletters and faculty meeting agendas. Have any trends appeared in which particular topics have been emphasized?
- Explore the academic emphasis of the district, county, or state. Is there a particular focus or mission already published?

With large staffs, committees can be formed to explore these topics in-depth. The purpose of the process is to identify and suggest areas for a collective staff mission. The area should be based on information about past performance. The following three questions may help in this process toward developing a shared vision:

- *What have we previously emphasized and focused on as a staff?*

- *What do we collectively believe is most important for our students?*

- *Based on concrete data, what appears to be the areas of greatest need for our students?*

4. Establish a mission statement for the school.

Any group of people working together to create an effective school must know where they are headed. Such vision creates a common clarity of purpose. When each member knows where the school community is headed, a firm belief and commitment in the direction evolves. The next step is to put in writing the direction the school site has chosen to focus upon. The statement defines the school's main purpose and establishes the overall direction of the staff. This step is often time-consuming but the end product is well worth the effort.

Vision creates a common clarity of purpose.

5. Accentuate the mission.

The finished mission statement must now be remembered by everyone on the staff. If the mission is not accentuated, the process will quickly be forgotten. Collectively choose your mission, and then collectively write the mission as a statement. Finally, publish the statement and keep it highly visible. The statement can be written on all school stationery and publications. Many schools place large plaques or bulletin boards containing the mission statement in highly visible locations around the school grounds. The mission chosen by the staff must now remain with the staff and community. Ask yourself, "Is everyone (staff, community, and students) aware of our mission?" If the answer is no, seriously analyze whether efforts to accentuate the organization's mission have been intense enough.

Once you get your whole staff in tune with that purpose, everything else falls into place. Purpose drives you. It means that collectively the staff will focus on the same issues. The ultimate success of the organization will be measured in terms of its ability to fulfill the vision.

Guideline Questions: School Mission and Major Focus

The following questions are provided as guidelines for the administrator to help determine if conditions are being fostered to create a major focus and mission for the school. Read each statement carefully. Check the appropriate column. There are no right or wrong answers.

	Regularly	Seldom	Never
1. I take the time to write my personal educational belief statement.	___	___	___
2. I act in accordance with my belief statement.	___	___	___
3. My staff members have a firm awareness of my beliefs.	___	___	___
4. I take the time to identify the personal belief systems of my staff.	___	___	___
5. My staff feels comfortable expressing their individual beliefs to me and to each other.	___	___	___
6. I analyze past performance data to determine what procedures have proven effective in enhancing student performance.	___	___	___
7. The staff and community are surveyed at least once a year to determine what they feel the primary focus of the school is (and should be).	___	___	___
8. Staff members are asked to explore and develop a shared vision as to what they believe is most important to their students.	___	___	___
9. A mission statement defining the main purpose and overall direction of the staff is established.	___	___	___
10. The mission statement of the school is published.	___	___	___
11. Everyone (staff, community, and students) is aware of the school's mission.	___	___	___

Action Plan:

Steps I will take to enhance the development of a major focus or mission for the school are:

- _____
- _____
- _____
- _____

Providing opportunities for joint decision-making and shared responsibility is the third esteem-building step to enhance a sense of mission. Numerous studies on effective schools have demonstrated the importance of actively involving the staff in the decision-making process. Research verifies that such a process enhances the staff's morale. L.D. Briggs, in his analysis of "high morale descriptors," found that "teachers who act autonomously in the decision-making process and play an active role in deliberations have a greater commitment in implementing decisions."[1] Patricia Duttweiler concluded from her exhaustive review of effective schools that one of the most effective ways principals can motivate teachers is by including them in the decision-making process.[2]

Staff morale is enhanced through active staff decision making.

On the other hand, research indicates that leaving teachers out of the decision-making process invites a lowering of their morale. When M.B. Morris examined the differences and similarities between schools perceived as "more satisfying" and "less satisfying" by teachers, he found that "in 'more satisfying' schools, teachers were far more likely to perceive themselves as having a part in the decision-making process than were teachers in the 'less satisfying' schools."[3] In addition, a study commissioned by the governor of Georgia (1981) to determine the reasons for the high attrition of teachers in that state verified that teachers want and need to have input in the direction and process of the school site. One of the survey questions researchers asked teachers who left the system was, "What could reasonably be done to get you back into public education in Georgia?" Though higher salary was listed as an important consideration, factors such as "giving teachers more voice in how things are done, allowing teachers to speak out, and giving teachers more authority" were also considered important.[4] Clearly, a desire to have a voice in how things are done at the school site is a primary source of motivation for teachers.

Despite the research verifying the need for joint decision-making, a recent survey polling 40,000 public elementary and secondary school teachers across the country found that the majority of teachers are not involved in this process. Based on the questionnaires, the Carnegie Foundation concluded that nationwide, teachers are not sufficiently involved in making critical decisions that affect them. Carnegie President Ernest Boyer stated:

"While most teachers help choose textbooks and shape curriculum, the majority do not help select teachers and administrators at their schools, nor are they asked to participate in such critical matters as teacher evaluations, staff development, budget, student placement, promotion and retention policies and standards of student conduct."[5] Having a "say" in the organization boosts staff morale, and helps in forming a critical perception interpreted as "our choice," and not solely "their decision." When decisions are developed through a collective effort, the result is a strong, unified commitment.

---

1. Briggs, L.D. "High Morale Descriptors: Promoting a Professional Environment." *The Clearing House for the Contemporary Educator in Middle and Secondary Schools.* vol. 59, 317.
2. Duttweiler, Patricia C. "Educational Excellence and Motivating Teachers." *The Clearing House for the Contemporary Educator in Middle and Secondary Schools.* vol. 60, 78.
3. Morris, M.B. "The Public School as a Workplace: The Principal as a Key Element in Teacher Satisfaction." *A Study of Schooling in the United States.* Dayton, OH: Institute for the Development of Educational Activities, 1978.
4. "Teacher Attrition Study: State of Georgia." Darden Research Corporation, Atlanta, GA: State Department of Education.

ESTEEM BUILDER #2

PROVIDE OPPORTUNITIES FOR JOINT DECISION-MAKING AND SHARED RESPONSIBILITY

Joint decision-making process demands open communication.

Developing professional unity and a joint decision-making process demands open communication between the administrator and staff. The development of this kind of "all-channel" communication involves "give and take" from all parties. All individuals must feel safe enough to risk offering ideas and opinions; the administrator, in turn, plays a primary role in the evolution of this sense of trust. The number of decisions staff members take part in varies enormously from school to school. Many sites attempt a total implementation of the process only to fail. Failure generally occurs when the foundation for the decision-making process has not been properly laid. Several prerequisites are required to help assure a more successful transition. The following points should be kept in mind:

1. **The process should be gradual.** The process of joint decision-making must be gradual. To jump from a total administrator decision-making model to an all-out joint approach is doomed to fail. Neither party is ready to assume their new roles of "shared deciders." A more successful alternative is to look at the types of decisions staff members currently make. Once this list has been assessed, it can gradually be added to, until both the administrator and staff feel comfortable in the routine.

2. **Lower-level decisions should precede higher-level decisions.** Joint decision-making should begin by confronting staff members with lower-level types of decisions. Ordering materials, creating bus and yard duty schedules, and arranging school-wide events are the kinds of choices with which to begin. As successes in the process and comfortableness in the method are evidenced, simpler decisions can be replaced with more difficult choices. Gradually, the administrator working together with the staff can decide on issues such as budget, student tracking policies, and administrator selection.

3. **Open communication between administration and staff.** Developing unity in the joint decision-making process demands open communication between administrators and staff. The relationship between parties must be secure enough so that all involved take an active part in the process. A prerequisite essential to the development of a sense of mission is the feeling of security. Conscious, deliberate plans must be made to increase this feeling.

4. **Give-and-take between parties.** True decision-making involves "give and take" from both parties. All individuals must be willing to listen to the opinions and ideas of others. The enhancement of Selfhood and Affiliation contribute greatly to this process. When individuals are aware of one another's uniquenesses (Selfhood) and feel a sense of cohesion and staff bonding (Affiliation), all parties can better understand the rationale for the choices being made jointly.

---

5. "Teachers Left Out of Vital Decisions." *EDCAL Bulletin,* September 1988, 2.

5. **Commitment to the process.** Another prerequisite essential to the decision-making process is that all parties must perceive that their decisions will be adhered to. This implies commitment to the process. The final decision may not be the first choice of the administration or individual staff members, but everyone will adhere to it because the choice was a joint decision.

6. **Democratic.** The dialogue in joint decision-making must necessarily include everyone. Therefore, during the process, it is critical to continually assess if all individuals are being listened to and heard. The process is threatened when a few individuals usurp the democratic process and become dictatorial. In this case, the process quickly turns from joint decision-making to one-sided, autocratic decision-making.

It is critical to continually assess if all individuals are being listened to and heard.

Guideline Questions: Decision-Making Policies (SEB 99)

An evaluation of the current decision-making process often can help determine the extent to which the procedure is being implemented. Below are listed some of the most common school decisions. Spaces are included to add additional decisions commonly made at the individual school site. Read each item and then check the decision-making body that most often decides that issue.

Decision	Decision-Making Bodies				
	District	Total Staff	Admin. Only	Admin. & Staff	Other
1. Ordering materials & supplies	___	___	___	___	___
2. Textbook selection	___	___	___	___	___
3. Yard duty schedule	___	___	___	___	___
4. Bus duty schedule	___	___	___	___	___
5. Mission statement of school	___	___	___	___	___
6. Standards of school conduct	___	___	___	___	___
7. Cafeteria rules	___	___	___	___	___
8. Piloting of new programs	___	___	___	___	___
9. Selection of school-wide events	___	___	___	___	___
10. Scheduling of school-wide events	___	___	___	___	___
11. Classroom visitation policies	___	___	___	___	___
12. Extent of parent involvement	___	___	___	___	___
13. Homework policies	___	___	___	___	___
14. Faculty meeting agenda	___	___	___	___	___
15. Student placement	___	___	___	___	___

Guideline Questions: Decision-Making Policies

Decision	Decision-Making Bodies				
	District	Total Staff	Admin. Only	Admin. & Staff	Other
16. Piloting of textbooks	___	___	___	___	___
17. Curriculum content	___	___	___	___	___
18. Staff development choices	___	___	___	___	___
19. Promotion & retention policies	___	___	___	___	___
20. Design of inservice programs	___	___	___	___	___
21. Grading policies	___	___	___	___	___
22. Student tracking policies	___	___	___	___	___
23. Selection of new teachers	___	___	___	___	___
24. School budget	___	___	___	___	___
25. Classroom budget	___	___	___	___	___
26. Teacher evaluation policies	___	___	___	___	___
27. Selection of new administrators	___	___	___	___	___
28. Selection of substitutes	___	___	___	___	___
29. Faculty meeting schedule	___	___	___	___	___
30. Other:	___	___	___	___	___
31. Other:	___	___	___	___	___
32. Other:	___	___	___	___	___

STAFF PROBLEM SOLVING   SEB 100

One of the strongest characteristics of effective teams is their ability to work together.

One of the strongest characteristics of effective teams is their ability to work together. Ideas and opinions are openly shared. Problems and concerns are safely voiced. Teams who work through obstacles as a group are enhanced in their collegiality. Staff members display a sense of "shared responsibility" when problems arise along with a greater willingness and openness to work together to solve a problem for the "good of the team." Individual self-esteem is also enhanced. Since they are supported in their efforts to work through problems, they perceive that their opinions and ideas count. Because they are given opportunities to do grade-level or staff-wide problem sharing, their feelings of self-empowerment are enhanced.

Administrators have tremendous power to create environments in which team problem solving can occur. By no means does this happen over night. Research suggests that most staff members have not been in situations where their ideas and solutions are asked for. To begin, therefore, by asking staff members to troubleshoot sophisticated school-related issues can prove disastrous. A safer practice is to provide the opportunity for group problem solving much more slowly. The process of asking staff members to share responsibility for group problem solving must be deliberate and ongoing.

The activities and exercises provided in this section are designed to help the administrator develop an effective "problem-solving team." They also are beneficial for another reason: individuals with low mission quite often are weak in problem-solving skills. Goals they may have set are frequently not attained due to an obstacle along the way. Instead of trying to remedy the problem by thinking of alternatives, the individual all too often gives up and quits. The possibility of self-esteem enhancement never transpires. These activities provide the opportunity for staff members low in mission to practice problem-solving strategies by working with a team who can model appropriate techniques to dealing with problems. In addition to these exercises, activities in *Esteem Builders* may be used with the staff, in particular:

The process of group problem solving must be deliberate and ongoing.

Code	Title	Page
N/A	Teach Problem-Solving Skills	222
M2	Problems	223
M5	Brainstorming	225
M6	Strategy Sheet of Solution Consequences	226
M9	Problem Map	228

SNAP GROUP PROBLEM SOLVING   SEB 101

Purpose: To allow teachers the opportunity to "problem shoot" issues and develop possible solutions.

Materials:
- Set of Snap Group cards (page 128). Run off on paper and cut in "cards" along the outside margins.
- Pencil or pen per group.
- Large chart paper and thick marking pen per group.

Procedure: Divide the group into smaller teams of four to five members. Distribute pre-printed Snap Group Cards to each group. Provide a few blank cards if teams ask to create their own set of problems. Explain that there are many issues confronting teachers that tend to lower their morale and self-esteem. Tell members that the problems listed on the cards are typical issues facing educators today. Emphasize that there are many other issues and that each group may discover problems that are not on the cards. Explain that the essential point needed for staff collegiality is to *deal with the problem and come up with possible solutions* so that the problem will not get out of hand.

Explain that the first part of the task is for each group to quickly choose one problem to deal with. They may choose a card or a member may volunteer a problem. The problem should deal with an issue related to staff morale and self-esteem that is impacting the school site. Emphasize that the groups have three minutes maximum to come to an agreement on the problem. Instead of allowing teams to choose their own problem, a variation is to ask them to turn the Snap Cards face down. Mention that all of the cards impact "our staff" at one time or another. The group shuffles the cards and then the recorder turns one card over. The card chosen is the one used during the Snap Group session. This variation reduces the amount of time needed for the activity. The facilitator should choose the variation most appropriate to the needs of the group.

Rules: Tell the group the rules for a Snap Group:

1. Each group will quickly choose a recorder. The recorder writes all solutions on a large chart paper with a thick marking pen so all members can clearly see the responses.

2. Groups sit in circles with four to five members.

3. Brainstorming rules apply (no evaluation or judgment of ideas...all ideas count...every idea is written down).

4. The group chooses a problem *(see above for variations to choosing the problem issue)*. The recorder quickly writes down the title of the problem at the top of the chart paper. Once the problem to be dealt with is identified, brainstorming begins.

5. Brainstorming is conducted clockwise. The person to the right of the recorder is the "starter" (the first person to talk). Every team member is given the opportunity to generate a solution to the problem. If members have an idea to share, they "snap" their fingers and then state a solution. The recorder quickly writes down the solution on the chart paper. If members do not have a solution at the moment, they quickly say "pass." The person immediately to their right takes a turn either "snapping" a solution or "passing" to the next person on their right.

6. Allow three to four minutes for brainstorming. The facilitator calls "time" and the brainstorming stops.

Variations: Choose one of the following variations. Each time the Snap Group activity is done, a different variation can be tried:

1. At the end of three to four minutes, each group may begin the process of eliminating solutions. First, ask groups to cross out ideas that are either unrealistic or uncontrollable. The group then selects their top three choices from the remaining solutions. Teams may use "The Strategy Sheet of Solution Consequences" (page 241 of *Esteem Builders*) to complete the steps in this section.

2. Each team chooses a reporter. The reporter quickly announces to the large group the

problem the team was dealing with in the Snap Session. The reporter then reads the solutions their team generated to the rest of the group.

3. Each team passes their list of solutions to the team immediately on their right. That team now has four minutes to read aloud the problem and all the possible solutions the last team generated, then *add to the list with solutions* their team generates.

Optional Activity: At the completion of the Snap Group activity, distribute copies of the student Esteem Builder Activity forms M5 Brainstorming (page 240) and M6 Strategy Sheet of Solution Consequences (page 241). Explain that the brainstorming activities members just performed in groups can also be done with students. Refer participants to the directions for brainstorming on pages 225-226 of *Esteem Builders*.

PROBLEM CARDS   SEB 102

Purpose: To aid staff members in developing strategies for improving school-related problems; to provide the opportunity for staff members to share successful strategies; to identify barriers to staff involvement.

Materials:

- 3" x 5" cards (about 8 per participant).
- Pen or pencil.
- "Strategies to Problems" form (6-8 per group). Extra copies should be available.

Procedure:

1. Distribute eight 3" x 5" cards to each participant. Ask participants to think of situations involving school they have had difficulty working with. *If desired, the situation can be narrowed down to a particular type of problem (i.e. involving parents or a student or a staff member. Each time the exercise is performed the situation can be varied).* Ask them to complete as many cards as they can in five minutes.

2. Ask participants to divide into groups of four to five members. Distribute eight to ten "Strategies to Problems" forms (page 129) to each group.

3. Ask each group to quickly choose a facilitator and a recorder. The facilitator shuffles the cards, reminds the group of the directions, and keeps the group on task. The recorder writes the group's ideas on the "Strategies to Problems" form. The recorder's job will be rotated.

4. Tell the group facilitator to collect members' completed cards, then shuffle and place them face down in the middle of the group. The facilitator turns over the top card and reads it aloud.

5. Starting with the person to the facilitator's right, each group member takes a turn stating one possible solution to the problem. Rotating clockwise, individuals continue stating solutions until everyone in the group agrees that another card should be pulled. The recorder writes the problem and records on the form all strategies the group verbalizes.

6. When the facilitator turns over a new problem card from the top of the pile, the recorder then relinquishes his or her duties and passes the job to the person on his or her left. The recorder uses the same form until no more space is available. A new form is then begun.

Variations: If desired, each group may choose one or two problems and describe the solutions they generated to the other participants. Another variation is for the large group facilitator to gather all the forms the smaller groups completed and type up a master list of problems and strategies. These lists are then distributed to the faculty at a later time.

TRIAD PROBLEM SHOOTING   SEB 103

Purpose: To discuss school-related problems among staff members; to provide an opportunity to generate solutions to obstacles confronting individual staff members.

Materials: "Triad Problem Shooting" form for each participant (page 130).

Procedure:

1. Ask the group to divide themselves into teams of three (triads). Ask triad members to "letter off" so that each member is *a different letter.* The first member of the triad is A, the second member is B, and the third member is C.

2. Distribute the "Triad Problem Shooting" form to each participant.

3. Explain the Triad Problem Shooting exercise to the group. Tell participants to think of a problem/obstacle they are faced with. Provide a few examples: a) a problem with a parent, b) a specific problem with a student, c) a problem with instructional materials, d) a problem with a colleague. Emphasize that no names of individuals should be used during the activity.

4. Ask each participant to *briefly* write the problem they are thinking about on their "Triad Problem Shooting" form.

5. Now explain the directions. Each member is assigned a role:
   A = Case Presenter
   B = Recorder
   C = Time Keeper

- The Case Presenter describes the problem they are confronted with to the other two team members. Tell the group that the Case Presenter should be very specific in describing the problem and identifying the exact behaviors or issues they feel are contributing to the problem.

- After the Case Presenter explains the problem, the Recorder uses the "Triad Problem Shooting" form to list ideas the group generates as possible solutions.

- The third member of the team, the Time Keeper, uses the "task time" scheme listed on the "Triad Problem Shooting" form to keep a close watch on the length of the group discussion:

  a) three minutes for the Case Presenter to present the case (the problem).
  b) three minutes for team members to ask the Case Presenter questions regarding the problem.
  c) three minutes are then spent as a triad generating solutions to the problem. All solutions are written on the form.
  d) three minutes for the triad to formulate a specific plan to deal with the problem.

- The next Case Presenter (person to the right of the current Case Presenter) then presents the case. The same procedure as before follows until all members of the triad have presented all four task components.

Variation: If time is limited, triad members may take turns presenting their case at other staff gatherings. This variation will require three different meetings until all members have presented their cases. At each faculty meeting, individuals remain with the same triad until everyone has had an opportunity to present their cases.

ESTEEM BUILDER #3

ENCOURAGE PERSONAL AND PROFESSIONAL GOAL-SETTING

*"There is no achievement
without goals."*
—ROBERT J. McKAIN

The third task in enhancing a sense of mission is to encourage effective goal-setting and then support individuals in attaining their goals. Motivation, on a professional as well as personal level, stems from what we expect from ourselves. Goals provide the direction and impetus to get there. Research emphatically verifies that peak performers use goals. A study in 1953 asked that year's graduating class at Yale University twenty questions. Three of those questions had to do with goals: "Have you set goals? Have you written them down? And, do you have a plan to accomplish them?" Only three percent of the class answered yes to all three questions. Twenty years later, in 1973, surviving members

Research emphatically verifies that peak performers use goals.

of the class of '53 participated in another study. Interestingly, the three percent who had written their goals at the time they graduated twenty years previously were more happily married, more successful, and enjoyed better health.[1]

INCREASING STAFF MOTIVATION

Goals spur us on to new heights and their successful attainment builds renewed confidence in ourselves to try even harder. Whatever the reason, the failure to reach the goal results in the loss of a sense of meaning and purpose and thus lowers the feeling of mission. To help the staff member enhance his/her success in attaining goals (and thereby enhance the feeling of mission), the esteem builder can take the following steps:

1. Aid the staff member in identifying meaningful goals.

An important principle in goal-setting is to set goals that are challenging but attainable. Three common reasons why people fail to reach their goals are:

- The goals are unrealistically high.
- The goals have no relevance to their lives.
- The goals are set too low.

Knowledge of previous performance in the area to be focused upon is essential.

Knowledge of previous performance in the area to be focused upon is essential. The administrator can be instrumental in facilitating the goal-setting process. Whether the goal is a personal goal important to the individual or a professional goal consistent with the mission of the organization, attaining the goal will enhance self-esteem. The administrator and staff member can take the following steps and work together to ensure greater success in achieving the goal:

- **Analyze the staff member's professional performance.** An appropriate time for this procedure might be during an evaluation. The administrator and staff member can then review teaching performance. Evaluations, test scores, and current observations are all helpful devices to refer to during the process. Teaching strengths and weaknesses should be determined.

- **Discuss and acknowledge effective teaching techniques.** The administrator should specifically point out the individual's strengths. The person might be asked what strengths they feel they possess.

Here are some areas I noticed you're particularly effective in.
What do you feel are your teaching strengths?

---

1. McCollum, Gardner M. *Goals—Vital to Success.* Cumberland, MD: Ops Inc., vol. II, no. 3, November 1986, 3.

- **Identify a professional area that needs improvement.** This area should be one that is measurable. The administrator can begin by asking the person what areas he/she feels need improving. The administrator can then either choose to agree (particularly if he/she believes this is an area that needs improvement) or suggest another area. Out of this honest dialogue a goal is determined.

What one area would you like to improve in?
Have you noticed an area that you'd like to work on this year?
Let's agree on one area to work on this year that would improve your teaching effectiveness.

- **Identify a personal goal for the individual.** In addition to identifying an area of professional improvement, it is important to recognize goals that are significant to the individual, goals that are more personal in nature. These goals might include trying a new curriculum, improving an image, attending professional development seminars in a special area, giving an in-service to a group, developing a skill or attempting a new approach to teaching. Keep in mind that individuals are far more committed to achieving the goal if they care about it personally. The strength of the "care element" should be discussed before any final decisions are reached.

> **Individuals are far more committed to achieving the goal if they care about it personally.**

Is there an area you'd like to personally work on this year?
Is there an area you'd like to learn more about this year?
What new teaching strategies or curriculum are you interested in?

2. Aid the staff member in writing the goal.

Gardner McCollum from the University of Alabama states that eighty-seven percent of us have no specific goals or plans for our lives, and of the remaining thirteen percent, only three percent have specific written goals. It is the latter who accomplish fifty to one-hundred times more than those who have goals but do not write them down.[2] To be effective, goals should be stated briefly and then written down. Doing so increases both clarity and commitment.

The critical part of this second step is to be exact, to help the person become very definite in what it is he/she wants to achieve. Remember, if a person sets out to do something in a general way, that's usually the way it will be done. Taking the time to help the individual write the goal(s) down on paper in specific, concrete terms means the individual knows exactly what is to be accomplished.

---

2. McCollum, Gardner M. *Goals—Vital to Success.* Cumberland, MD: Ops, Inc., vol. II, no. 3, November 1986, 3.

- **Outline Steps to Successful Goal-Setting**

Effective goal-setting consists of five components. As the goal is written together, continually check to see whether the five SMART elements are being met. A "Personal Goal Contract" is provided on page 126 to assist the administrator and staff members in writing an individual goal which follows the SMART elements:

SMART GOALS © Borba (SEB 104)

- **S**pecific
- **M**easurable
- **A**chievable
- **R**ealistic
- **T**ruthful

S = Specific. The goal should be written in very specific, concrete terms. A **what** (what are you trying to accomplish?) and a **when** (when do you plan to achieve it?) are included in these brief statements:

I will increase the reading scores to 80 percent of my third grade class by May 30, 1992.

I will present a 30-minute in-service to the staff on self-esteem enhancement by October 5, 1992.

The goal should specifically state what you're attempting to achieve and then set a definite timetable for reaching it.

People need a measuring stick to evaluate their progress.

M = Measurable. There should be a way to evaluate whether the goal was attained. People need a measuring stick to evaluate their progress. As the goal is read ask, "How will the individual know when they have succeeded?" There are many ways to record progress. The most successful measuring devices have the characteristics of being *visual, individual, and ongoing*. A teacher who has set a goal of trying to arrive on time in her classroom might use an index card to chart her arrival time each day. In this way, she could clearly see the progress toward her goal during a month's time by referring to the times she has written down. A language arts teacher who sets a goal of "improving the written performance of students" might choose to record her goal performance each week by filing a sample of each student's writing into individual folders.

Both teachers are *measuring* their progress toward their goals using effective but different measuring devices. Each device is *visual*, allowing the teacher to clearly see their past and present progress; *individual*, so that the teacher is measuring his or her goal only in reference to personal progress; and *ongoing*, since each teacher consistently recorded progress at set intervals. Each device is successful because it instantly gives the teacher evidence of his or her progress.

A = Achievable. Goals that are challenging but attainable get the best results. The goals should be broken into easily achievable objectives. So often goals are not achieved because the level of aspiration is either too high or too low. In neither case will self-esteem be enhanced. The most successful goals are usually set *slightly higher than the last goal*. Suppose a teacher's reading test scores for his fourth-grade students last year were sixty-eight percent. For the teacher to set a goal this year that "all students will read at the ninety-five percent level by June" would in all probability be an unachievable goal. it would be much more appropriate for the goal to be written so that it is slightly higher than the previous goal, such as "eighty-five percent of the students will read at the seventy-five percent level by June." The goal is now more achievable for the teacher because it is based on his past teaching performance.

> **The most successful goals are usually set *slightly higher than the last goal*.**

R = Realistic. The individual must have personal control over achieving the goal. Often, goals are written but their attainment is totally unrealistic because the individual does not have the power to reach the goal. Teachers, for instance, are often very concerned about their students' environments. Issues such as employment, educational background, and personal lifestyles are areas the educator has no control over. Writing a goal to improve such areas would be fruitless. The individual must ask, "Do I have control or power over achieving this goal?" If the answer is no, the goal should be rewritten.

T = Truthful. An individual is more motivated to achieve goals that are meaningful to him/her. Therefore, the goal should be one that has significance to the individual. The person must care about the goal. A question he/she should answer is, "Do I really want to work toward the attainment of this goal?" If the answer is no, chances are great that the goal won't be attained.

3. Provide support, offer feedback, and monitor progress.

Once the goal is written, the administrator's esteem-building role is to monitor progress toward attainment of the goal and then offer support on a continuing basis. Informal meetings should be arranged periodically between staff members and the administrator. Specific feedback from the administrator regarding personal progress is always valuable. When individuals give up striving after the goal, it's usually because they're not sure what to do in order to improve their performance or they're unaware of progress that has already been made. This may also be a good time to review whether the goal was set too high; if so, rewrite it at a more achievable level. Above all, staff members should be supported for failures as well as achievements. This process can be extremely rewarding. As the relationship between the administrator and staff members grows, security and trust are enhanced. As each goal is met with success, personal competence grows as well.

4. Celebrate goal attainment and set new goals.

When the goal is attained, a celebration is in order. The goal-setting process should never stop here, though. This is the time to acknowledge the achievement and then begin the goal-setting process again. Each success enhances personal competence.

Guideline Questions: Goal-Setting Procedures (SEB 105)

The following questions are provided as guidelines for the administrator to help determine if conditions are being fostered to promote effective goal-setting procedures. Read each statement carefully. Check the appropriate column. There are no right or wrong answers.

	Regularly	Seldom	Never
1. I use the teacher evaluation process as a means to set and clarify expectations.	_____	_____	_____
2. I help staff members identify their teaching strengths and weaknesses.	_____	_____	_____
3. I help staff members select goals that are consistent with the mission or direction of the school.	_____	_____	_____
4. I work with staff members in selecting goals that are of personal significance to them.	_____	_____	_____
5. I encourage staff members to write down professional and personal goals.	_____	_____	_____
6. I check the effectiveness of the written goal with individual staff members to determine if the goal is specific, measurable, achievable, realistic and truthful.	_____	_____	_____
7. I provide staff members with specific feedback as to their goal-setting progress.	_____	_____	_____
8. I make it a point to celebrate when a staff member achieves a goal.	_____	_____	_____
9. When a staff member achieves a goal, we meet to write the next goal.	_____	_____	_____

GOAL MAP   SEB 106

Goal-setting effectively enhances performance and self-esteem.

Research clearly validates that goal-setting effectively enhances performance and self-esteem. While it is widely acclaimed as a useful way to enhance mission, goal-setting is far from a common practice. Staff members often find goal-setting tedious because they are not familiar with the actual process. The Goal Map (page 131) is a procedure that will familiarize staff members with the procedures involved in goal-setting. One of the greatest obstacles to goal-setting is that individuals too often begin by setting goals that are too lofty or simply will take too long to achieve. While a teacher's goal might be "to be a highly effective teacher," for the beginning teacher such an outcome is not likely to occur. The teacher needs to understand that "steps" must be taken in order to achieve goals. The long-term visionary goal might be "to be a highly effective teacher." In order to achieve such a vision, the key question to ask is, "What steps do I need to take in order to get there?" These steps are called "short-term goals."

Distribute the goal to the staff. Ask individuals to think of their goals in terms of steps. Ask them to also think of two categories: 1) personal goals (i.e. improve cooking skills, acquire more patience, learn to ski), and 2) professional goals (i.e. make science lessons more relevant to students, implement cooperative learning structures in the classroom, learn the principles of positive reinforcement so as to help disruptive students be more attentive). The targets within these two areas are written as "long-term visionary goals."

Ask individuals to think of their goals in terms of steps.

Next, ask participants to identify the steps needed along the way in order to achieve the desired outcome. These are then written as smaller goals beginning with the first thing that needs to be accomplished (today!). The immediate goal (what should be accomplished in a one or two week period) is written next. The third and final step in the process is to think of a longer range goal, of what should be accomplished in about two months time. Emphasize that many long-term goals take years to achieve, and only if the individual clearly keeps that goal in mind. Olympic athletes, for instance, often take ten years to reach their goal of winning a gold medal. They never deviate from that long-term vision, but continue to add daily, weekly, or monthly short-term goals to their schedules. As they perfect their skills, each year they get closer to their desired outcome.

It is often helpful to present your own personal goal to the group, giving examples of all the steps you have taken in order to get closer to your vision. You could also use an example of a teacher who chose as his/her professional goal to become more proficient in the skills of cooperative learning. The steps to this attainment might be:

Present Moment: Sign up for an in-service in cooperative learning. Order materials on cooperative learning theory and practice.

Immediate Goal: Read the first book on cooperative learning.

Longer Range: Attend the cooperative learning training. Try cooperative learning lessons once a week.

Long-Term Goal: Use the principles of cooperative learning daily in my classroom.

Reflection: Four steps were described for the esteem builder to guide staff members toward attainment of their goals. Identify a staff member who you believe could benefit from a greater sense of mission. Describe what you will specifically do in each step for building mission to help the individual reach a goal:

Staff Member's Name _____

1. Aid the staff member in identifying meaningful goals.

I will _____

_____

_____

2. Aid the staff member in writing the goal.

I will _____

_____

_____

3. Provide support, offer feedback, and monitor progress.

I will _____

_____

_____

4. Celebrate goal attainment, then set new goals.

I will _____

_____

_____

MISSION ESTEEM BUILDERS   SEB 107-126

1. *Agenda Topics (SEB 107).* Post an open faculty meeting agenda a week prior to the event. Allow staff members to write agenda topics.

2. *Staff Survey (SEB 108).* Survey the staff as to how often they perceive they have the opportunity to share ideas and opinions.

3. *Brainstorming Rules (SEB 109).* At a staff gathering, teach the rules for brainstorming. Post the rules in the staff lounge. Encourage staff members to use the brainstorming process as a technique for generating alternatives to a problem, question, or issue. (Refer to page 225 in *Esteem Builders* to review the brainstorming procedure.)

4. *Brainstorming Sessions (SEB 110).* Hold brainstorming sessions as a regular part of staff gatherings. Pose a problem, review the rules for brainstorming, then divide the large groups into smaller teams and ask them to brainstorm solutions.

5. *Problem Box (SEB 111).* Place a Problem Box in the staff lounge. Staff members can jot down any problems at the site they feel need addressing.

6. *Problem Box Cards (SEB 112).* Encourage teachers to write (anonymously if desired) a school problem they're having on a 3" x 5" index card. Ask them to describe the situation and then place the card in a designated Problem Box (kept in a central location). Take a few minutes during each faculty meeting to read the problems submitted on the cards and then ask the group to brainstorm solutions to the problems.

7. *Room Whip (SEB 113).* Begin a faculty meeting with a "whip" around the room in which each staff member responds to the statement: "One thing I want to try is..."

8. *Attitude Boosters (SEB 114).* Write a few "attitude boosters" on construction paper and hang them in the faculty room, such as:

"All the resources we need are in the mind." Theodore Roosevelt, Jr.

"Most people don't plan to fail; they fail to plan." John L. Beckley

"The man who does things makes many mistakes, but he never makes the biggest mistake of all—doing nothing." Benjamin Franklin

"The only people who never fail are those who never try." Ilka Chase

"Only those who dare to fail greatly can ever achieve greatly." Robert F. Kennedy

"Show me a thoroughly satisfied man and I will show you a failure." Thomas Alva Edison

"Ninety-nine percent of the failures come from people who have the habit of making excuses." George Washington Carver

"He who has never failed has never tried." Emmett Lecompte

9. *Goal Sharing (SEB 115).* Periodically at faculty meetings ask participants to share their goals with a partner. At a future meeting, the same partners can again be paired to ask each other about their goals and support one another in attaining them.

10. *Valuable Input (SEB 116).* Ask...ask...ask for teacher input in decision-making and planning.

11. *Committee Recommendations (SEB 117).* With larger staffs, set up a committee to make recommendations regarding larger decisions (budget expenditures, scheduling, etc.).

12. *Celebration Sheets (SEB 118).* Keep an ample supply of printed "Celebration Sheets" (page 132) on hand so you can write a note of congratulations to someone who has achieved a goal.

13. *SMART Process (SEB 119).* Teach the process of goal-setting at a faculty meeting using the SMART process.

14. *Goal Folders (SEB 120).* Store staff members' personal and professional goals in individual folders.

15. *Involvement in School Decisions (SEB 121).* Survey your staff by asking the question, "Which one school decision would you like to be included in that you are not included in now?" The administrator can go further than just finding out what decision the staff wants to be included in by acting on or implementing this information whenever reasonable and possible.

16. *Mission Statement (SEB 122).* Print your school's mission statement on a variety of communication forms: newsletters, stationery, business cards, plaques, and note cards. Make sure the statement is readily visible.

17. *Risk Taking (SEB 123).* Encourage risk taking and always support effort.

18. *Personal Creed (SEB 124).* Encourage staff members to develop a personal creed and write it down: "This is what I believe in…"

19. *Collective Creed (SEB 125).* Encourage staff members to develop a collective creed and write it down: "This is what we believe in…"

20. *Esteem Builder Activities (SEB 126).* Activities in *Esteem Builders* can easily be adapted for adults. In particular the following activities have been used successfully with staffs to enhance the feeling of mission.

Code	Title	Page
M1	What I Like…What I Want to Change	223
M2	Problems	223
M5	Brainstorming	225
M6	Strategy Sheet of Solution Consequences	226
M17	Overcoming Obstacles to Goals	233
M19	Daily Goal-Setting	234
M21	Record of Weekly Goals	234
M29	Goal Award Grams	236

Purpose With Responsibility: Building Mission
SUMMARY

A sense of mission is the fourth feeling staff members with high self-esteem possess. Administrators can aid staff members who are lacking in mission by taking the following steps:

---

1. Develop the major focus, direction, or mission of the school.
2. Provide opportunities for joint decision-making and shared responsibility.
3. Encourage personal and professional goal-setting.

Keeper

The most important idea about the concept of mission I want to remember is:

_____
_____
_____
_____
_____
_____
_____
_____
_____
_____

One way I will apply this idea in my relationship with my staff is: _____

_____
_____
_____
_____
_____
_____
_____
_____
_____

PERSONAL GOAL CONTRACT

High-achieving individuals tend to be goal-oriented and motivated by the vision of what they want to accomplish. Effective goals have five components. As the goal is written, continually check whether the five **"SMART"** elements are met.

> **S** = Specific
> **M** = Measurable
> **A** = Achievable
> **R** = Realistic
> **T** = Truthful

Write three personal or professional goals you want to accomplish within the next year:

_____

_____

_____

_____

Choose the goal you want to accomplish immediately. Write the goal using the five components of "SMART" goal-setting.

MY GOAL: I will: _____

_____

_____

_____

> **SPECIFIC:** *The goal should be written in very specific, concrete terms. A **"what** (what is it you're trying to accomplish?) and a **"when"** (by when do you plan to achieve it?) are included in the brief statement.*

DATE: I plan to start this goal on: _____

DATE: I plan to achieve this goal by: _____

> **MEASURABLE:** *There should be a way to evaluate whether the goal was attained.*

I will evaluate my success in accomplishing this goal by: _____

_____

_____

_____

Esteem Builders' Complete Program
Jalmar Press, Rolling Hills Estates, CA

ACHIEVABLE: *Goals that are challenging but attainable get the best results. The goals should be broken into easily achievable objectives.*

The steps I need to take to achieve my goal are:

Step a: _____

Step b: _____

Step c: _____

Step d: _____

Who or what I need to help me achieve my goal: _____
_____
_____
_____
_____

Reread the goal you wish to achieve. Answer the following questions:

_____ Do I have control over achieving this goal?

_____ Is it totally within my power to accomplish this goal?

List any circumstances that may impede the attainment of your goal: _____
_____
_____
_____
_____

REALISTIC: *The individual must have personal control over achieving the goal. Do you?*

Do I have the power or control to deal with these circumstances? If you answer "no" to any of these questions, reread the goal to seriously determine if this is the best choice or if you should rethink your goal.

TRUTHFUL: *Individuals are more motivated to achieve goals that are meaningful to them.*

Finally, ask yourself: "Do I really want to work toward the attainment of this goal?"

Signature: _____ **Date:** _____

SNAP GROUP CARDS

Staff members do not feel appreciated and recognized by other staff members.	**All staff members are not committed to enhancing self-esteem.**
Staff members do not feel a strong sense of belonging with one another.	**Staff members do not readily see the need of a self-esteem program.**
Staff members do not interact positively with one another.	**Staff members cannot readily identify students with low self-esteem.**
Staff members do not openly share ideas and materials with one another.	**Staff members do not communicate positively with one another.**
Staff members do not know what other staff members are doing within each others' classrooms.	**Staff members do not have a feeling of school pride.**
Staff members do not feel they are making a difference in the lives of their students.	_____ _____ _____ _____

STRATEGIES TO PROBLEMS

Problems	Strategies

Esteem Builders' Complete Program
Jalmar Press, Rolling Hills Estates, CA

TRIAD PROBLEM SHOOTING

ROLES:

        A = Case Presenter;   **B = Recorder;**   **C = Time Keeper**

TASK TIME:

        3 minutes: Case Presenter to present their case.

        3 minutes: Questions to the Case Presenter from the triad.

        3 minutes: Brainstorming solutions as a group to the problem.

        3 minutes: Traid formulates a specific plan for the problem.

THE PROBLEM:

_____

_____

_____

_____

POSSIBLE SOLUTIONS TO THE PROBLEM:

_____

_____

_____

_____

_____

_____

_____

_____

THE PLAN:

_____

_____

_____

_____

_____

_____

_____

Esteem Builders' Complete Program
Jalmar Press, Rolling Hills Estates, CA

GOAL MAP

PERSONAL GOALS   PROFESSIONAL GOALS

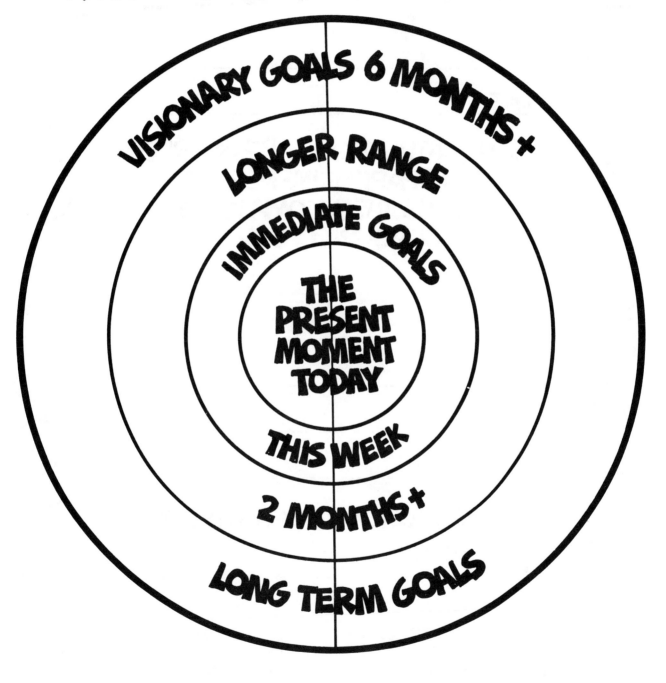

VISIONARY GOALS 6 MONTHS +

LONGER RANGE

IMMEDIATE GOALS

THE PRESENT MOMENT TODAY

THIS WEEK

2 MONTHS +

LONG TERM GOALS

Esteem Builders' Complete Program
Jalmar Press, Rolling Hills Estates, CA

CELEBRATION

TO _____

DATE _____

CONGRATULATIONS ARE IN ORDER!
IT'S APPARENT WE NEED TO
CELEBRATE THE ACCOMPLISHMENTS
OF YOUR GOAL OF

_____

_____

_____

_____

I KNOW IT TOOK A LOT OF HARD WORK!

SIGNED _____

Esteem Builders' Complete Program
Jalmar Press, Rolling Hills Estates, CA

ACTION PLAN FOR ENHANCING A SENSE OF MISSION

Take time to think through your action strategies. What will you personally do to enhance the sense of Mission for your staff? The importance of this planning cannot be overemphasized.

In an effort to enhance the feeling of mission in my staff, I will implement the following ideas and actions:

To develop the major focus, direction, or mission of the school as a staff, I will:

1. _____
_____

2. _____
_____

3. _____
_____

To provide opportunities for joint decision-making and shared responsibility among staff members, I will:

1. _____
_____

2. _____
_____

3. _____
_____

To encourage individual staff member's personal and professional goal setting, I will:

1. _____
_____

2. _____
_____

3. _____
_____

Date of Commitment: _____

Follow-up Date: _____

Esteem Builders' Complete Program
Jalmar Press, Rolling Hills Estates, CA

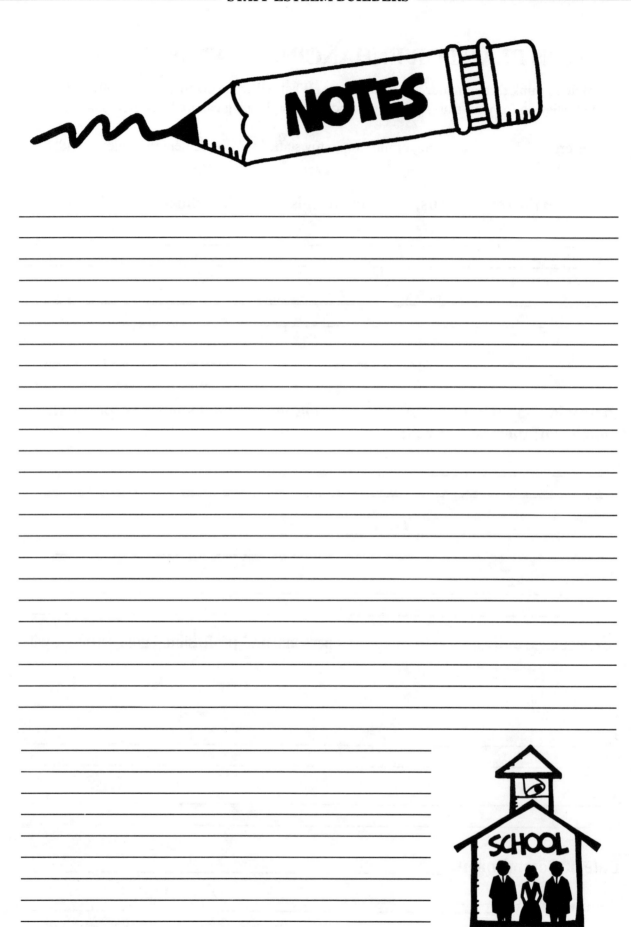

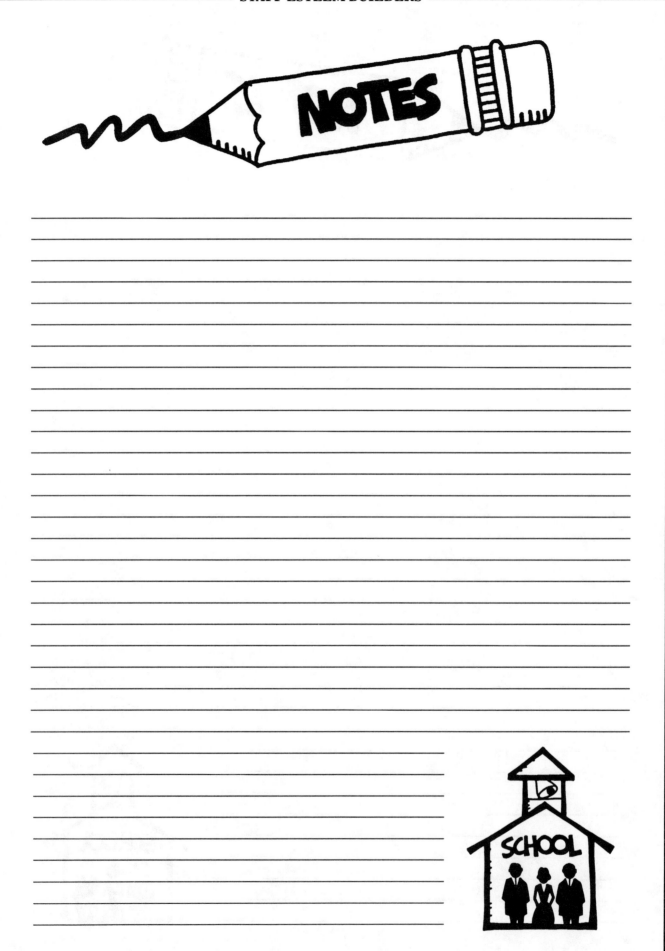

6

Building Competence and a Sense of Personal Efficacy

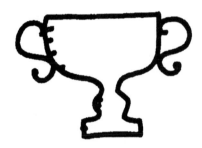

STAFF ESTEEM BUILDERS

- Set High and Achievable Expectations
- Provide Opportunities to Recognize and Demonstrate Individual Competencies and Strengths
- Monitor Progress and Provide Specific Feedback
- Help Individuals Recognize They Do Make a Difference
- Competence Esteem Builders

STAFF COMPETENCE BUILDERS
CONTENTS

Competence: *A feeling of success and capableness in things regarded as important or valuable; aware of strengths and able to accept weaknesses; a sense of empowerment and self-efficacy over the direction of one's life.*

LOW COMPETENCE INDICATORS

- is reluctant to contribute ideas or opinions, may depend on others
- has difficulty accepting weaknesses and identifying strengths
- is a poor loser, magnifies any loss or failure
- discredits achievements
- easily discouraged, has difficulty recognizing progress

HIGH COMPETENCE INDICATORS

- willing to take risks and try something new
- accepts weaknesses and recognizes strengths
- turns mistakes into learning opportunities and tries again
- takes pride in achievements
- works on improving areas of low capability
- accepts feedback

6

Building Competence and a Sense of Personal Efficacy

Whether you think you can or whether you think you can't... you're right!

—HENRY FORD

The fifth and final component of self-esteem is competence. Generally, individuals acquire this feeling following frequent successes, particularly in areas considered important or highly valued. The feeling continues to grow after individuals have accomplished a personal or professional goal they set out to obtain. Each accomplishment in which individuals relied upon their own resources and capabilities instills a sense of personal power. Each successful goal is another internal validation that "I'm a worthwhile individual," and so self-esteem is further enhanced. These individuals recognize they have a sense of personal responsibility and control over the direction of their lives.

Self-esteem is only empowering when it is *applied*. For individuals merely to have good feelings about themselves can be ineffective, unless those feelings are used to their advantage. One of the main reasons individuals with high self-esteem are so effective in life is that they are able to make their feelings of competence work for them, and thereby increase their potential even further. Webster defines the verb "to mobilize" as meaning "to put into action." High self-esteem individuals use this same principle, and that's one of the main reasons why these staff members are so capable. *They have learned to empower themselves and put their ideas into action.* Here are individuals who can use their potential as educators to the fullest because they reinforce and acknowledge themselves internally. Here are individuals who have acquired a sense of "self-efficacy." As staff members, they are no longer dependent on other's encouragement and praise. These educators have a firm sense of direction in their individual professional roles as

Self-esteem is only empowering when it is *applied*.

— 141 —

staff members, they are no longer dependent on other's encouragement and praise. These educators have a firm sense of direction in their individual professional roles as well as in their positions as team members. Because they have a sense of competence, they are able to mobilize themselves into productive action.

The administrator's role in the enhancement of competence is primarily one of facilitator rather than commander. The esteem builder serves as a guide who provides materials and moral support. Support may involve brainstorming ways to overcome obstacles, offering advice as a consultant, checking on evaluation outcomes, providing in-service opportunities or allocating special funds. While the administrator may offer suggestions and advice, in the end individuals must create their own paths. Personal competence will not be enhanced if individuals rely too heavily on direction from the administrator or depend too much on the manager's ideas or opinions.

The staff member must develop their own sense of competence.

At times it may seem easier to say, "This is how you should do it." or "Do it this way." Such autocratic direction, though, is counterproductive and not conducive to building individuals' personal confidence. The staff member must develop their own sense of competence or power.

LOW AND HIGH COMPETENCE INDICATORS

A staff member who feels incompetent may be recognized by the following behavioral characteristics:

- is reluctant to contribute ideas or opinions, may depend on others for decisions and direction;

- has difficulty accepting weaknesses and identifying strengths;

- is unwilling to take risks, feeling "I may fail";

- relies on the same material, techniques, or approaches;

- tends to act helpless and is dependent in areas where he/she can or should be competent;

- is a poor loser, magnifies any loss or failure;

- tends to use negative self-statements regarding accomplishments and may discount or discredit any achievement;

- easily discouraged, has difficulty recognizing progress;

- says "What's the use?" and gives up easily;

- makes little use of test results or evaluation devices demonstrating past performance.

These behaviors greatly diminish a feeling of competence. On the other hand, a staff

Although I've never attempted this before, I'm willing to give it a try.

It can be risky to confront, but sometimes we need to do it anyway.

I'm good at a lot of things, although sometimes I take on too much at one time.

Sometimes I blow up without thinking. I'm working on this all the time.

If I make a mistake, I'll try it a different way.

I have lots of ideas on that topic that I'd be willing to share.

I completed my thesis and I'm proud of my accomplishment.

I think I'm a really good parent.

List individuals exhibiting behaviors indicating possible *low competence:*

_____ _____

_____ _____

_____ _____

_____ _____

_____ _____

List individuals exhibiting behaviors indicating possible *high competence:*

_____ _____

_____ _____

_____ _____

_____ _____

_____ _____

ESTEEM BUILDER STEPS TO ENHANCING COMPETENCE

Competence can be enhanced. The following are the four steps esteem builders can take to increase an individual's personal sense of competency:

1. **Set high and achievable expectations.**
2. **Provide opportunities to recognize and demonstrate individual competencies and strengths.**
3. **Monitor progress and provide specific feedback.**
4. **Help individuals recognize they do make a difference.**

SET HIGH AND ACHIEVABLE EXPECTATIONS

"Confidence is contagious.
So is lack of confidence."
—VINCENT T. LOMBARDI

The kind of expectations an administrator sets is a critical aspect in self-esteem enhancement.

Leadership methods vary greatly, but one constant among great leaders is a commitment to superior work. A "hands-off" approach does not work at home any more than in the classroom or office. An administrator who cares about the staff cares about how successful they are, and shows this by devoting much time and energy to helping them learn to be effective. A laissez-faire attitude, on the other hand, conveys the message: "Feel free to do what you choose. This school is not worth caring about." The kind of expectations an administrator sets is a critical aspect in self-esteem enhancement. Are they ones that are self-enhancing or self-defeating? Are they set at a reasonable level so that staff members will want to stretch and commit themselves to reaching them, or are they positioned so high that individuals throw up their hands in frustration and say, "Why bother?"

David C. McClelland, a psychologist at Harvard University, has done extensive research on what he terms "achievement motivation." McClelland finds that the best-motivated people like to have not only clear-cut objectives but also objectives that are attainable. In an exhaustive series of experiments with adults, McClelland learned that people who stay consistently motivated are hooked on what he calls *accomplishment feedback*. Such individuals want to have their capacities stretched but they also need to have regular successes. The research clearly showed that motivated individuals keep working because of the continuous satisfaction they receive in their ability to meet short-term goals. Alan Loy McGinnis sums up the important lesson leaders must learn from McClelland's work: "In pressing for excellence, we must be careful to have goals that are both challenging and realistic, and we must devise a graded progression of objectives, so that our people can enjoy the regular feedback of success."[1]

The administrator can assume a critical leadership role in enhancing the personal competency of staff members. The expectations the leader sets for his or her staff directly affect their teaching effectiveness. The administrator should expect the best from the people he or she leads and aspire toward a commitment to excellence. To expect less is to expect incompetence. At the same time, expectations must be realistic and achievable. They should be challenging but also provide an opportunity for success and the enhancement of competence. The esteem builder must first consciously assess the expectations set for the staff and then provide the resources, encouragement, and support necessary to achieve the desired results.

Reflection: Expectations that are clearly stated and attainable are the kind of expectations David C. McClelland from Harvard University finds are the most motivating. Take a moment to reflect upon the expectations you set for your staff. Do they meet these two criteria? First, list the expectations you have for staff members. Next, read each written

---

1. McGinnis, Alan Loy. *Bringing Out the Best in People*. Minneapolis, MN: Augsburg House, 1985, 68.

expectation and assess the item in two ways by asking: 1) "Have I clearly stated my expectation to each staff member?" For example, if an outsider were to walk onto the school campus and randomly poll staff members with the question, "What expectations does your administrator have for you?" would staff members be able to answer with specific issues? and 2) "Is the expectation attainable for each member? Have I taken the time to break the expectation down into smaller components so the individual can become successful?"

My Expectations for My Staff	Clearly Stated	Attainable

Action Plan: One step I will take to help ensure that my expectations for my staff are both clearly stated and attainable is:

_____

_____

_____

Guideline Questions: High and Achievable Staff Expectations (SEB 127)

The following questions are provided as guidelines for the administrator to help determine if conditions are being fostered that set high and achievable expectations for the staff:

	Regularly	Seldom	Never
1. Do all staff members clearly know what is expected of them?	_____	_____	_____
2. Do all staff members clearly know how to attain what is expected of them?	_____	_____	_____
3. Do I devote time and energy helping staff members be effective?	_____	_____	_____
4. Do I set expectations that are both realistic as well as challenging?	_____	_____	_____
5. Do I involve individuals in the process of setting personal and professional expectations?	_____	_____	_____
6. Are the majority of my staff members successful at reaching the expectations that are set?	_____	_____	_____
7. Do I verbally express faith and confidence in individuals' abilities to accomplish tasks?	_____	_____	_____
8. Do I provide emotional and/or material support necessary to help individuals reach the set expectations?	_____	_____	_____

ESTEEM BUILDER #2

PROVIDE OPPORTUNITIES TO RECOGNIZE AND DEMONSTRATE INDIVIDUAL COMPETENCIES AND STRENGTHS

---

*"If you want to get the best out of man, you must
look for the best that is in him."*
—BERNARD HALDANE

The key to creating success and "winners" is to discover the hidden talent of each individual staff member.

One of the best ways to motivate individuals is to help them concentrate on images of themselves succeeding. The old adage that "Nothing succeeds like success" has been found by major companies to be a powerful technique. In their best-selling book studying the best-run companies in America, *In Search of Excellence,* Peters and Waterman found that successful organizations capitalize on that adage. Good companies design their systems to reinforce the notion that their employees are winners. As Peters and Waterman state, "The systems in the excellent companies are not only designed to produce lots of winners; they are constructed to celebrate the winning once it occurs."[2] Such a system creates a strong formula for success. The key to creating success and "winners" is to discover the hidden talent of each individual staff member.

STRENGTH AID   SEB 128

Philosopher Elbert Hubbard once said, "There is something that is much more scarce, something finer far, something rarer than ability. It is the ability to recognize ability." All people have hidden talents; it's up to the best motivator to unleash those hidden capabilities. People need an atmosphere in which they can specialize, discover their distinctiveness, and capitalize on their skills. Self-esteem enhancers recognize that each individual has unique talents. The real difference between an effective and an ineffective team is whether its members are aware of their talents and then (provided they are aware) whether they have the opportunity to demonstrate those skills. Esteem builders can be instrumental in this process of unleashing other persons' hidden talents. One technique an esteem builder can use to help an individual gain a greater sense of competence is identified by the acronym AID. There are three parts to a "Strength AID" (© Borba) that the esteem builder should keep in mind.

The first step is to identify a specific **Strength (S)** the individual actually possesses. Then help that person become **Aware (A)** of the skill. Keep in mind that low-competent individuals frequently are unaware of the talent or deny that it exists. To be most effective, the skill or talent should be one that can be observed at the site. For example, if the individual possesses a strong equestrian talent, it is probably not the most effective talent to acknowledge since horseback riding is rarely a skill demonstrated at the school site. A talent in art, science, or physical education, or a personality strength such as loyalty, determination, or perseverance might be more practical to address. Once the esteem builder has determined

---

2. Peters, Thomas J. and Robert H. Waterman. *In Search of Excellence.* New York: Harper & Row, 1982, 77.

what talent to stress, his or her job is to help the individual become aware of the skill. Draw attention to the talent in a written or verbal form: "I noticed what an outstanding lesson you gave today in science. You have such a command of astronomy. Now we can capitalize on your talent in our science meetings."

The second part of the AID technique is to tell the individual exactly what they can do to **Improve (I)** in the skill. Again this improvement could be written or verbal, but it is important that the esteem builder be highly specific in this feedback. Once the individual is aware of his/her skill, competence is enhanced when the staff member knows how to be even more proficient in the skill. A suggestion for improvement might be: "Your teaching lesson in astronomy could improve if you allowed students to create their own star charts. Concrete experiences help students grasp the concept on a level they can understand."

The final element of AID is to provide the opportunity for the staff member to **Demonstrate (D)** his/her strength to others. One of the greatest competence builders is for someone else to recognize the individual's talent and to acknowledge him/her for it. Too often a low competence individual hides his/her talent from others. The astute esteem builder finds the opportunity for the talent to be displayed so that other staff members recognize their colleague's skill. The Strength AID technique is explained in greater detail in the section that follows.

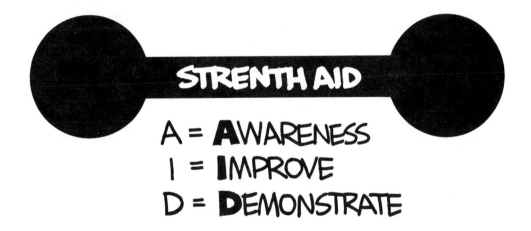

AWARENESS

The first step toward enhancing competency is to help individuals become aware of their strengths. These strengths may be professional or personal but they are always individual. To enhance personal competency, individuals must recognize the special competencies they have that distinguish them from other staff members. The administrator should always consciously be looking for such talents. A few of the many opportunities to discover individuals' strengths include: classroom observations, test scores, committee work, comments from parents, students, or colleagues and interactions with students and parents. Individual staff members' names and strengths can be noted on an ongoing form, which can serve as an invaluable record-keeping device. Though possibilities for strengths are endless, a few examples are provided:

- *Physical Appearance:* neat, attractive, etc.

- *Personality:* likable, friendly, open, etc.

- *Cognitive Abilities:* logical, curious, quick, creative, knowledgeable, etc.

- *Relationship with Colleagues:* warm, open, accepting, etc.

- *Relationship with Students:* warm, caring, empathetic, etc.

- *Teaching Performance:* knowledgeable, student-oriented, prepared, etc.

- *Motivation:* hard-working, prompt, persevering, etc.

- *Special Interests and Talents:* athletic, artistic, gourmet, etc.

Individuals now need to form an image in which they literally "see" themselves as competent in certain talents.

Once talents are discovered, the individuals who possess them must become aware of what these discoveries are. An administrator must not assume others perceive they are talented in the areas he/she has pinpointed. Individuals now need to form an image in which they literally "see" themselves as competent in certain talents. With staff members who have low self-esteem, this process can be time-consuming. Here are a few suggestions in helping these individuals become aware of an identified strength:

- **Put compliments in writing.** Send Strength Grams or notes especially designed for commending an observed strength. "I just wanted you to know I observed a special strength you obviously possess. It is..."

- **Be specific.** Always tell the individual exactly what they did right. Beyond just identifying the strength, tell the person specifically what you observed them doing which keyed you into that talent. "I wanted you to know I was very impressed with your ability to work with James yesterday. You have a talent in communicating with at-risk youngsters. You knelt down at his level, talked very calmly and demonstrated a lot of caring." Detailed commendations such as this one have far more impact than vague pats-on-the-back. Specific praise reinforces an individual's specific behavior and lets that person know you've really noticed and thought about them.

- **Commend Verbally.** In cases where you don't have the opportunity to write specific notes of praise, take a few minutes to pull the person aside and tell them exactly what you observed. Don't overlook the power of delivering the message personally.

- **Evaluate Strengths.** Every evaluation session should include a discussion of the staff member's personal strengths and talents. Ask individuals what talents they think they possess. Tell them exactly what strengths you've observed about them.

IMPROVEMENT

Staff members have become aware of an earned and deserved talent; now help them recognize how they can become even more proficient in the talent. Many individuals are aware of a talent or strength, but they never take the time to develop it any further. Competency increases as individuals stretch their capacity. Take the time to help the person know exactly what they can do to improve in that strength or talent. There are several ways to do this:

1. Provide the opportunity for individuals to attend seminars or in-servicing in a particular professional topic they wish to explore.

2. Help staff members track their current performance in a particular skill so that they now have a measuring stick with which to assess their growth.

3. Set aside time for conferencing with individuals about their present performance and what they can do to improve. Set a long-term as well as several short-term goals for improvement.

4. Celebrate each person's improvement.

5. Encourage individuals to observe other colleagues who can effectively model the desired skill.

6. Help individuals locate resources (books, tapes, persons, etc.) that can provide them with information on the skill.

7. Encourage staff members to pair up with a colleague who desires to improve in the same area. Colleagues could then support one another.

DEMONSTRATION

The final step in this process is to provide opportunities for individuals to demonstrate an identified strength or competency. Without this opportunity, the sense of competency cannot be enhanced. Demonstrating the skill in front of others can be an extraordinary vehicle for enhancing competency. Not only will the esteem builder be acknowledging the talent but the possibility is opened up for other staff members to ackowledge the skill. To have colleagues commend individuals' talents ignites the success cycle even further. As C.C. Colton aptly stated, "Applause is the spur of noble minds." Some ways the administrator can provide opportunities for staff members to demonstrate a strength include:

Provide opportunities for individuals to demonstrate an identified strength or competency.

• Ask individuals to demonstrate their skills at a faculty meeting.

• Encourage persons to conduct a mini-in-service for parents or teachers in which the skill is demonstrated.

• Commend individuals and the skills they possess at a faculty gathering. Invite the newspaper to document these skills.

• Hold a Strength Fair at which faculty members demonstrate their skills and talents.

• Set up a "brag board" on the wall of the faculty room where staff members can share talents and skills. Set up a bulletin board with a caption such as "Our Brag Board." Encourage staff members to pin up articles, photographs, news clippings, etc. that depict the competencies of their colleagues. Samples of lessons and student work could also be included.

- Assign various faculty members the role of "expert" in the skill or talent they possess.

- Ask faculty members to share their skills at a faculty meeting.

Knowledge of strengths builds feelings of competence.

Reflection: The principles of enhancing individuals' awareness of their strengths and talents are critical. Too many staff members wallow in self-doubts and never recognize their skills and assets. Knowledge of strengths builds feelings of competence; it helps staff members build a feeling of being effective in their role as teachers. Take a moment to reflect on your current behaviors. How do you let individual staff members become aware of their strengths, talents, and assets? Write specific methods you use currently on the left side of the T-bar below. Now think of ways you let individual staff members demonstrate their talents to others. List all the ways in which you currently help staff members display their talents to others on the right side of the T-bar.

CURRENT WAYS	
Awareness of Strengths	**Demonstration of Talents**

Reflect one step further. How can you expand on your current behaviors? What are new ways you could begin implementing to help staff members become aware of their strengths? Add these to the left side of the T-bar below. Finally, reflect upon additional methods you could employ to help staff members demonstrate their talents to others. Write these on the right side of the T-bar.

NEW WAYS	
Awareness of Strengths	**Demonstration of Talents**

Put an asterisk next to the one item in each category you will implement. What will you do differently?

Guideline Questions: Individual Competencies and Strengths (SEB 129)

The following questions are provided as guidelines for the administrator to help determine if conditions are being fostered that provide opportunities for individual staff members to recognize and demonstrate their individual strengths and competencies.

	Regularly	Seldom	Never
1. Do I work at creating an atmosphere in which staff members can specialize, discover their distinctiveness, and capitalize on their skills?	_____	_____	_____
2. Do I consciously look for the talents of each staff member?	_____	_____	_____
3. Do I write down the talents and skills I've discovered about each staff member?	_____	_____	_____
4. Do I write or tell staff members about the talents I've observed?	_____	_____	_____
5. Do I tell the individual exactly what I observed that keyed me into their talent?	_____	_____	_____
6. Do I make it a point during evaluation sessions to discuss the evaluee's personal strengths and talents?	_____	_____	_____
7. Do I let individuals know exactly what they can do in order to improve their talents?	_____	_____	_____
8. Do I provide support (resources, funding, seminar information, personnel) to help individuals develop their talent?	_____	_____	_____
9. Do I encourage staff members to pair up with or model individuals with similar talents?	_____	_____	_____
10. Do I provide opportunities for individuals to demonstrate the identified strengths and competencies?	_____	_____	_____

ESTEEM BUILDER #3

Monitor Progress and Provide Specific Feedback

---

*"Some are kissing mothers and some are scolding mothers,
but it is love just the same, and most mothers
kiss and scold together."*
—PEARL S. BUCK

The third step esteem builders can take to enhance competence is to monitor the progress of individual staff members and then provide them with specific feedback telling them exactly what they are doing right or what they need to do in order to improve. People need to be recognized for a job well done; they also need to be told, when needed, how to do the job more effectively. The enforcement of high standards requires that we let individuals know when they are not meeting those standards. Not to do so lowers our own standards as well as other individuals' level of competence. Self-esteem is lowered when expectations are set too high. Likewise, self-esteem is reduced when the expectations for competent performance are set far below what individuals are capable of reaching. Both settings can rob others of a heightened sense of competence.

Effective feedback is vital to the evaluation process.

The evaluative relationship between administrator and staff members can be an excellent vehicle for enhancing self-esteem and the sense of competence. The evaluation process by its nature is designed to improve instruction. Such a process will be greatly enhanced if the staff member comes to the evaluation as a "willing, and receptive partner." If we are not careful, the very feedback we hope will improve performance could also deter performance. There is an art to giving effective feedback that not only improves an individual's behavior in the future but at the same time builds self-esteem. An "Effective Feedback Action Plan" is provided on page 166. Effective feedback is vital to the evaluation process. The evaluative relationship between administrator and staff members can be an excellent vehicle for enhancing self-esteem and the sense of competence. To ensure that the feedback is conducive to esteem enhancement, it is critical that the evaluation process be well planned. Use the form to create an action plan *before* conferencing.

Below are suggestions for ways the esteem builder can provide "effective criticism" that protects the staff member's self-esteem and still gives concrete feedback to improve performance. These steps, as outlined on the "Effective Feedback Action Plan," include:

EFFECTIVE FEEDBACK STEPS   (SEB130)

1. Do It Immediately
2. Check the Facts
3. Begin Positively
4. Be Specific and Use Data
5. Be Descriptive and Not Evaluative
6. Explain the Need for Improvement
7. Provide Redirection
8. Follow-Up

---

1. **Do It Immediately.** Don't put off the meeting; instead arrange an individual conference as soon as convenient. The danger in waiting is that the behavior can become more serious, and then it becomes more difficult to change.

2. **Check the Facts.** Before continuing any further, be sure to have the facts right. Always be able to support your statements with data. Ask yourself:

   Do I have all the information I need?
   Am I sure of my statements?
   What kinds of facts do I have to back up my statements?
   Have I looked at this problem from all angles?
   Am I really ready to confront the individual with the problem?

3. **Begin Positively.** Stay calm during the process. Confronting someone in an angry tone will just trigger anger in the other person. The goal is not to antagonize the person but to make him/her receptive to the information you are about to give. Beginning with a positive statement helps set a calmer, more positive tone for the evaluation. The positive anecdotal notes you have kept on file concerning individual staff members can now become excellent resources to pull from. Ask yourself:

   Are there positive characteristics about this individual I could mention?

   These positive characteristics are where you begin.

4. **Be Specific and Use Data.** Tell the individual exactly what he/she is doing that needs to be improved or changed by pinpointing particular aspects of the person's behavior. Give specific and not general examples of his/her behavior.

   General: "You're always late."
   Specific: "I noticed you've been at least 10 minutes late to the last three faculty meetings."
   General: "You're never prepared."
   Specific: "The last two times I observed your classroom, your lessons were not prepared."

   "You had to take out five minutes from the reading lesson to locate the worksheets. I noticed you also had to quickly read the teacher's manual to determine the directions for the task while your students waited."

Facts and data help back up your statements. Specific data also helps the individual recognize you've thought this evaluation process through and have taken the time to document what you're saying. Aim for only *one* behavior change per conference. More than one item will be too overwhelming for an individual with low competence. The goal is to be specific and create a plan by the end of the conference for the individual to change his/her behavior.

Aim for only *one* behavior change per conference.

5. **Be Descriptive and Not Evaluative.** Remember to criticize the individual's behavior and *not the individual*. Also avoid analyzing an individual's motives. "You are lazy" is an evaluation. "You took two hours to prepare a simple reading exercise" is a description.

6. **Explain the Need for Improvement.** Be sure the person clearly knows why the behavior is a problem. The person must walk away from the session recognizing why his/her behavior needs to improve. Without this awareness, changing the behavior is difficult. Beginning your message with an "I statement" and then telling the individual how you feel about the behavior as well as its effects is a powerful communication technique. Thomas Gordon in his book, *Leader Effectiveness Training (L.E.T.)*, suggests using the following three-part formula for sending I-messages:[3]

Behavior + Feelings + Effects

All three elements (behavior, feelings, and effects) should be in your message but not necessarily in that order. Two examples are provided below:

I am very concerned about your tardiness to meetings because you are missing critical information as well as setting an unprofessional image for your colleagues.

Behavior: tardiness to meeting; *Feelings:* very concerned; *Effects:* missing information, setting an unprofessional image for colleagues.

I am uneasy about your lack of lesson preparation. It is greatly reducing your teaching effectiveness and keeping your students off task far too much.

Behavior: lack of lesson preparation; *Feelings:* very uneasy; *Effects:* reducing teaching effectiveness, students off task.

> The most important part is helping the individual learn what to do in order to improve their performance.

7. **Provide Redirection.** The most important part of the process is helping the individual learn what to do in order to improve their performance. This is the time when a dialogue between the two of you is crucial. The goal is to correct the action by providing redirection.

Dr. Sidney B. Simon in his book, *Negative Criticism And What To Do About It*, recommends that during the feedback process with a staff member regarding their performance, the person providing the feedback should ask the following three questions:

1. *What did you like about what you did?*
2. *In what ways would you change it the next time you do it?*
3. *In what ways can I help you? Would you like support from me?*

Simon suggests that questions of this kind are more positive in nature and therefore better received by the staff member. Being more constructive than critical is always a better technique. Together, come to an agreement as to what will be done, how it will be done and when it will be done. Ideally, these steps should be written down.[4]

---

3. Gordon, Dr. Thomas. *Leader Effectiveness Training (L.E.T.): The No-Lose Way to Release the Productive Potential of People.* New York: Bantam Books, 1977.

4. Simon, Sidney. *Negative Criticism: And What To Do About It.* Hadley, MA: Values Associates, 1978.

8. **Follow-Up.** The final step will not take place during the feedback session, but at a future session. Before the end of the session, arrange a time to meet again. Emphasize that you will *always* be available to talk about the issue. Mention that improvement usually does not take place over night and often a number of sessions are needed. Close the meeting on a *positive* note. You may wish to have the individual repeat key points discussed during the session to make sure he/she heard your message clearly.

Close the meeting on a *positive* note.

If done correctly, effective feedback conveys to the individual that incompetence will not be sanctioned. "I know you can do better, and this is how you can do it."

Guideline Questions: Effective Feedback (SEB 131)

The following questions are provided as guidelines for the administrator to help determine if conditions are being fostered to monitor staff progress and provide feedback.

	Regularly	Seldom	Never
• Do I let staff members know when I am pleased with their performance?	_____	_____	_____
• Do I monitor the progress of staff members through procedures such as classroom observation, test scores, informal discussions and parent evaluation?	_____	_____	_____
• Do I review staff members' performances on a regular basis, allowing the persons being reviewed to be directly involved in the process?	_____	_____	_____
• Do evaluated individuals clearly know the guidelines for how they will be evaluated prior to the process?	_____	_____	_____
• When a staff member's performance is ineffective do I immediately schedule an individual conference?	_____	_____	_____
• Do I support my critical statements with specific and adequate data?	_____	_____	_____
• Do I hold evaluation sessions in private?	_____	_____	_____
• Do I begin the session calmly, without showing anger?	_____	_____	_____
• Do I begin the evaluation session with a positive statement regarding an individual's performance?	_____	_____	_____
• Do I tell an individual *specifically* what I do not like about his/her performance?	_____	_____	_____

Guideline Questions: Effective Feedback (SEB 131)			
	Regularly	**Seldom**	**Never**
• Do I make sure the person clearly knows why I see his/her behavior as a problem?	_____	_____	_____
• Do I use "I messages" that tell the individual how I feel about the behavior as well as the effect of his/her behavior?	_____	_____	_____
• Do I help the individual learn what to do in order to improve ineffective behavior?	_____	_____	_____
• Do I arrange for a follow-up meeting to determine progress in correcting the behavior?	_____	_____	_____
• Do I follow through and hold the follow-up meeting?	_____	_____	_____

Action Plan: Write three action strategies you will begin implementing to monitor progress and provide specific feedback for your staff members:

1. _____
_____
_____
_____
_____
_____

2. _____
_____
_____
_____
_____
_____

3. _____
_____
_____
_____
_____
_____

ESTEEM BUILDER #4

HELP INDIVIDUALS RECOGNIZE THEY DO MAKE A DIFFERENCE

"When you cease to make a contribution, you begin to die."
—ELEANOR ROOSEVELT

We all must believe we can be effective in our professional role. It is particularly critical for teachers to recognize they do make differences in the lives of students. Theodore Sizer, a former dean of education at Harvard University, stated that the most important factor in job satisfaction for teachers is recognizing they make a difference. The National Center for Education Information (1986) confirmed this when they surveyed American teachers and found the top reasons why people teach. These reasons included: "a chance to use their minds and abilities," "a chance to work with young people," and "an appreciation for a job well done."

The morale of the education profession is at an all-time low, and understandably so. Teachers are constantly slapped with news releases and media coverage pointing out their ineffectiveness. Again and again the educational profession is blamed for all the problems of our youth. There has never been a time in education when teachers have been faced with such great obstacles. Parent support is at an all-time low, budget constraints are rampant, class sizes continue to rise, risk factors in students are increasing at the same time that expectations of teachers are at their highest. More than ever, teachers need to know they can have a positive impact on students' lives.

The administrator can play an instrumental role in helping staff members recognize how powerful they are as "difference makers." Some of the many ways staff members can be made aware of their contributions include: sending notes mentioning specific moments that have created differences for students, publicly acknowledging a teacher's achievements, or holding evaluation sessions with individuals whose test scores, observations or other objective data demonstrate teaching effectiveness. Whatever the method used to let teachers know about their effectiveness and impact on their students, the critical point is that the administrator consciously work at helping staff members recognize they can make a difference!

> **The administrator can play an instrumental role in helping staff members recognize how powerful they are as "difference makers."**

Ways to Show Staff Members They Make a Difference (SEB 132-146)

1. **Written Hearts (SEB 132).** Before a staff gathering, cut out construction paper hearts and write the name of each staff member on a different heart. Colleagues can then anonymously pull the name of a staff member out of a bag or box. Ask participants to take a few minutes to write something that tells the person whose name they chose why he/she is effective as an educator or how he/she makes a difference. Write the statement about the person on his/her "heart." Participants may present their colleague with the heart before the meeting convenes or place it in the individual's box so that he/she can read it at a later time.

2. **Whip (SEB 133).** Before a faculty meeting, ask staff members to share one special moment they had with their class that day (or during the week) by responding to an open statement such as: "One activity that was successful for me was..." Allow each staff member one minute to respond. Other whip possibilities are for teachers to share a moment when they know they made a difference or to describe a technique that's working effectively with their students. Begin whips by making open statements such as: "A moment that made a difference for a student was..." or "A technique that's working for me to improve a student's behavior is..." Variations on these include: "A special (or fun) moment in the classroom this week was..." or "A favorite lesson I did this week was..." The facilitator must emphasize that sharing should be quick, taking no more than a minute or two. The whip can be a fast way for staff members to acknowledge one another's efforts.

3. **Paired Sharing (SEB 134).** At a faculty gathering, ask participants to pair up (the activity could be varied by dividing the group into teams of four). Ask each team to choose a "starter" (the person who talks first). Explain to the group that team members will have a few minutes to share a moment they know they made differences in the lives of their students. Emphasize this does not have to be an "earth-shattering" difference—any moment will do. Each team member describes the moment while the rest of the team listens to the explanation without interruption. At the conclusion of the description, all team members applaud the speaker and the person on the "starter's" left assumes the role of speaker. Continue the activity until all members on the team have shared.

4. **"You're Significant" Buttons or Badges (SEB 135).** Present to each staff member a button or badge inscribed with a saying such as: "Significant Other," "I'm a Difference Maker," or "I'm proud to teach."

5. **Inspirational Teachers' Awards Banquet (SEB 136).** Ask each student in the school or district to write down the name of an elementary, middle and/or high school teacher who made a difference in their life. Collect the ballots. With a support group, plan a special banquet for nominated teachers. This could be hosted at a local restaurant or in a school cafeteria. Invite the students who supplied the names of the teachers to the event. Create a certificate or plaque for each nominated teacher. At the conclusion of the banquet, ask each student to come to the front of the room and award his/her special teacher the certificate. *Idea suggested by Stockton Unified School District, Stockton, California.*

6. **Parent Letter Campaign (SEB 137).** The Esteem Builder Team or administrator is usually in charge of the parent letter campaign. It is important to try and keep teachers unaware of the activity. Create an open letter to all the students' parents asking them to write, if they choose, a personal letter to any teacher(s) who has made a difference for their child. Explain that all the letters should be delivered to the teachers on the same day *(and specify this day!)*. An excellent time to do this activity is on Teacher Appreciation Day. *Idea suggested by Dr. William Knight, Principal, Newport Mesa School District, Newport Beach, California.*

7. **Personal Business Cards (SEB 138).** Print up a set of business cards for each staff member. Print not only their name, school, and address on the cards, but also the words, "I Am Proud to Be an Educator," or a similar statement.

8. **Central Office Acknowledgments (SEB 139).** Send notes acknowledging teachers' accomplishments to the Central Office. Be sure to make a copy of the letter to hand to the individual.

9. **Teacher Appreciation Day Assembly (SEB 140).** Invite students from nearby schools who have graduated to come to your school at a set date and time. Hold a large school assembly with all staff members, students and parents in attendance. Ask the returning students to tell how a staff member at that school site made a difference in their lives. *Idea suggested by Robert Reasoner, Moreland School District, San Jose, California.*

10. **Essay Contest: "A Teacher Who Made a Difference" (SEB 141).** Invite all students to write an essay about a teacher they had who made a difference in their lives. The essay must describe how they feel about that individual and what they remember about the teacher. Completed essays can be judged and winning entries published in the school and community newsletters. In addition, authors could read selected essays at a school assembly. All essays could also be displayed on bulletin boards throughout the school building.

11. **Student Interviews (SEB 142).** A week before Teacher Appreciation Day ask volunteers to interview students about their current teachers. Students are asked, "Tell me why your teacher is special?" or "What is one thing that makes your teacher special?" Cut out a large red, construction paper apple for each student. Each student's response (one or two sentences) is written on the "apple." The student may sign their statement. Completed apples may be used in a variety of ways: create a personal book for each teacher by stapling his/her students' apples together, staple all the apples on a large bulletin board or display case, or hang the apples of each teacher's students on a large tree trunk made from brown construction paper. *Idea suggested by Hayward Unified School District, Hayward, California.*

12. **Teacher Quotations (SEB 143).** Quotations about teacher effectiveness and how they create differences for students is a powerful tool. Print a favorite quote on stationery for teachers to use, or on smaller strips of paper placed in individual staff boxes, or even on larger pieces of tagboard hung around the faculty room. The inspiring quotations on page 168 offers many to choose from.

13. **Appreciation Grams (SEB 144).** Provide an ample supply of awards or appreciation grams (page 172) along with pens near staff members' boxes. Post a sign encouraging colleagues to write to each other: "Write a note to a staff member letting them know how they made a difference."

14. **You Make the Difference Cards (SEB 145).** Run off a large supply of "You Make the Difference" Cards on light-colored construction paper (page171). Cut along the borders to create individual cards. At a staff gathering, explain how important it is

for colleagues to support each other and let each other know he/she is making a difference. Distribute several cards to each participant. Provide a convenient location at the school site where additional cards may be obtained if needed. Explain that as staff members observe a colleague "making differences," they are to sign their own name on the back of a card, write the recipient's name on the front of the card, and either give it to the individual or place it in his/her box. Staff members should write on the card specifically what they saw someone doing that made a difference. A variation to this activity is to collect the completed cards and place them in a "lottery bowl" (any container) on the faculty room table. Once a week have a staff drawing by pulling a few cards from the lottery bowl. Winning "difference makers" can receive prizes such as items donated by local businesses. *Idea suggested by the Self-Esteem Design Team (Marion Goldstein, Michael Vocatura, and Helen Samuels) from Rocky Mountain Elementary School, Colorado.*

15. **Books Celebrating Teachers (SEB 146).** There are many powerful books affirming the role teachers have a "difference makers" for students. A few are listed below:

America's Best Classrooms: How Award-Winning Teachers Are Shaping Our Children's Future by Daniel and Terry Seymour. An inspiring expedition into the hearts and minds of thirty teachers, all winners of the Teacher of the Year Award. Wonderful success stories of teachers who are winning in classrooms every day (Princeton, NJ: Peterson's Guides, 1992).

Among Schoolchildren by Tracy Kidder. One year in the teaching career of a powerful, devoted fifth-grade teacher. A clear description of how one good teacher can make a difference in a child's life and in our society (Boston, MA: Houghton Mifflin, 1989).

Escalante: The Best Teacher in America by Jay Mathews. It is rare to find another teacher who has produced such spectacular results in such a difficult setting and who offers so many encouraging answers to some of the most important social and educational questions of our time. Here is his life and an explanation of his success (New York, NY: Holt & Co., 1988).

I Am a Teacher: A Tribute to America's Teachers by David Marshall Marquis and Robin Sachs. Seventy outstanding teachers are interviewed and photographed. This book clearly shows nothing is more important than outstanding teachers (New York, NY: Simon & Schuster, 1990).

My Great Aunt Arizona by Gloria Houston. This is written as a children's picture book, but adults who read it fall in love with it. A true story of the author's great aunt, Arizona, who grows up to become her teacher and influences generations of school children (New York, NY: Harper Collins, 1992).

Small Victories: The Real World of a Teacher, Her Students and Their High School by Samuel G. Freedman. A Manhattan high school is overcrowded and ranked among the worst ten percent of high schools in New York State. How do ninety-two percent of its graduates go on to higher education? The answer lies in dedicated teachers, one of whom, Jessica Siegel, is the subject of this book (New York, NY: Harper & Row, 1990).

Reflection: Helping teachers recognize they impact students' lives is critical toward enhancing personal efficacy. In what ways could you let teachers know they do make a difference? List these ideas in the space below. Now put an asterisk next to the one item you plan to implement.

_____

_____

_____

Guideline Questions: Awareness of Teacher Efficacy (SEB 147)

The following questions are provided as guidelines for the administrator to help determine if conditions are being fostered that provide staff members with an awareness that they make differences in the lives of their students.

	Regularly	Seldom	Never
• Do I consciously work at helping staff members recognize their effectiveness?	_____	_____	_____
• Are staff members encouraged to acknowledge one another's professional effectiveness?	_____	_____	_____
• Is time provided at faculty meetings for staff members to share effective techniques they've tried with students?	_____	_____	_____
• Do I tell individual staff members about the specific techniques they are using that are effective?	_____	_____	_____
• Do I make it a point to tell individual staff members comments others have made concerning their effectiveness?	_____	_____	_____
• Do I encourage parents to acknowledge teacher effectiveness?	_____	_____	_____
• Are students provided with opportunities to tell teachers how they impacted their lives?	_____	_____	_____

COMPETENCE ESTEEM BUILDERS   SEB 148-176

1. *Teacher's Pride (SEB 148).* Set up a Teacher's Pride Bulletin Board. Highlight special projects and ideas currently being used in classrooms.

2. *Buttons and Badges (SEB 149).* Present to staff members buttons or badges inscribed with statements such as: "Significant Other," "A Teacher Who's Making a Difference," and "I'm Proud to Teach."

3. *Scrapbook (SEB 150).* Keep a scrapbook of school-wide and classroom happenings that highlight teachers' efforts, gains, and competencies.

4. *Local Newspapers (SEB 151).* Ask the local newspaper to chronicle special school and class happenings, particularly ones demonstrating teacher competencies, efforts, and moments that validate that the staff member has made a difference.

5. *Celebrations (SEB 152).* Celebrate staff members' achievements and accomplishments. Celebrations can be as elaborate as a dinner or luncheon to acknowledge special efforts or as simple as asking colleagues to give deserving individuals a ten-second standing ovation. Whatever the technique, find the time to celebrate and acknowledge staff victories.

6. *Brag Board (SEB 153).* Set up a Brag Board in the faculty room where individuals can "brag" about their own personal or professional achievements. Encourage staff members to brag about the achievements of their fellow colleagues as well: "I just wanted to let you know I noticed an incredible lesson the other day that Sally was doing with her second grade students. Ask her about the cooperative learning lesson she is doing in her math program. From Margaret."

7. *Success Grams (SEB 154).* Have certificates or success grams available for staff members to validate one another's successes.

8. *Experts (SEB 155).* Assign teachers the role of "expert" in a particular subject or expertise. Ideally, each staff member will become an "expert" in an unique area. Make sure other staff members recognize these individuals and their expertise.

9. *Mini-Workshops (SEB 156).* Allow staff members to conduct "mini-workshops" or short in-service sessions at faculty meetings on professional development days in areas they are particularly accomplished.

10. *Brag Sessions (SEB 157).* Plan one-minute Brag Sessions at faculty meetings. Individual staff members acknowledge one thing they're doing with their students that has been effective.

11. *Strengths and Weaknesses (SEB158).* Encourage individual staff members to examine their personal strengths and weaknesses. Emphasize that we all have things we are proud of about ourselves as well as things we would like to change.

The "Strengths and Weaknesses" form found in *Esteem Builders* on page 309 could be used during this self-reflection activity.

12. *Graphs (SEB 159).* Encourage staff members to track their individual teaching performance on graphs. This is an excellent way for individuals to evaluate their growth.

13. *Personal Expectations (SEB 160).* Allow individual staff members the freedom to set their own expectations regarding a new area they wish to enhance their skills or become more proficient in.

14. *Shared Resources (SEB 161).* Encourage staff members to utilize each other's resources.

15. *Progress Evaluation (SEB 162).* Develop ways to monitor the progress of individual staff members as they work toward their goals. Plan time to meet with them individually to evaluate their progress and see what kind of support they need.

16. *Needed Support (SEB 163).* Make a point of asking individual staff members what kind of support or resources they need in order to accomplish their objectives.

17. *Self-Evaluations (SEB 164).* Create opportunities for staff members to monitor and assess their own progress. Encourage individuals to create their own techniques for evaluation.

18. *Clear Expectations (SEB 165).* Routinely meet with individual staff members to discuss exactly what you expect from them. Staff members should clearly know what is expected of them and how they can go about meeting these expectations.

19. *List of Strengths (SEB 166).* Create a list of all staff members' names. Identify at least one personal and one professional strength of each staff member. List these strengths next to the individual's name.

20. *Commendations (SEB 167).* Routinely send verbal or written commendations to individual staff members specifically identifying strengths or skills you observed about them. Commend individual staff members for achievements at faculty gatherings.

21. *Ways to Improve (SEB 168).* Take the time to help individual staff members not only know what their strengths are but also exactly what they can do to improve in that strength or talent.

22. *Seminars (SEB 169).* Provide opportunities for individuals to attend seminars or in-servicing in a particular professional topic they wish to explore.

23. *Modelling (SEB 170).* Encourage staff members to observe colleagues who can effectively model the desired skill or talent individuals wish to improve in.

24. *Colleague Support (SEB 171).* Encourage staff members to pair with colleagues who wish to improve in the same skill or who demonstrate a similar talent. Colleagues could then support one another.

25. *Strength Fair (SEB 172).* Hold a Strength Fair or Hobby Day where staff members demonstrate their skills or talents (to one another or to students).

26. *Special Moments (SEB 173).* At faculty gatherings, ask staff members to share a special moment they had with their class that day.

27. *Compliments (SEB 174).* Emphasize to staff members the importance of validating one another's moments of "making a difference." Encourage the staff anytime they hear someone else complimenting a fellow colleague to personally tell the staff member.

28. *Certificates and Grams (SEB 175).* A number of certificates and grams are provided in *Esteem Builders* for educators to use with their students. Many of these certificates can easily be run off on colored copy paper for staff members to use with one another. Some of the forms that can be used include:

Code	Title	Page
C1/2	Hobby Day Award	293
C4	Attention!	295
C5	Strength Award	296
C34	News Flash	307
C38	Hanging Award	288
C39	Positive Wristbands	315
	Staff Warm Fuzzy	386

29. *Esteem Builder Activities (SEB 176).* Educators have successfully used many activities in *Esteem Builders* on themselves in an upgraded version to enhance the feeling of competence. Not only is this technique a fun way for staff members to find out about each other, but it also helps build staff esteem. Activities you may wish to try are:

Code	Title	Page
C1	Hobby Day Checklist	291
C2	My Interest	292
C8	Strength Barbells	298
C16	I Can	299-300
C26	Accomplishment Banner	284

SUMMARY

A sense of competence is the fifth and final feeling individuals with high self-esteem possess. This is a critical feeling for educators because of their strong desire to feel as though they are making differences for their students. Competence can be enhanced. The following are the four steps esteem builders may take to increase competency among staff members:

---

1. Provide opportunities to recognize and demonstrate individual competencies and strengths.
2. Set high and achievable expectations.
3. Monitor progress and provide specific feedback.
4. Help individuals recognize they do make a difference.

Keeper

The most important idea about the concept of competence I want to remember is:

_____

_____

_____

_____

_____

_____

_____

_____

_____

One way I will apply this idea in my relationship with my staff is: _____

_____

_____

_____

_____

_____

_____

_____

_____

EFFECTIVE FEEDBACK ACTION PLAN

Name of individual: _____

1. Do It Immediately:

Date and time of scheduled conference: _____

Date individual verifies attendance: _____

2. Check the Facts:

___ Do I have all the information I need?

___ Am I sure of my statements?

___ Have I looked at this problem from all angles?

___ Am I really ready to confront the individual with this problem?

Facts I plan to use to back up my statements: _____

_____

_____

_____

_____

3. Begin Positive:

Positive characteristics about this individual I could mention are: _____

_____

_____

_____

_____

The positive statement about the individual I plan to start with is: _____

_____

_____

_____

Esteem Builders' Complete Program
Jalmar Press, Rolling Hills Estates, CA

4. Be Specific and Use Data:

Examples of the individual's behavior I plan to give that tell him/her exactly what I do not like:

_____
_____
_____

5. Remember:
Be descriptive and not evaluative! Use facts. Describe the behavior and not the individual's motives.

6. Explaining the Need for Improvement:
How I will let the person clearly know why I see the behavior as a problem.

Behavior + Feelings + Effects

"*I am* (how I feel about their behavior): _____

about (site the behavior that bothers you...what specifically are they doing wrong?) _____
_____

because (site the effects the behavior has on their performance) _____
_____

7. Provide Redirection:
What the individual could do to improve the behavior:
Possible Solutions to the Behavior: _____
_____
_____
_____

"What did you like about what you did?"
"In what ways would you change it the next time you do it?"
"In what ways can I help you? Would you like support from me?"

8. Follow-Up:
Possible dates and time for follow-up sessions:

Date: _____ Time: _____

Date: _____ Time: _____

Permission to Reprint for Classroom Use.
© 1993 by Michele Borba

— 167 —

Esteem Builders' Complete Program
Jalmar Press, Rolling Hills Estates, CA

IT IS THE SUPREME ART OF THE TEACHER TO AWAKEN JOY IN CREATIVE EXPRESSION AND KNOWLEDGE.

ALBERT EINSTEIN

WHO TEACHES ME FOR A DAY IS MY FATHER FOR A LIFETIME.

CHINESE PROVERB

EVERYONE WHO REMEMBERS HIS OWN EDUCATIONAL EXPERIENCE REMEMBERS TEACHERS, NOT METHODS AND TECHNIQUES. THE TEACHER IS THE KINGPIN OF THE EDUCATIONAL SITUATION. HE MAKES OR BREAKS PROGRAMS.

SIDNEY HOOK

WHILE WE TEACH, WE LEARN.

SENECA

IF YOU CAN READ THIS... THANK A TEACHER

BUMPER STICKER

KINDERGARTEN TEACHER: ONE WHO KNOWS HOW TO MAKE THE LITTLE THINGS COUNT.

ANONYMOUS

THE MAN WHO CAN MAKE HARD THINGS EASY IS THE EDUCATOR.

RALPH WALDO EMERSON

A TEACHER IS ONE WHO MADE TWO IDEAS GROW WHERE ONLY ONE GREW BEFORE.

ELBERT HUBBARD

A TEACHER IS LIKE A CANDLE WHICH LIGHTS OTHERS IN CONSUMING ITSELF.

RUFFINI

Esteem Builders' Complete Program
Jalmar Press, Rolling Hills Estates, CA

APPRECIATION GRAMS

"A teacher affects eternity; he can never tell where his

influence stops."   *Henry Adams*

To: _____

From: _____

Date: _____

_____

_____

_____

_____

_____

_____

_____

_____

I just wanted to let you know what an influence you are!

"DIFFERENCE MAKER AWARD"

Date: _____

To: _____

From: _____

"I just wanted to let you know

_____

_____

_____ "

YOU'RE MAKING A DIFFERENCE!

Remember:
1. Give a student a pat-on-the-back every day.
2. Give a colleague a pat-on-the-back every day.
3. I make a difference to someone every day.

Esteem Builders' Complete Program
Jalmar Press, Rolling Hills Estates, CA

YOU MAKE THE DIFFERENCE LETTERS

The following letter may be sent to the staff explaining how the *You Make the Difference* program works. Decide which dates (ideally, one each month) will be the dates of the card drawings. Fill these dates in the letters. Attach a set of *You Make the Difference* cards (SEB 145) with each letter.

Dear Staff:

The Self-Esteem Committee wants you to know that *YOU MAKE THE DIFFERENCE!* You make the difference for kids, and you can make the difference for each other. We all need that extra bit of recognition, and it feels as good to give it as it does to receive it. Attached is a sheet of *"You Make the Difference!"* cards. Let your colleagues know you appreciate their good deeds, new ideas, or in the true spirit of self-esteem, recognize someone for the intrinsic value we *all* possess. Hand cards out freely to other staff persons. Here's how - on the line on the front, write the person's name you are recognizing; on the back, please note how this person makes the difference, and remember to sign your name (see example below). When you receive a card, read it and then put it in the box in the staff lounge. Five names (a total of 15) will be drawn at the P.T.O. meetings on _____, _____ and _____. Watch for prizes, but most of all, watch for the recognition and value you all deserve. We all make the difference, let's tell each other so!

Please make it your goal to hand out the attached 12 cards over the next three months. Extra cards are available in the school office. Parents will be participating also. Information will be coming soon.

With warm regards and the utmost in self-esteem,

BECAUSE YOU
GREET STAFF
MEMBERS
WITH A SMILE
EACH DAY!
THE SELF-ESTEEM
COMMITTEE

You Make the Difference letters written by Helen Samuels, parent; and Marion Goldstein, parent; from Rocky Mountain Elementary School Self-Esteem Design Team; Westminster, Colorado.

Esteem Builders' Complete Program
Jalmar Press, Rolling Hills Estates, CA

YOU MAKE THE DIFFERENCE LETTERS

The following letter may be sent to the parents explaining how the *You Make the Difference* program works. Decide which dates (ideally, one each month) will be the dates of the card drawings. Fill these dates in the letters. Attach a set of *You Make the Difference* cards (SEB 145) with each letter.

Dear Parents:

Our school has identified enhancing staff self-esteem as a goal for this school year. A self-esteem program is currently being implemented to increase positive feedback and recognition between staff members. We are very happy to offer parents the opportunity to be involved as well. Think about the last time you wanted to thank a staff member for something wonderful your child brought home, for that extra bit of effort or for a job well done. Did you do it? Well, we are going to make it easy for you to follow through with all those "thank yous" that have been left unsaid.

Attached are three *"You Make the Difference!"* cards. Present them in person to the staff member you wish to recognize or send them to school with your child. If you need more than three (we hope you will!), you or your child can pick up more in the school office. Here's how it works: On the line on the front, write the staff person's name you are recognizing; on the back, note how this person makes the difference and remember to sign your name. See the example below. When a staff person receives this card, he/she will read it and will then put it in a box in the teacher's lounge. Five names (a total of 15) will be drawn at the parent meetings on _____, _____ and _____. Prizes will be awarded by the Self-Esteem Committee, but please know that you, as parents, can give the very important gift of the kind of recognition that all staff members deserve. They all make the difference! Let's tell them so!

Thank you!
Your Self-Esteem Committee

Because your energy and enthusiasm has really made a difference for Joshua. Sincerely, Sue and Joe Anderson

You Make the Difference letters written by Helen Samuels, parent; and Marion Goldstein, parent; from Rocky Mountain Elementary School Self-Esteem Design Team; Westminster, Colorado.

Esteem Builders' Complete Program
Jalmar Press, Rolling Hills Estates, CA

Esteem Builders' Complete Program
Jalmar Press, Rolling Hills Estates, CA

ACTION PLAN FOR ENHANCING A SENSE OF COMPETENCE

Take time to think through your action strategies. What will you personally do to enhance the sense of Competence for your staff? The importance of this planning cannot be overemphasized.

In an effort to enhance the feeling of Competence of my staff, I will implement the following ideas and actions:

To ensure that I set high and achievable expectations among staff members, I will:

1. _____
_____

2. _____
_____

3. _____
_____

To monitor progress and provide specific feedback for individual staff members, I will:

1. _____
_____

2. _____
_____

3. _____
_____

To encourage individual staff members to recognize they do make a difference, I will:

1. _____
_____

2. _____
_____

3. _____
_____

Date of Commitment: _____

Follow-up Date: _____

Esteem Builders' Complete Program
Jalmar Press, Rolling Hills Estates, CA

BEHAVIOR FOCUS

TASK: Analyze your own behavior toward staff members. Consider your strengths as well as areas you could improve.

BEHAVIOR STRENGTHS (Esteem Enhancing to Staff)	**BEHAVIORS TO IMPROVE** (Esteem Defeating to Staff)

TASK: SELF-COMMITMENT

Choose one area you'd like to improve that you feel may be impeding the self-enhancement of your staff. Write a goal to yourself as to what you plan to do and when you plan to start.

I am making a contract with myself to: _____

I will accomplish this goal by doing: _____

The first step I will take is: _____

Signed: _____ **Date:** _____

Esteem Builders' Complete Program
Jalmar Press, Rolling Hills Estates, CA

STAFF SELF-ESTEEM ACTION PLAN

The enhancement of staff self-esteem must be a deliberate, planned process. The importance of an administrator developing an action plan cannot be overemphasized. Take time to think through the specific techniques, ideas, and strategies you plan to implement to enhance the self-esteem of your staff.

To enhance the self-esteem of my staff, I will implement the following actions:

To enhance the feeling of security among my staff, I will:

1._____
2._____
3._____

To enhance individual staff member's feeling of selfhood, identify, or uniqueness, I will:

1._____
2._____
3._____

To enhance a feeling of staff affiliation and cohesiveness, I will:

1._____
2._____
3._____

To enhance staff members' sense of mission or purpose, I will:

1._____
2._____
3._____

To enhance staff members' sense of personal competence and efficacy, I will:

1._____
2._____
3._____

Esteem Builders' Complete Program
Jalmar Press, Rolling Hills Estates, CA

7

Staff Team
Building Activities

TEAM BUILDING ACTIVITIES

• Activities to Build Positive Self-Esteem and
Team Bonding Among the Staff

TEAM BUILDING ACTIVITIES
CONTENTS

Team Building Activities: *To help the esteem builder in directing the staff to begin team building, the following Team Building Activities are offered in this chapter of* **Staff Esteem Builders**. *All of these activities are designed to enhance staff collegiality and affiliation.* **The majority of these activities can be used to enhance any of the five feelings of self-esteem;** *however, they have been categorized under a specific feeling, in case the esteem builder needs an activity best suited for enhancing a specific feeling component.*

7

Staff Team Building Activities

It takes a village to raise a child.
—OLD AFRICAN PROVERB

Ideal staff environments are characterized by a strong sense of affiliation and cohesiveness. Here is a place where staff members enjoy being with one another. Sharing of teaching ideas and materials is a common practice. Individuals know about one another personally; they know each other's personal interests, names of family members, hobbies and summer vacation destinations as well as teaching strengths and grade-level preferences. Collaborative efforts are common. Staff members feel safe observing in one another's rooms and asking for support. Such an environment also connotes a "turned on team." Individual staff members work for the good of the school and toward the realization of collective efforts. Though their individual classrooms and students are important to them, these staff members are also willing to devote much time and effort to school functions and group causes.

Such environments do not happen by chance. In fact, they are deliberately and purposely planned. Administrators have enormous power in creating such atmospheres. They can create opportunities for individuals to find out about each other. They can structure activities which deliberately emphasize team building concepts. They can encourage staff members to try staff peer processes such as team teaching, peer coaching, and grade-level sharing. They can also support and acknowledge team-building efforts. In short, the administrator is essential as both a model and facilitator in enhancing the team-building environment. He or she takes deliberate, purposeful steps to create a workplace where its members not only trust one another but also enjoy being with one another.

Staff bonding connotes a feeling of "team affiliation" or togetherness. In order to care about one another, educators first need to find out about each other. The activities that follow are designed to provide individuals with opportunities to discover the "personal side" of their colleagues. A large selection of exercises that have been successfully used with teachers are provided to choose from. Each activity is a slightly different variation with a similar objective: _to provide an opportunity for staff members to find out about_

> **Ideal staff environments are characterized by a strong sense of affiliation and cohesiveness.**

— 181 —

one another. They are designed to be used at any staff gathering or faculty meeting. When choosing the activity keep in mind the following points:

- Read the activity thoroughly to familiarize yourself with its structure.

- Some activities require a few materials, all of them commonly found in a school building. Have all materials necessary for the activity on hand prior to the task.

- Begin with the activity you think the staff would respond to the best. A few of the activities involve risk-taking and a stronger level of colleague trust. As a rule, it is best to begin with "less threatening" tasks that are also fun. Always be aware of the comfort level of the participants. If you notice resistance or tension, try a safer task. Staff members must be helped to feel safe doing these activities. Always allow participants the right to pass.

- Make sure that you participate in the activity with the staff. One of the most critical roles an administrator assumes is the role of "model." By sharing yourself personally, you allow a trusting relationship to develop between you and your staff members.

One of the most critical roles an administrator assumes is the role of "model."

POINTS TO CONSIDER IN STAFF BONDING:

- reinforce and celebrate togetherness and cohesiveness;

- create opportunities to recognize individual staff uniquenesses...to find out about each other;

- accentuate activities to bond the staff as a group;

- recognize and acknowledge team-building efforts;

- encourage and support team building processes;

- make sure there are opportunities for *just plain fun* as a group.

SURVEYS   SEB 177-179

Purpose: To provide the opportunity for participants to find out about each other; to increase the energy flow at an in-service by having participants stand and do a quick, purposeful activity.

Materials:
- 1 copy of the "Get Acquainted Checklist" or another survey of your choice for each participant (all participants should receive a copy of the *same* survey).
- pencils or pens for each participant.

Procedure: Duplicate any of the following surveys found at the end of this chapter:

- SEB 177 Get Acquainted Checklist (page 208).
- SEB 178 Warm-Up Bingo (page 209).
- SEB 179 Interviews (page 210).

Or use a survey found in *Esteem Builders*. Surveys that have been successfully adapted from student activities to adult exercises include:

- S17 Time for Friends (pages 60 & 75).
- S19 Name Exchange (page 61).
- S23 Find a Friend (pages 62 & 79).

Explain the procedure to the group as a whole (directions to the activity are found on either the top of the form or in *Esteem Builders*) and provide a time limit (generally no more than ten minutes). It is usually helpful to also specify that a different participant's name should be found for each of the questions.

It's often fun to provide the winner with an inexpensive door prize (i.e. a box of chalk, a set of colored markers, a new whistle). At the completion of the activity, tell participants that the same type of activity can easily be done with their students. Provide a few sample copies of "get-acquainted activities" teachers can use with their students, or refer participants to the following pages in *Esteem Builders:*

Code	Title	Page
S17	Time for Friends	60
S18	Name Bingo	60
S19	Name Exchange	61
S20	Personality Trivia	61
S22	Interest Search	62
S23	Find a Friend	62

TEAM BUILDING ACTIVITIES   SEB 180-185

Purpose: To emphasize the development of the staff's interpersonal skills; to provide opportunities to develop listening and other communication skills; to create opportunities to find out about each other.

Materials: No special materials are needed for the following team-building activities. A large room for the activities is strongly recommended. Chairs and tables can be pushed aside to create more space if needed.

Procedure: Note: As in all the other activities, it is strongly recommended that the facilitator take the time to become thoroughly familiar with the directions of the exercise before attempting it with the group. Whenever possible, practice the activity with a smaller group of individuals before actually doing the task.

• *Knots (SEB 180).* Staff members stand shoulder to shoulder in groups of four to eight. *The larger the group the more difficult the task. It is best to first demonstrate the task using a small group of individuals and then expand the number when some groups desire a "challenge."* Ask everyone to close their eyes. This part of the task could be optional. Each group could vote on whether they wish to do the activity with eyes closed. Tell each person to hold the hands of two other team members who are not standing directly next to one another. The group's task is now to "untangle the knot" until a smooth "untangled" circle of group members forms. Emphasize that ideally no one may let go of anyone else's hand during the activity.

Extension Activity. A task director could be assigned to each team to ease the exercise. The first group to complete the activity could then become consultants for other groups.

• *Faculty Lineups (SEB 181).* Staff members form one long line around the room based on how they fit into the line. Identify where the beginning and end of the line are to be. They must quickly interview people in the line to find out what position they belong in. Possibilities include:

1. number of years as an educator;
2. number of different grade levels taught;
3. number of siblings;
4. number of states lived in;
5. number of children.

• *Face to Face Interviews (SEB 182).* Use only one question each time an interview session takes place. Every ten seconds staff members walk up to another colleague and ask the same question. Some possibilities for questions include:

1. What is your favorite hobby?
2. Where is your favorite place to go?
3. Why do you think self-esteem is important?
4. What staff in-service would you like to attend?
5. What one change would you like to see happen in education?
6. What is your favorite movie?
7. What is your favorite TV show?
8. What thing do you love to do that you don't do enough?
9. What do you wish you had more time for?

• *Inside-Outside Circles (SEB 183).* Staff members create two circles (same number of individuals...one circle on the inside of the other). The inner circle moves counterclockwise; the outer circle moves clockwise. Circles move to the next individual, the interview question is asked, and the rotation continues. Some questions that could be asked include:

1. What is one thing you'd like me to know about you?
2. What's an accomplishment outside of education you're proud of?
3. What are you afraid of?
4. What makes you happy?
5. What is your favorite grade level to teach?
6. What is your favorite part of teaching?

• *Voting...What's Your Opinion? (SEB 184).* Participants are asked a question and reminded there are no right or wrong answers. At the same moment, each participant indicates their answer using the same designated signal such as:

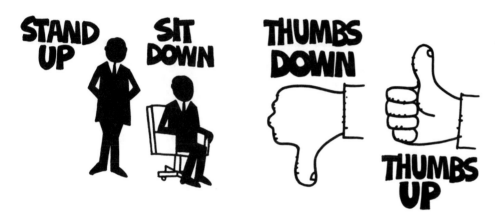

• *Find Your Counterparts (SEB 185).* Participants are directed to ask one question of the other persons in the room such as: "Find all the other members of this room who are born in the same month as you are and stand by them. You have one minute to do so." Additional questions could include: same number of siblings as you...lived in the same number of different places as you...have same number of pets as you do. The list is endless.

STAFF WELCOME   SEB 186

Purpose: To greet new members of the staff and say hello to returning staff members.

Materials: Personal (store-bought or handmade) invitations to be sent to staff members announcing the date and time of the Staff Welcome event.

Procedure: The Esteem Builder Team and/or site administrators meet at a convenient time to plan a staff get-together. Ideally, the gathering will be held either before school starts or anytime the first month of school at a time convenient to the majority of the staff. A few ideas to be considered are:

- an after-school wine and cheese social (at someone's house);

- dinner, lunch, or brunch at a restaurant;

- potluck at someone's house;

- an after-school dessert (at the school site or nearby at someone's house);

- a staff breakfast (at a school site);

- staff retreat (at a nearby location);

- staff gathering at a special event (play or other program).

MUG FILE   SEB 187

Purpose: To increase the opportunity for individual staff recognition; to enhance the feeling of staff affiliation.

Materials:
- A 3" x 5" or 4" x 6" card for each participant; an index card box to store the completed cards.
- A large monthly school calendar with each date depicted in a box so that at least one to two inches of writing space are provided.
- A large facsimile of the information below recreated on a large piece of chart paper.

<u>MUG FILE</u>

NAME:	
PHONE NUMBER:	
HOME ADDRESS:	
POSITION:	**ROOM NUMBER:**
SIGNIFICANT OTHERS:	
CHILDREN'S NAMES:	
BIRTHDAY:	**ANNIVERSARY:**
FAVORITE HOBBY OR INTEREST:	
ANY UPCOMING SPECIAL EVENTS:	

Procedure: Distribute index cards to staff members. Display the completed chart with the information copied from the Mug File. (This could be hung in the staff room or completed during a staff meeting.) Ask staff members to complete the card using the information from the chart. Explain that the card will be kept in a box and made available only to staff members (or a Sunshine Committee formed to recognize individual staff members).

Collect all the completed cards. Use the information from the cards to list important dates (birthdays, anniversaries, upcoming weddings or trips) on a large calendar. Next to the date written on the calendar, note the name of the staff member as well as the name of the event. Hang the calendar in the faculty lounge or other central location. Recognize the event as a staff on the date it occurs with a card, personal note, flowers, helium balloon or other means.

POSITIVE NAME TAGS   SEB 188

Purpose: To provide staff members with an opportunity to get acquainted and find out more about each other.

Materials: A 3" x 5" index card and thin-tipped marking pen for each participant.

Procedure: Provide participants with a card and pen. Ask them to boldly print their first name in the middle of the card. Individuals are then to think of about five words that describe themselves. Emphasize that all words must be positive and that any category is acceptable. Allow two to three minutes for writing.

Next, ask the group to quickly form partners. Encourage participants to find someone they may not already know. Ask each team to determine who will be the first speaker. Explain that partners are to introduce themselves to the other using the descriptive words on their name tags. Listeners may not interrupt until their partners indicate they have finished their self-descriptions. Listeners may then ask questions or comment on the descriptions. Partners then exchange roles of listener and describer and the activity is repeated. Allow about seven to ten minutes for introductions. As a follow-up activity, partners could join another pair. Partners quickly introduce one another to the other pair using their partner's name tag.

SMILE PIN   SEB 189

Purpose: To enhance a positive school environment.

Materials: A smile pin or button for each participant. These can be purchased from a button maker, ordered from a catalogue, or created from a school-owned button maker.

The pin could also be made from a heavy piece of tagboard or poster board that has a safety pin attached to the back. The face of each pin should depict a smile or some kind of positive saying. Many schools use their school mascot or school name on the pin.

Procedure: Distribute a smile pin to all staff members at the first staff meeting. Explain that during the first week, pins are to be passed to other staff members only. During subsequent weeks, pins will be passed to students and students will pass them to other students. The staff could brainstorm ways to "earn" the pin. Some possibilities include:

- smiling at another person;
- giving someone a compliment;
- helping another person;
- sharing or being cooperative;
- saying something positive to another person.

During the second week, staff members will pass pins to students demonstrating any of these behaviors. The students will then pass them to other students. The student pin passing activity should be no longer than a week. A rule for the activity could be that no pins may be taken home. All pins are to be stored in the students' homeroom and retrieved the next day. *Idea suggested by Darlene Daugherty, principal, Littleton School District, Littleton, Colorado.*

GRAFFITI BOARD   SEB 190

Purpose: To enhance a positive working environment and increase a sense of staff trust.

Materials:
- Cover an existing staff bulletin board with plain butcher paper or pin up a light-colored piece of poster board.
- Colored marking pens.

Procedure: The Esteem Builder Team or a staff member creates a Graffiti Board in the faculty room to generate comments among the staff. The board could have captions such as: "Comments" or "Thank you" or "Did you know..." Provide pens near the board. Encourage staff members to write positive comments about other staff members. The board can be left up for about a week and made again if there is enough interest among the staff.

SECRETS   SEB 191

Purpose: To build staff cohesiveness; to provide opportunities to discover personal traits about each staff member.

Materials: 3" x 5" cards (one per participant).

Procedure: Randomly distribute a 3" x 5" card to each participant at a staff gathering. Ask individuals to think of a statement about themselves that no one else on the staff knows (i.e. the state they were born in, the college they went to, a place they once lived or visited, a special trip, etc.). Emphasize that the "secret" should be something they feel comfortable sharing. Explain that the statement is to be printed on only one side of the card. Encourage participants to disguise their handwriting somewhat so that their unique handwriting does not reveal who the author is. Explain that the cards will be left in a convenient location during the week (such as on a faculty lounge table or hung up on a faculty bulletin board). Throughout the week, encourage staff members to read the cards and try to guess which staff member belongs to each secret. Staff members should then write the name of the individual they think corresponds to the secret on the back of each card.

At a following faculty meeting or staff gathering, each secret is read to the group by the activity facilitator. The staff member who wrote the secret then reveals his/her identity to the group.

Variation: At the end of the week, ask staff members to write their name on the front of their secret. Cards are then collectively hung on a large tagboard poster or bulletin board in the faculty lounge for staff members to read at their leisure.

ROOM PLAN   SEB 192

Purpose: To provide staff members with the opportunity to find out about one another's early childhood; to create a discussion tool for staff members to talk about the personal self.

Materials: SEB 192 Room Plan (page 211); marking pens, colored pencils, or crayons.

Procedure: Ask participants to quickly form pairs. Provide each person with a copy of the SEB 192 Room Plan form and distribute pens, crayons and/or pencils among the group. Now ask participants to think about their childhood. In particular, ask them to think about a favorite room during their childhood. Explain that the room could be a bedroom or family room in their own home, or a room in some other location such as a classroom or grandparent's kitchen. Emphasize there are no right or wrong answers. The room should represent a special positive memory that they wish to pass on to others.

Ask participants to think about what that room looked like. What was in it? What color was it? Where were the windows, the doors, the furniture? Explain to participants that when they are ready they are to draw their favorite room. Emphasize that artistic merit does not count! Provide five to ten minutes for drawing, or until participants have completed their pictures. Ask them to take turns explaining their favorite room to their partners.

I LIKE POSTERS   SEB 193

Purpose: To enhance awareness of individual staff members' interests, likes, and enjoyments.

Materials:

- 12" x 18" light-colored construction paper for each team.
- Several different colored marking pens.
- A watch with a second hand.

Procedure: Ask the group to quickly form groups of four (not more than five). Distribute paper and pens to each team. Ask each group to quickly decide who will start the activity (the "starter"). Explain that the first part of the activity will take four minutes. The team's starter holds the paper and pens, and writes "I like" at the top of the paper. Team members take turns saying "I like..." and then filling in the sentence stem with something they personally like or enjoy. Individuals quickly write down their own response and then pass the paper to the person on the right (i.e. "I like chocolate," "I like skiing," "I like cooking," etc.). The paper continues to be passed clockwise for four minutes. Remind the group there should be no interruptions or questions during the activity and that all responses are valid. Encourage participants to come up with responses different from those their teammates have shared.

At the end of four minutes, ask each group to quickly pass their "I like page" back to the "starter." Explain that the starter's new job is to quickly reread all the responses to the team. The team must then come up with a team name based on what interests their team has in common. Finally, the team is to use the back of their paper to create a team sign based on their team name. Emphasize that the team should have not only the team name on the page but the members' individual names. Words, symbols, or pictures may be included in the poster. Allow ten minutes for making the poster. Provide a few minutes for each team to share their poster and rationale for their team name to the group. Hang up the posters in the staff lounge. Variations on this topic are endless, such as "I am...," "I love...," "I look forward to...," "I wish...," or "I hate...."

NAME COLLAGES   SEB 194

Purpose: To provide the opportunity for staff members to find out about each other on a personal level.

Materials: 1 sheet of 12" x 18" light-colored construction paper or poster board for each team; ample supply of colored marking pens and glue.

Optional: Stickers, letter templates, or letter cut-outs.

Procedure: Ask the group to quickly divide into partners. Encourage participants to work with someone they may not know well. Distribute paper and pens to each team. Letter templates or cut-outs may be displayed on a table if desired. Explain that the first task each team has is to write their first names in large block letters on the paper. Emphasize there is no right or wrong way to do the task; encourage creativity. Letters may be hand-drawn, drawn with templates or glued on using the letter cut-outs provided. Both partners' names must appear on the same side of the paper.

The second task is for the partners to interview one another to determine what they have in common *besides education*. Discovered commonalities are somehow to be displayed on the poster. Mention that the commonalities can be depicted by any means, such as words, pictures, symbols or any decoration desired. Emphasize that both partners must contribute to the finished product. Allow fifteen minutes or so for partners to complete their collages. When collages are finished, ask each team to share their products with the rest of the group and describe discovered commonalities. Hang up the finished products.

NAME TAG EXCHANGE   SEB 195

Purpose: To increase the feeling of selfhood; to provide staff members with the opportunity to find out about each other's backgrounds and personal interests.

Materials:
- 4" x 6" index cards
- Pins
- Thin-tipped black marking pens for each participant.

Procedure: During a staff get-together, training or staff meeting, distribute an index card and pen to each participant. Ask participants to listen to the following directions and then print their responses to the questions on their name tags on the location to be described.

1. Hold your card vertically.

2. Print your first name in the middle of card.

3. Circle your name.

4. Along the top side of the card, print the state in which you were born.

5. Along the bottom side of the card, print the name of your favorite TV show.

6. Along the left-hand side of the card, print the number of siblings you have.

7. Along the right-hand side of the card, print the name of your favorite ice cream flavor.

8. Immediately under your name, print your favorite hobby or interest.

Note: There are no right or wrong questions for this task. The main point is that the questions, which can easily be varied, should always be nonthreatening.

When everyone has completed their cards, ask them to pin it on themselves. Explain that they now have ten minutes to mingle with each other, reading and commenting on one another's name tags.

To vary this activity, change the rules. Say, "Your job in the next ten minutes is to find as many colleagues as you can who share the same answers as you. When you find someone who shares *any* answer that is the same, you are to initial one another's cards next to the corresponding category." For this variation, participants should hold their cards so that they can easily be signed by others in the group.

Allow a few minutes following the activity for discussion.

BABY PICTURE GUESS WHO   SEB 196

Purpose: To enhance a feeling of staff awareness and positivism.

Materials:

- A bulletin board or large poster with the caption "Guess Who?"
- A roster of all staff members' names.
- A marking pen.
- A baby picture of each staff member.

Procedure: A week or two prior to the activity, ask staff members to bring a baby picture of themselves to school. Emphasize that they should not show anyone at the school site the picture and their name should not be included on the front of the picture. Pin each picture on a bulletin board or poster. With a marking pen, write a different number on the board under each photograph. Instructions for the activity could be included on the bulletin board or poster.

Explain that the object of the activity is to try and guess which baby picture belongs to which staff member. Encourage staff members to take a staff roster and write the number of the baby picture which corresponds to the name of the staff member they think it belongs to. Allow a few days for all staff members to complete the roster, then publish the results. Write the real name of the staff member under each picture. A variation of this activity is to let the students also guess who is who. Special prizes such as movie passes, a children's literature selection, a favorite teacher's resource as well as inexpensive door prizes could be awarded to the winners.

IDENTITY SHIELD   SEB 197

Purpose: To enhance staff members' awareness of themselves and each other.

Materials: SEB 197 Identity Shield (page 212).

Procedure: During a staff meeting or any other all staff get-together, distribute a copy of the SEB 197 Identity Shield form to each participant. Explain that the Identity Shield is to represent four aspects of each participant's life. Emphasize that these should be four areas that individuals would like to share about themselves that may help other staff members find out more about their individuality. Possible areas could be: family, childhood, education, travel, interests, teaching goals, favorite foods, etc. The group could decide which four areas they would like to address on the forms. Allow staff members approximately five minutes to draw a picture in each section. Ask the group to quickly form partners. Explain that each person has three minutes to share their shield with a partner. They also may ask their partners one question about the information on their shield.

Variation: A variation to this activity is to have participants create large identity shields from poster board. Finished shields may then be hung along school walls for students to enjoy. For this activity, refer participants to "My Identity Shield" form (page 132 in *Esteem Builders*).

PARTNER HANDPRINTS   SEB 198

Purpose: To increase the awareness of individual staff member's unique strengths and attributes.

Materials: 12" x 18" light-colored construction paper per team; colored marking pens.

Procedure: Invite participants to quickly find a partner. Encourage everyone to choose someone they may not know well already. Explain that the first part of the activity is to trace their partner's handprint on the paper. Distribute construction paper and pens to each team. Emphasize that both of their partner's handprints should fit on the paper and both handprints should be on the same side. Each person's name should be printed inside their handprint near the bottom of their palm. Allow a few minutes.

Explain that the second part of the activity is an interview. Participants are to take five minutes to interview their partners. Interviewers are to find out at least five different personal strengths, interests, or attributes about their partners, then write the answers in one of the five finger outline shapes of their partner's handprint. At the end of ten minutes, ask interviewers to quickly share with the group a few details they discovered about their partners. You may wish to hang up the finished products.

BIRTHDAY RECOGNITION   SEB 199

Purpose: To recognize individual staff members on their birthdays.

Materials:

- 3" x 5" index cards (one per staff member).
- Index card box to store cards.
- Store-bought or computer-generated birthday cards.

Procedure: At the beginning of each year, ask each staff member to fill out a 3" x 5" card with the following information:

- Name
- Phone number
- Birthday
- Significant others' names, children's names
- Hobbies, interests, favorites such as colors, music, food, etc.

Ask staff members to return the cards to a designated location (administrator's box, a particular staff member's room, or to an Esteem Builder Team member). Each year designate a person(s) responsible for maintaining the card file. This could be the responsibility of the Esteem Builder Team. The Birthday Committee will be responsible for putting the birthday card information for that week's birthdays in the weekly bulletin, hanging up a "Happy Birthday" poster in the faculty room and/or asking staff members to sign a birthday card for the individual. Summer birthdays can be recognized in June. The birthday staff member could be given special privileges such as: an administrator or staff member relieves the person of yard duty, or an administrator relieves the member from their classroom so that he/she may visit other classrooms. *Idea suggested by the Stockton Unified School District Self-Esteem Support Team.*

INTEREST SEARCH   SEB 200

Purpose: To learn about the interests of fellow staff members.

Materials: S22 Interest Search (page 78 of *Esteem Builders*).

Procedure: During a staff meeting or staff get-together distribute copies of the S22

Interest Search form to participants. Provide three minutes for individuals to fill in the "My Favorite" column on the left-hand side of the form. Then allow five to ten minutes for staff members to find others who have the same interests. At the completion of the activity, provide time for the group to share their results with one another if appropriate.

POSITIVE FINDERS   SEB 201

Purpose: To enhance a positive staff environment; to recognize the positive deeds of others.

Materials:

• Names of each staff member written on separate strips of paper.
• Container to place all the names in (basket, bag, or hat).

Procedure: At a staff gathering or faculty meeting, describe the Positive Finders activity. Explain that staff members who choose to do the activity will pull the name of a staff member from a container. Emphasize that everyone will pull a different name and that all names should remain secret. Mention that the role of the name puller is to look for positive, good, friendly deeds that the individual performs during the next week.

At the next staff gathering, "positive finders" report to the group positive deeds they observed the person doing. (Examples: "I noticed this week that Mary was spending a lot of extra hours after school in her classroom," or "I heard Kelly on the playground helping two students work through a difficult conflict. She was using excellent reflective listening skills," or "I overheard two parents talking in the parking lot. They were commenting on how much they appreciated Greg's caring attitude towards kids."

STAFF APPRECIATION & MESSAGE CENTER   SEB 202

Purpose: To provide staff members with an opportunity to extend appreciation towards one another. To increase communication and sharing as a staff.

Materials:

• A large bulletin board.
• Marking pens and poster board or colored butcher paper.
• A string cut into a 24" length.
• Pins or tacks.
• Library pocket cards (one per staff member).

Optional: Recognition Grams (page 69 in *Esteem Builders)*. Duplicate a large quantity of the forms on bright-colored copy paper and cut along the lines.

Procedure: Create a bulletin board space to be used in a faculty lounge or other central location where all staff members gather. Cover the board with colored butcher paper and divide the board into two spaces. On one side create an area where staff members can write comments to one another expressing their appreciation. Attach a long string to a marking pen and pin it on the board. Encourage staff members to use the area to write notes to each other or to the entire staff. As the space becomes crowded, new butcher paper can be added.

On the second half of the board, allow space for a Staff Message Center. Attach a library pocket for each staff member. On the pocket write the name of each individual with a marking pen. A photograph, quote, or baby picture of the staff member could also be added to decorate the front of the pocket. Make a larger library pocket for note cards cut into 3" x 5" lengths. The Recognition Grams found in *Esteem Builders* could be used for this purpose. Duplicate large quantities of the forms and leave them in the larger library pocket. Encourage staff members to write notes to one another using the forms.

RECOGNITION GRAMS   SEB 203

Purpose: To increase the feeling of support and positivism among the staff.

Materials: Duplicate Recognition Grams on page 69 of *Esteem Builders* on bright-colored ditto paper and cut them along the margins.

Procedure: At a staff gathering or faculty room, explain the procedure for using the Recognition Grams. Explain that the grams will be left in convenient locations in the faculty and staff room. Encourage staff members at any time to fill out a Recognition Gram whenever they would like to compliment or thank someone. The note can either be put in that person's mailbox or given directly to him/her. A particularly interesting way to make the grams available is to purchase a few plastic napkin holders. Store the grams inside the napkin holders and attach a string with a tied pencil or pen to each holder. Place the holders along faculty tables.

COMMON POINTS   SEB 204

Purpose: To provide the opportunity for staff members to learn about each other and identify common interests among staff members.

Materials: A2 Common Points (page 190 of *Esteem Builders)*.

Procedure: At a staff meeting or other staff get-together, distribute copies of the A2 Common Points form to participants. Explain that the staff is allowed ten to fifteen minutes to find two people per item who have the same interest as they do. At the conclusion of the activity, allow time for participants to share information they have found out about other staff members.

PLAYING FAVORITES   SEB 205

Purpose: To help staff members learn about themselves and each other.

Materials: SH20 Playing Favorites (page 133 of *Esteem Builders).*

Procedure: At the beginning of a week, distribute copies of the SH20 Playing Favorites form to each staff member. Encourage the staff to fill out the form and then return it to the facilitator (or Esteem Builder Team members). The facilitator then cuts the names off of each paper and assigns each one a different number for later identification. He/she keeps a roster of all staff members and their assigned number to be referred to later. Papers are posted in the staff lounge or some other central location. By the end of the week, staff members are to guess which paper describes which person. At the conclusion of the activity, the facilitator attaches the names of the staff members to each paper. Prizes can be awarded to the individuals who make the most correct guesses. *Idea suggested by the Stockton Unified School District Self-Esteem Support Team.*

CANDY BAR ACKNOWLEDGERS   SEB 206

Purpose: To recognize staff members for their positive team building (or individual) efforts; to provide staff members with the opportunity to acknowledge one another and strengthen their communication network.

Materials:

* SEB 206 Candy Bar Acknowledgers (page 213).
* Candy bars corresponding to the form selected (i.e. if you plan to use the "You're a Lifesaver" acknowledgment, you will need a package of Lifesavers for each acknowledgment you plan to give out).

Procedure: Duplicate SEB 206 Candy Bar Acknowledgers on cardstock or construction paper and cut out the form selected. The acknowledger is then glued, stapled, or taped to a corresponding candy bar as identified on page 213. The acknowledgers may be used in a number of ways:

1. as treats for all staff members, distributed at the beginning of a faculty meeting or left in their boxes to recognize them for their joint efforts;

2. as a form of appreciation for a particular deed, given by one staff member to another;

3. as an acknowledgment to a team, grade-level group, or special committee for outstanding efforts.

GOOD EGG AWARDS   SEB 207

Purpose: To increase positive interaction among staff members; to provide staff members with the opportunity to recognize the positive deeds of others.

Materials:

- Colored ditto paper cut in large egg shapes.
- A basket to hold the paper eggs.
- Pencils or pens stored in the basket.

Variation: The eggs could be made onto a ditto page with the caption "Good Egg Award" written on the form along with a few lines for writing.

Procedure: Place the paper eggs in a basket. Stick a few pens or pencils in the basket and place it on a table in the faculty lounge. Another basket may be placed near staff letter boxes. Encourage staff members to write to each other recognizing special efforts, deeds, or positive behavior. The completed egg notes commenting on jobs well done are placed in teachers' boxes.

STAFF MEETING WHIPS   SEB 208

Purpose: To provide opportunities for staff members to find out about each other.

Materials: None needed; a stop watch is desirable.

Procedure: "Whip" is the name of an activity in which everyone quickly shares their response to a question or open-ended sentence stem. Generally, one person facilitates the activity by quickly pointing to people either randomly or in succession. Whip activities are also great ways to either begin or end meetings. They also could be used as an energizer during a meeting. They need not be lengthy—in fact, one person could act as a timekeeper so that the activity does not extend the time limits. In this way, participants find out about each other in a very short time.

The facilitator first decides on the "whip" question or sentence stem for the meeting. This may be written on a blackboard or chart paper. Tell the group the question or sentence stem and encourage them to quickly think about their response. Remind participants that everyone who chooses will quickly respond to the question or sentence stem. If participants are sitting in a circle, no facilitation is needed. A designated "first person" begins and then the circle moves either clockwise or counterclockwise with each person quickly filling in their response. If the seating arrangement is more random, explain that you will quickly point to people. Finally, remind participants that no interruptions or questions are allowed during the set "whip" time. At the end of the activity, time could be provided for participants to ask others to elaborate on their responses if desired. Suggestions for "whip" questions include:

- One thing I'm looking forward to trying this week is _____.
- One thing I'm looking forward to doing this weekend is _____.
- One thing that worked well for me this week was _____.
- This week I wish I'd _____.
- I'm really happy that _____.
- I wish _____.
- If I'd only known years ago _____.
- A fun thing that happened this week was _____.
- A funny thing that happened this week was _____.
- The best thing about this week was _____.
- I'm seeing progress with _____.
- A person I really wanted to thank but couldn't was _____.
- A special thing that happened to me was _____.
- Tonight I'm really looking forward to _____.
- Something I just did that I'd like you to know about is _____.
- One thing I'm doing at home that's fun is _____.
- Did you know _____?
- One thing I'm trying is _____.
- I'm looking forward to _____.
- Does anybody have _____?
- Something I'd like to learn about is _____.
- I'm really proud of _____.
- Something I'd like to brag about is _____.
- I made a difference by _____.
- I wish we _____.

- A great movie, book, or place to go is _____.
- I just want to share that _____.
- I'm feeling really _____.
- To relax these days I _____.
- I'm sure glad I _____.

WEBBING   SEB 209

Purpose: To provide an opportunity for staff members to find out about each other.

Materials: A skein of yarn.

Procedure: Staff members stand in a large circle, arm's length apart from one another. The circle should contain no more than fifteen members. For large faculties, smaller circles with ten to fifteen members may be formed. Each circle needs a skein of yarn that has been prewound into a ball. One person in the circle assumes the role of "starter" by holding the yarn and beginning a sentence whip. Whip possibilities are endless and could include:

- One thing I'm looking forward to this year is _____.
- I love to teach _____ because _____.
- I can contribute to the team by _____.
- One of my fondest memories of teaching is _____.
- One moment I made a difference for a student is _____.
- One thing I'd like you to know about me is _____.

The whip statement should be the same for all the circles and used throughout the duration of the activity. The starter states the whip, personally responds to the statement, then he/she holds onto the end of the yarn and tosses the ball to a colleague across the circle. The catcher then holds onto a length of yarn, responds to the whip, and tosses the remainder of the ball to the other side of the circle. By tossing the ball of yarn from side to side of the circle, a web of yarn forms. Emphasize that a length of yarn should be held each time a participant catches the ball. Continue the activity until a complete web is formed. When all members of the circle have had a turn, the "web" can then be "dewebbed" either by tossing and rewinding the ball in reverse form or by reversing the web with another statement.

COMPLIMENT BOOK   SEB 210

Purpose: To provide the opportunity for staff members to compliment and recognize one another.

- For each participant, provide one 1-1/2" three-ring binder.
- Dividers with the name of each staff member written on the dividers.
- Binder paper (five to ten sheets inserted behind each divider).
- Permanent marking pen.

Book Assembly: Write the words "Compliment Book" on the cover of the binder. Insert the dividers inside the binder with the name of a different staff member written within each divider tab (dividers may be alphabetized by name). Attach a long string to one of the rings and tie a pencil to the string. Finally, insert binder paper behind each divider.

Procedure: Explain at a staff meeting or staff gathering that the purpose of the Compliment Book is to increase staff members' correspondence with one another. Emphasize that so often their schedules are so tight or different from other staff members that they may not have many opportunities for communication. Explain that the Compliment Book will be left in a convenient and private location that is easily accessible to staff members (i.e. by staff mailboxes, on the front ledger or counter, on a table in the staff room). Encourage staff members to take the time and write notes to one another. Notes could include questions, compliments, thank you's or needs.

SCHOOL WANT AD POSTER   SEB 211

Purpose: To increase school pride and enhance awareness of positive school attributes.

Materials:

- Large chart paper or 12" x 18" light-colored construction paper or poster board for each participant.
- Thick marking pens.

Procedure: Divide the group into teams of four. Distribute chart paper and pens to each team. Ask each team to choose a recorder. Tell each group they will have five minutes to brainstorm positive attributes about the school. Emphasize that the attributes should be as concrete as possible (i.e. friendly place, caring place, supportive staff). At the time completion, explain that the next task is for teams to look over their lists. Each team now must create a Want Ad Poster for their school explaining why their school is special and unique. Emphasize the following rules for the Want Ad Poster:

1. Each team must create their own want ad without looking at any other team's poster.

2. The finished product should read like a want ad found in a newspaper ad.

3. Words, pictures, or symbols may be included on the poster.

4. All print should be written on only one side of the paper.

4. All print should be written on only one side of the paper.

5. Posters are created on the chart paper using ink pens (stickers, magazine cut-outs, photographs or any other medium may also be included).

6. Completed want ads will be read to the entire group.

Allow fifteen minutes for the project. Hang up the completed want ads and let each group read their product to the rest of the group.

STAFF LOUNGE DECORATING PARTY   SEB 212

Purpose: To create a place conducive to relaxation and staff belonging.

Materials: Any materials (furniture, posters, paint, equipment) that could create a more relaxing and attractive staff lounge.

Procedure: At a staff gathering, discuss for a few minutes if staff members feel the staff lounge is a place that enhances staff communication as well as personal comfort. If the majority of staff members feel it doesn't meet those requirements, discuss what kinds of *reasonable* things could be done to improve the appearance of the room and create a more inviting place. Funds are probably limited for this venture, so continue to stress the word "reasonable" throughout the discussion. Often staff members have items at home that they are willing to donate to the cause. Community members or local businesses also could be called upon to donate items. Such items might include:

- Fresh paint
- Curtains
- Wallpaper
- Tables arranged for communication
- Fresh flowers
- Staff message center
- Exchange of ideas board
- Pictures
- Plants
- Tape recorder for music

- Coffee machine

- Sofa or soft chairs

- Fewer or more tables

- Quotation or attitude posters

- Clean-up committee

Suggest holding a Staff Lounge Warming Party where decorating can take place. Perhaps staff members would be willing to rotate a few duties (such as cleaning up or arranging for fresh flowers).

SECRET PALS   SEB 213

Purpose: To increase the sense of staff cohesiveness; to provide an opportunity for staff members to acknowledge one another.

Materials: SEB 213 Secret Pal (page 214).

Procedure: Announce to staff members at a faculty meeting that for a specified period of time the staff will be doing a new activity called Secret Pals. Tell the group that participation is purely voluntary, but everyone is encouraged to take part since the activity is a great deal of fun. Ask participants to fill out the SEB 213 Secret Pal form. The completed forms are then turned upside down on a table. Each participant randomly pulls the form of another staff member; this person now becomes their secret pal.

For the duration of the activity, staff members periodically do secret deeds for their pal. These deeds could include purchasing inexpensive gifts, putting flowers or apples on their desk, providing classroom ideas or writing notes of acknowledgment. The information provided on the completed form helps staff members choose special treats for their pal. For instance, the pal may indicate he/she enjoys Milky Way candy bars; the staff member who pulls that person's name could then surprise the pal with this item in his/her box.

The activity may last any length of time (usually no more than one month). Pals try to keep their identities secret for as long as possible. On the final day of the activity, the secret pals announce themselves to their colleagues. The announcements can be made at a faculty meeting.

DREAM SPHERES   SEB 214

Purpose: To provide staff members with the opportunity to focus upon their visions of an effective school; to allow participants to hear one another's visions.

Materials: Marking pens and crayons in plentiful supply; at least one stapler for each group of four participants. Duplicate the circle on page 215 on various shades of light-colored cardstock for each participant. Keep extra copies available for participants who wish to start over on their drawings. Extra circles may also be needed to create spheres. Ideally, the balls should be precut.

Optional (but highly recommended): *Together* by George Ella Lyon. This is a delightful picture book that can be used for all ages. Written in rhyme and accompanied by wonderful pictures, the book carries an important message about the value of working together (New York: Orchard Books, 1989).

Procedure: Begin by reading the book *Together* by George Ella Lyon to the group. If the book is not available, describe the power of working together and how much more effective it is to work collectively instead of individually. Emphasize to the group the benefits of knowing one another's beliefs and goals. Distribute a precut circle to each participant. Ask the group to think about their dream for an effective school. Some variations of the question include:

• What is your own professional goal for the year?
• Where would you like to start in the esteem-building implementation process?
• What would your "dream school" look like?
• What one new idea or technique would you like to implement in your classroom this year?

There are dozens of possibilities. It is important to choose one question that *all* staff members will address. Ask participants to somehow depict their answers to the question onto the ball. Explain that they may use pictures, words, or symbols to describe their feelings. Emphasize that these ideas will be shared later with the group and that no one should be concerned about artistic talent.

Next, ask participants to count off into teams of twelve. For example, the first person would say "one," the next person "two" and continue in numerical sequence until twelve is reached. The next person would then become "one."   Ideally, each team should be comprised of twelve members since a completed sphere has twelve circles. Depending on the size of the group, blank circles may be inserted into the sphere to equal twelve items. As each team of twelve (or smaller, if blank circles will be used to make up for missing individuals) is formed, ask them to locate their group somewhere in the room where they will have a large enough space to create a circle. The group then folds the five lines in each circle outward. Each folded edge is joined to another colleague's folded circle edge. Stapling continues until all edges of each participant's circle have been stapled somewhere to the rest of the group's folded bedges. Each team has now created a sphere, as shown on the following page:

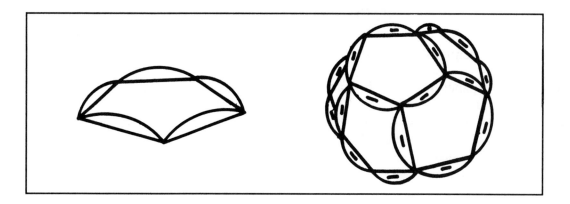

Fold the five flaps, as shown in the first drawing, then staple the twelve circles together to form a ball, as shown in the second drawing.

For the final part of the activity, ask each group to form a circle. One person holds the stapled sphere and begins the discussion by saying, "My dream is…" and completes the statement by describing what they drew or wrote on their circle. This person then gently tosses the sphere to an individual across from them in the circle. The activity is completed when each individual has had the opportunity to verbalize their dream.

Extension Activity: For this activity, form larger circles consisting of another group of twelve. Two spheres are then tossed alternately around the circle until everyone has had a turn voicing their dream and hearing the dreams of others.

Completed circles should be saved so that staff members can refer to one another's comments. Punch a hole in the top of one of the edges of each sphere. Tie a length of yarn to the hole and then hang the sphere from the ceiling of the faculty room.

NEWS FLASH   SEB 215

Purpose: To recognize staff members' accomplishments.

Materials: Duplicate on bright-colored paper copies of the C24 News Flash recognition gram (page 307 of *Esteem Builders*).

Procedure: Distribute copies of the C24 News Flash award to site administrators. Additional copies can be made available to staff members. Encourage administrators and staff members to use the News Flash Certificates as often as appropriately possible. Certificates can be put in mailboxes or handed directly to staff members.

STRENGTH MEDALLIONS   SEB 216

Purpose: To identify the strengths and competencies of fellow staff members.

Materials: A paper medallion for each participant.

Medallion Assembly: Cut a 6" circle from a golden-colored piece of posterboard. Punch two holes 1/4" from the edge of the circle. Attach a 20" piece of yarn through the two holes and tie the string together at the top to create a large loop. The loop should be large enough to slip over an adult's head. With a thin-tipped black marking pen, write the words "Strength Medallion" across the front of one side of the circle.

Procedure: Explain to the group that too often we underestimate our competencies and talents. Emphasize that for the next activity, deliberate "bragging" is not only called for but desirable and highly appropriate. Ask participants to take a medallion and a pen. Invite them to think about special talents they possess that make them unique as individuals. Ask participants to write a few of these talents on their medallions using one or two words to describe the skill. Allow a few minutes for this writing.

Then ask everyone to slip their medallions over their heads and wear them with the talents visible to others. Tell everyone that the next section of the activity involves "quiet walking and reading." Each person needs a pencil. The task as a group is to spend the next five minutes walking around the room quietly reading others' medallions. If a participant reads a talent listed on a colleague's medallion and agrees that he/she does possess that talent, the staff member may place a check mark in pencil next to the talent on the individual's medallion. If the individual has not written a talent that a staff member knows he/she possesses, the staff member may add the talent to the medallion. Emphasize that individuals may include talents on their medallions that they have not demonstrated at the school.

At the end of five minutes, ask participants to quickly divide into groups of four. Ask teams to choose a "task director" whose job is to keep teams focused on the assignment and make sure everyone has a turn. Each team member is to share one of the talents he/she (or a colleague) described on their medallion. Any team member may at this time ask a question of another team member. *Idea suggested by Sherry Yabu, Santa Clara County Office of Education, Santa Clara, California.*

"TEACHERS MAKE A DIFFERENCE" POSTERS   SEB 217

Purpose: To visually accentuate for educators that they do make life-touching differences in students' lives; to reaffirm for staff members a sense of efficacy; to reinforce their feeling that "you can make a difference!"

Materials: Selected copies of "Teachers Make a Difference" posters (pages 216 to 230). Duplicate these on cardstockweight paper of various colors.

Procedure: One of the main reasons educators have chosen their profession is to make a difference in students' lives. It is important for esteem builders at the school site to continually remind staff members that they can and do have a positive impact on their students. A series of quotes on the positive impact teachers have in classrooms provided in this chapter may be used in a variety of ways:

1. Place posters with quotes on faculty room walls to visually remind staff members of their potential positive impact with students.

2. Periodically place a quote on the desk of a teacher who has made a noticeable difference for a student. Include a personal note on the card, such as, "I just wanted to congratulate you on the powerful job you're doing with your students. Their behavior has greatly changed and everyone comments on what a difference you're making. Thank you from all of us!"

3. Many principals include a quote from a poster on the cover of a set of staff handouts.

There are countless ways an administrator can use the posters and the esteem-building quotes they contain, thus continually reminding staff of the impact they have on the lives of students.

GET ACQUAINTED CHECKLIST

TASK 1: You have 10 minutes during which you must get as many initials as possible of people in this room who fit the descriptions given below. Try to find a different person for each category.

_____Someone whose birthday is the same month as yours.

_____Someone who's taken an in-service on cooperative learning.

_____Someone who wears glasses.

_____Someone who wears the same size shoe as you.

_____Someone who has tried Cross-Age Tutoring.

_____Someone who water skiis.

_____Someone whose favorite color is the same as yours.

_____Someone who has black hair.

_____Someone who likes the same TV show as you.

_____Someone who has appeared in a play.

_____Someone who doesn't like Mexican food.

_____Someone who is about the same height as you.

_____Someone who likes to play baseball.

_____Someone who has the same last initial as you.

_____Someone who has the same color eyes as you do.

_____Someone who has been in education about the same time length as you.

_____Someone who has the same number of siblings as you.

_____Someone who has blonde hair.

Esteem Builders' Complete Program
Jalmar Press, Rolling Hills Estates, CA

WARM-UP BINGO

TASK: FIND SOMEONE IN THIS ROOM TO MATCH EACH DESCRIPTION. HAVE THEM SIGN THE SQUARE. TRY TO FIND DIFFERENT PEOPLE FOR EACH BOX.

B I N G O

SAME BIRTHDAY MONTH	BROWN EYES	LIKES BASEBALL	IS AN ONLY CHILD	SAME HAND SIZE AS YOU
IS WEARING RED	HAS A FISH	PLAYS FOOTBALL	ABOUT AS TALL AS YOU	HAS BEEN ON AIRPLANE
LIKES MUSHROOMS	SPEAKS 2 or MORE LANGUAGES	HAS BUCKLE SHOES	WEARING GREEN	BLUE EYES
WON AN AWARD	SAME NUMBER SIBLINGS	HAS SAME MIDDLE INITIAL	SAME HAIR COLOR	SAME SHOE SIZE
HAS BEEN OUT OF U.S.	HAS BEEN IN A PLAY	LIKES TO PLAY CARDS	HAS A SISTER	WEARING A BELT

Esteem Builders' Complete Program
Jalmar Press, Rolling Hills Estates, CA

INTERVIEWS

DIRECTIONS: Begin the activity, by quickly writing your own responses to each of the statements under the "Side 1" (You) column. Your task is now to find a member of the group that matches your response for each column. The identified person then signs his or her name in the space marked "Side 2" (Others) column. A person should not sign your paper more than twice.

	SIDE 1 (YOU)	SIDE 2 (OTHERS)
Your home state:		
Your birth month:		
A musical instrument you play:		
Your favorite dessert:		
Number of children:		
Your shoe size:		
A nonprofessional magazine you read:		
Your hobby:		
Your favorite vacation spot:		
Number of siblings:		
Your favorite TV show:		
Type(s) of your pet(s):		

Esteem Builders' Complete Program
Jalmar Press, Rolling Hills Estates, CA

ROOM PLAN

THINK ABOUT A FAVORITE ROOM OF YOUR CHILDHOOD.
WHAT DID IT LOOK LIKE? THINK ABOUT SOME OF YOUR
FAVORITE CHILDHOOD MEMORIES. DRAW THE ROOM.
NOW EXPLAIN THE ROOM TO A PARTNER.

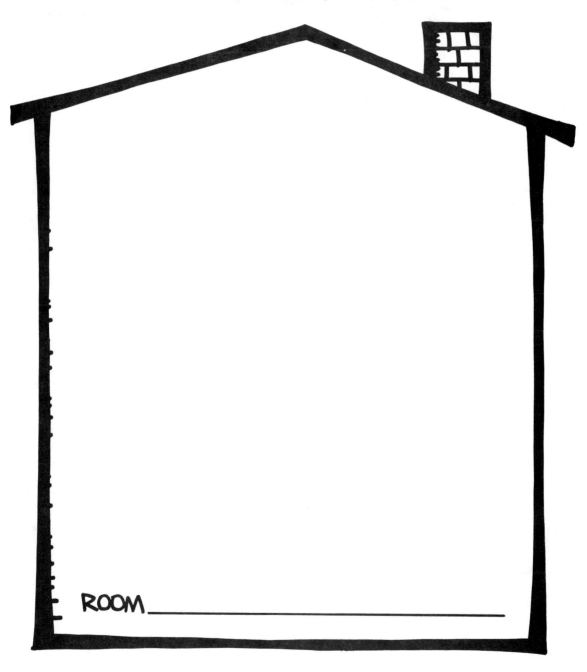

ROOM _____

Esteem Builders' Complete Program
Jalmar Press, Rolling Hills Estates, CA

IDENTITY SHIELD

Esteem Builders' Complete Program
Jalmar Press, Rolling Hills Estates, CA

Attach to a package of Lifesavers.

Attach to a Milky Way Bar.

Attach to a Three Musketeer Bar.

Attach to a Hershey's Kiss.

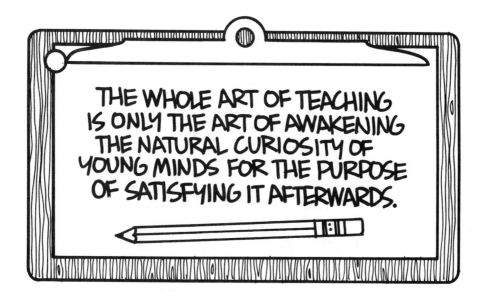

Esteem Builders' Complete Program
Jalmar Press, Rolling Hills Estates, CA

SECRET PALS

This form is to be filled out if you'd like to participate in the Secret Pal activity. The answers you provide about yourself will be randomly given to another staff member. Your answers are meant to help your "Secret Pal" provide you with fun goodies each day. Enjoy!

Fill out those items that are appropriate to you. Feel free to add information not included.

Name: _____

Birthday: _____ Anniversary: _____

Fill in your Favorites:

Flower: _____

Books/Author: _____

Hero or Idol: _____

Composer/Music: _____

Color: _____

Hobby/Interest: _____

Candy: _____

Snack: _____

Magazine: _____

Team: _____

Colors/House: _____ Kitchen: _____ Bathroom: _____

Places you would like to travel: _____

Something you forgot to bring with you: _____

Anything else _____

Esteem Builders' Complete Program
Jalmar Press, Rolling Hills Estates, CA

DREAM SPHERES

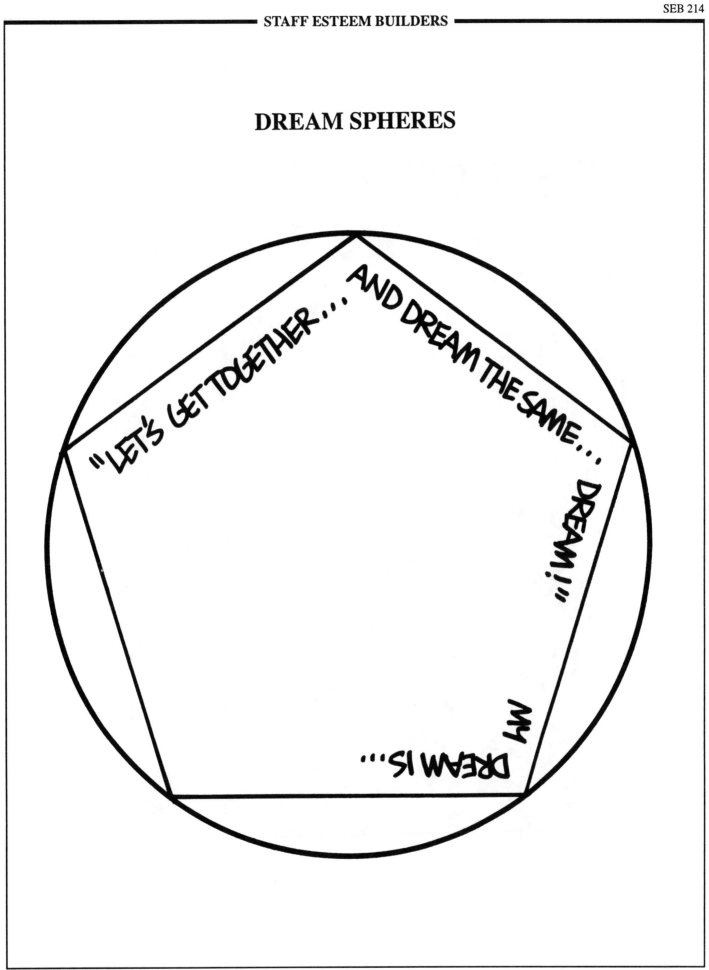

Esteem Builders' Complete Program
Jalmar Press, Rolling Hills Estates, CA

KINDERGARTEN TEACHER:
ONE WHO KNOWS HOW TO MAKE THE LITTLE THINGS COUNT.

ANONYMOUS

Esteem Builders' Complete Program
Jalmar Press, Rolling Hills Estates, CA

I ALWAYS FELT THE TRUE TEXTBOOK FOR A PUPIL IS THE TEACHER

MAHATMA GANDHI

Esteem Builders' Complete Program
Jalmar Press, Rolling Hills Estates, CA

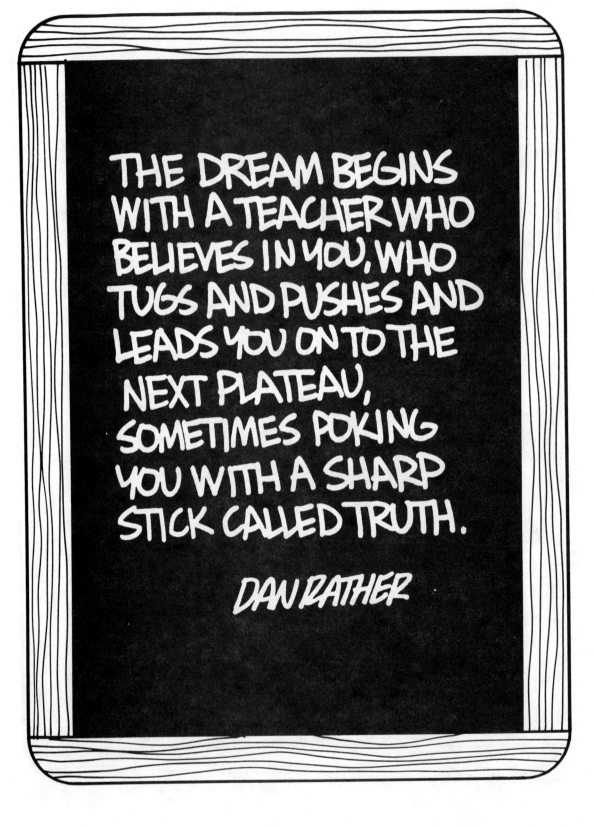

THE DREAM BEGINS WITH A TEACHER WHO BELIEVES IN YOU, WHO TUGS AND PUSHES AND LEADS YOU ON TO THE NEXT PLATEAU, SOMETIMES POKING YOU WITH A SHARP STICK CALLED TRUTH.

DAN RATHER

Esteem Builders' Complete Program
Jalmar Press, Rolling Hills Estates, CA

Esteem Builders' Complete Program
Jalmar Press, Rolling Hills Estates, CA

Esteem Builders' Complete Program
Jalmar Press, Rolling Hills Estates, CA

IN A COMPLETELY RATIONAL SOCIETY, THE BEST OF US WOULD ASPIRE TO BE TEACHERS AND THE REST OF US WOULD HAVE TO SETTLE FOR SOMETHING LESS, BECAUSE PASSING CIVILIZATION ALONG FROM ONE GENERATION TO THE NEXT OUGHT TO BE THE HIGHEST HONOR AND THE HIGHEST RESPONSIBILITY ANYONE COULD HAVE.

LEE IACOCCA

Esteem Builders' Complete Program
Jalmar Press, Rolling Hills Estates, CA

THE WHOLE ART OF TEACHING IS ONLY THE ART OF AWAKENING THE NATURAL CURIOSITY OF YOUNG MINDS FOR THE PURPOSE OF SATISFYING IT AFTERWARDS.

ANATOLE FRANCE

Esteem Builders' Complete Program
Jalmar Press, Rolling Hills Estates, CA

EVERYONE WHO REMEMBERS HIS OWN EDUCATIONAL EXPERIENCE REMEMBERS TEACHERS, NOT METHODS AND TECHNIQUES. THE TEACHER IS THE KINGPIN OF THE EDUCATIONAL SITUATION. HE MAKES AND BREAKS PROGRAMS.

SIDNEY HOOK

Esteem Builders' Complete Program
Jalmar Press, Rolling Hills Estates, CA

A TEACHER IS ONE WHO MADE TWO IDEAS GROW WHERE ONLY ONE GREW BEFORE.

ELBERT HUBBARD

Esteem Builders' Complete Program
Jalmar Press, Rolling Hills Estates, CA

Esteem Builders' Complete Program
Jalmar Press, Rolling Hills Estates, CA

A TEACHER WHO CAN AROUSE A FEELING FOR ONE SINGLE GOOD ACTION, FOR ONE SINGLE GOOD POEM, ACCOMPLISHES MORE THAN HE WHO FILLS OUR MEMORY WITH ROWS ON ROWS OF NATURAL OBJECTS CLASSIFIED WITH NAME AND FORM.

GOETHE

Esteem Builders' Complete Program
Jalmar Press, Rolling Hills Estates, CA

WHO TEACHES ME FOR A DAY IS MY FATHER FOR A LIFETIME.

CHINESE PROVERB

Esteem Builders' Complete Program
Jalmar Press, Rolling Hills Estates, CA

IT IS THE SUPREME ART OF THE TEACHER TO AWAKEN JOY IN CREATIVE EXPRESSION AND KNOWLEDGE.

ALBERT EINSTEIN

Esteem Builders' Complete Program
Jalmar Press, Rolling Hills Estates, CA

ALL OF US WHO MAKE MOTION PICTURES ARE TEACHERS - TEACHING WITH VERY LOUD VOICES. BUT WE WILL NEVER BE ABLE TO MATCH THE POWER OF THE TEACHER WHO IS ABLE TO WHISPER IN A STUDENT'S EAR.

GEORGE LUCAS

Esteem Builders' Complete Program
Jalmar Press, Rolling Hills Estates, CA

WHILE WE TEACH, WE LEARN.

SENECA

Esteem Builders' Complete Program
Jalmar Press, Rolling Hills Estates, CA

8

Team Building:
Increasing Staff Collegiality

TEAM BUILDING STEPS

- Individual Security: The Getting Acquainted or Searching Stage
- Individual Identity: The Defining Stage
- Team Affiliation: The Team Identity and Bonding Stage
- Team Mission: The Commitment Stage
- Team Collegiality: The Competence and Synergy Stage

TEAM BUILDING ACTIVITIES
CONTENTS

8

Team Building: Increasing Staff Collegiality

*"The achievements of an organization are the result
of the combined efforts of each individual."*
—VINCE LOMBARDI

In the last decade, research in organization effectiveness has concentrated on one area in particular: the concept of *team building*. Individuals in the business world frequently use expressions such as "teamwork" and "team player." Kenneth Blanchard sums up the critical role effective team building can play in an organization's optimal performance by stating: "Never before in the history of the workplace has the concept of teamwork been more important to the functioning of successful organizations. With the rapid social, technological and informational changes that are occurring, our society is faced with stresses never before encountered. Our organizations are more complex and more competitive. No longer can we depend upon a few peak performers to rise to the top to lead. If we are to survive, we must figure out ways to tap into the creativity and potential of people at all levels."[1]

Lately, though, expressions common to team building are being used not only in the corporate world but in the educational arena as well. School district managers are recognizing that the premises of effective team building are also conducive to promoting top performance in school staffs. Maximum productivity at a school site is achieved when individuals are transformed into a turned-on, committed group of staff members. As the football coach, Vince Lombardi, stated: "The achievements of an organization are the result of the combined efforts of each individual."

The process in which individual workers support one another, collaborate in their efforts toward shared goals, and communicate openly with one another is called *team building*. Effective teams do not happen by chance. In almost all cases, a leader has helped them develop into a cohesive group of staff members. An effective team is defined as a group that has, as its highest priority, the accomplishment of team goals. Members may have

The process in which individual workers support one another, collaborate in their efforts toward shared goals, and communicate openly with one another is called *team building*.

---

1. Blanchard, Kenneth, Ph.D. Introduction to *The One Minute Manager Builds High Performing Teams* by Kenneth Blanchard, Donald Carew and Eunice Parisi-Carew. New York: William Morrow and Co., 1990, 6.

strong personalities, possess highly-developed and specialized skills, and be committed to a variety of personal objectives; but, for them, the most important business at hand is that the group succeed in "reaching the goal that its members, collectively and with one voice, have set."[2]

BENEFITS OF EFFECTIVE TEAMS

Working as a team has benefits for both the school as a whole and the team members (or staff). The box below depicts some of the most important benefits which result from work as a team:

> **BENEFITS OF EFFECTIVE TEAMS**
> 1. **Optimal Productivity**
> 2. **Collegiality**
> 3. **Open Communication**
> 4. **Stronger Commitment**
> 5. **Pooled Resources**
> 6. **Enhanced Decision-Making**
> 7. **Increased Staff Morale**

- **Optimal Productivity.** Research in staff-cooperative ventures clearly substantiates that working together results in greater productivity than does working alone. Since the group is committed to succeeding together, they therefore have a heightened concern for achieving a quality product. The product now has the stamp of "our team" on it; it is no longer an individual project. How much more powerful, for instance, is a self-esteem program in which all staff members are committed to the concept than for an individual classroom teacher to attempt implementing such a program school-wide. Reinforcement of the esteem concepts is more far-reaching as well as consistent since all staff members share the same goals. The team works collaboratively to try and ensure that each member produces the best possible work.

- **Collegiality.** One of the primary benefits of team building is that it helps generate a feeling of collegiality among the staff. Here is a staff who, because they've had the benefit of working together in successful team encounters, has developed a respect toward each other. Colleagues listen to one another and take each other's beliefs seriously (though not always agreeing). Collegiality arises from the trust that has been built up within a group. Such a feeling is next to impossible to create unless frequent opportunities to work together have been provided and encouraged. Individual competitiveness in the staff is reduced since people are more willing to collaborate and invest in a team effort.

---

2. Quick, Thomas L. *Successful Team Building*. New York: American Management Association, 1992, 3.

- **Open Communication.** Another benefit of team building is that it helps keep the communication network among staff members open. Information flows more freely since individuals have developed a feeling of trust toward one another. Ideas and opinions are shared on a more consistent basis.

- **Strengthened Commitment.** Individuals who have shared successes and personal experiences with one another become more committed toward one another. As their team achievements grow, members feel a stronger commitment to the team itself; they don't want to let it down. As a result, their sense of responsibility to the team increases.

- **Pooled Resources.** As team members work together, their knowledge of one another's strengths and talents increases. The level of trust toward each other rises, and individuals become more willing to share their skills with the team. Work is actually easier because resources are being pooled. Effective teams are comprised of members who recognize the unique talents and skills each person can contribute toward the accomplishment of team goals.

- **Enhanced Decision-Making.** It has been proven time and time again that a group of individuals working together will generate many more options and ideas than one member working alone. This means that decisions made by a team are usually better than what even the brightest person in the work group could come up with alone.

- **Increased Staff Morale.** Effective teams develop feelings in their members that are critical to self-esteem. These include feelings of trust and security, individual identity (recognizing the unique strengths and capabilities of individual members), affiliation or belonging, mission or purpose and team competence or team empowerment. Meeting these esteem needs enhances the overall morale of the staff.

EFFECTIVE TEAMS © Borba

- Trust
- Empowerment
- Affiliation Needs
- Mission
- Success

CHARACTERISTICS OF EFFECTIVE TEAMS

The most effective teams generally have five characteristics in common. Using the first letters in the word TEAMS will help you remember what these characteristics are:

T = Trust. The first characteristic of an effective team is that individual members trust one another. They are willing to share ideas freely amongst all members of the group because they feel safe and secure with one another. Communication is always open in effective teams. Open communication allows individuals to feel free to express differing opinions. Because a sense of trust has been fostered in the group, each member recognizes that all ideas will be respected.

E = Empowerment. Effective teams recognize the strengths of individual members, and they capitalize on one another's capabilities and uniquenesses. Effective teams also recognize that they became effective because they pooled their resources and shared their knowledge. Though each member has a unique personality and their own agenda to fulfill, no one single person "makes the team" work. Instead, the team is a collective of individual personalities and strengths. In such a group, staff members retain *ownership* for their ideas and recognize the unique roles they play in order to help the team succeed. Everyone assumes active participation in the team and shares leadership roles. The team provides its members with a sense of *empowerment*. Individuals feel a sense of personal empowerment because they are an integral part of the team structure; in addition, they feel a collective sense of power being part of a successful team.

A = Affiliation. Another distinguishing characteristic of effective teams is that they support one another and collaborate as a group. Its members have a strong feeling of connectedness and affiliation. Because they've taken the time to know each other personally, a sense of belonging has developed. Team members who have created a feeling of affiliation are more committed to one another. Individuals feel appreciated and respected by other team members. They generally enjoy working together as a group because their affiliation needs are successfully being met.

Effective teams know where they are headed.

M = Mission. Effective teams know where they are headed. They have a clear knowledge of each other's individual beliefs as well as of the team goals they've set for themselves. Shared goals give the team a sense of purpose and direction. Their team efforts are more focused since goals provide them with a means to measure their progress. Effective teams have clearly identified what they want to achieve together and the goals allow them to take action.

S = Success. Everyone needs to feel a sense of accomplishment from their efforts. Effective teams acknowledge their collective successes and celebrate them together. Achievement comes after hard work, not before. Shared celebrations help create an even stronger sense of team bonding. Together team members worked toward the accomplishment of their goals and now together they celebrate their hard work.

TRUE TEAMWORK

It is difficult to comprehend the tremendous impact an effective team can have on both organizational productivity and emotional growth unless an individual has personally experienced such membership. Once a person has experienced or witnessed the positive results, there's no backtracking…the commitment of this individual toward the team building concept can surmount impossible odds.

I experienced the epitome of an effective team in my own community of Palm Springs, California, in July 1991. The incident centered around a tragic accident involving a bus load of Girl Scouts who had gathered from all parts of the world to tour the United States together. The last part of their tour was a trip to the top of a mountain range on the Palm Springs Tram. The girls had just completed the tram ride and were on their way back down a steep grade when the bus driver lost control of the vehicle. The bus flipped over and crashed into the mountain. Some died in the wreckage, and many of the girls and their leaders suffered life-threatening injuries. Each moment added to the seriousness of the injuries. Many lives were saved that day due to the effectiveness of a team that had prepared for just such a moment. The triage unit from the Palm Springs hospitals went into action as soon as they received a call alerting them to the accident. As a result of their efforts, the number of deaths and the severity of the injuries were greatly reduced. Their efforts were successful because of their constant practice in team building. The teams had these five factors in common:

1. **Headed by a strong leader.** At the helm of that team was one of the strongest leaders around. Dr. Alan Fleckner is one of the country's best authorities in emergencies requiring triage response. He is also one of the best authorities on how to create an effective team. Within minutes of the crash, he was in a helicopter flying over the sight, organizing a team, and relaying critical information on a shortwave radio to hospital personnel.

2. **Shared a common goal.** The triage unit clearly had a purpose for their organization and that was to work together to maximize their efforts in saving lives. Each member was committed to that goal and had a clear knowledge of the team's purpose.

3. **Practiced.** One of the reasons why the team was so successful on the day of the crash is that they had practiced working together countless times before. Team building is never an overnight success. Each member must learn to feel comfortable working with the other members. Each member must recognize the other members' strengths and talents. At the peak of an emergency, the team knew they could rely on one another because they had spent hours and hours practicing their roles.

   Team building is never an overnight success.

4. **Capitalized on one another's strengths.** One of the reasons teams are so effective is that they can be so much more productive working together than working alone. Each member of the triage unit knew the specialties and talents of the other members. Each

member also clearly knew their own strengths and contributions to the group. During the height of the emergency, the team called upon one another's talents because they *already* recognized them.

5. Committed. Each member of the team gave 100 percent to their life-saving efforts during the emergency. They could do so because they were wholeheartedly committed to their task. Whether the team is working in an emergency or practice setting, their efforts are always "all-out" because they believe in their mission.

STEPS TO TEAM BUILDING

Team building is critical in creating an effective school environment. The school administrator can play a central role in making the difference between a turned-on or a burnt-out team. Such turned-on teams do not happen by chance. Team building must be deliberately and consistently planned. The development of a team begins with an awareness of the process required for its acquisition. Team building is a progressive process that always involves the same critical five steps which must take place *sequentially*. The team building steps are:

Step 1. Individual Security: *The Getting Acquainted or Searching Stage.*
The first step in team building is to help members get acquainted with one another. This stage is crucial because it lays the foundation for trust. New members walking into a "predefined" team are particularly low in security. The culture and rules of the team have already been defined and the new member can feel very isolated. Each member needs to feel that he or she is being personally invited to join in the group. This is often a *searching* stage where each member tries to figure out just how he or she "fits" into the group. During this time, members frequently have a lot of questions about the expectations of the group as well as the other individuals in the group.

Step 2. Individual Identity: *The Defining Stage.*

In the first stage, members ask questions that are generally "overall" organizational issues. In the second stage, members want to know more about the unique personalities of the staff; they want to define who the individuals are within the group. Before individuals can feel comfortable with one another in the role of "team member," they need to first feel comfortable with one another in the role of "team member," they need to first feel comfortable with one another as individual members. Teams flourish when they recognize one another's strengths and talents and capitalize on them. The triage unit in Palm Springs was successful in their task largely because every member was fully aware of what the other members could contribute. When individuals take on the task of "doing it all," they break down the team. Individual members of the group begin to feel, "Why should I bother? He or she is going to do it all anyway," or "He or she feels they know all the answers." One person "doing it all" leads to group fragmentation. It can also lead to a few individuals assuming the role of "power heads" while others become the "powerless." The second stage is critical because it helps individuals define how they will play on the team. It is a time of finding answers to the question, "What can I contribute?"

Teams flourish when they recognize one another's strengths and talents and capitalize on them.

Keep in mind that individuals at this stage usually are still not "risk takers." For most of us, it is difficult to readily admit our strengths and capabilities to others we have just met. A strong recommendation at this stage is to start slowly and informally. It is safer to begin discussions on the level of an interest or hobby by asking questions such as, "What do you enjoy doing in your spare time?" or "What is your favorite vacation spot?" or "What is your favorite subject to teach?" than to begin with, "What are your greatest strengths and talents?" Activities on the level of personal interests help individuals define who they are as individual team members without taking undue risks.

Step 3. Team Affiliation: *The Team Identity and Bonding Stage.*

This is the first time that individuals actually assume the role of "team." Members of the group begin the process of actually working together. In Stage 2 the team was, in actuality, comprised of a group of individuals, as illustrated below:

In Stage 3 those individuals begin to pool their resources and work side by side as a team. Sharing of ideas and resources is more common at this stage. Individuals can work as a team because they feel as though they are wanted or "included." They also know each other personally. Personal knowledge about individual team members creates a stronger feeling of team commitment. This team has had the opportunity to work together for a longer period of time. Support for one another is more evident, as is support for the team as a whole. No longer is this group a "collection of individuals" (as shown previously in Stage 2). This group is working together toward a common goal. Stage 2 individuals assume roles in the group that basically still serve themselves. Stage 3 individuals assume roles that help serve the team, as illustrated below:

Step 4. Team Mission: *The Commitment Stage*.
The effectiveness that comes from working as a group becomes evident during the fourth stage. By now, team members know not only the personalities and interests but one another's beliefs. Working toward the accomplishment of a team goal is the team's objective. They have a clear direction and purpose to their gathering. Time on task is more common when the team gets together because everyone clearly understands their mission. Open communication at this level is critical. Without the give and take of ideas, the outcome can be dissension among individual team members. The team must recognize that while they do not have to agree with one another's opinions, it is important to listen to every member's ideas.

Step 5. Team Collegiality: *The Competence and Synergy Stage*.
The fifth and final stage of team building is the stage of team collegiality. Generally, this team has experienced the accomplishment of a goal. Such achievements refuel their commitment to more team goals as well as to one another. After they have accomplished one of their goals, their desire to work toward the completion of others is even stronger. Members work well together, and they support one another. Individual competition is greatly reduced since collaboration is the aim. In such a collaborative group, collegiality has been achieved because members trust one another. The group pools their resources and talents because they fully know one another's strengths and talents. They've worked hard to achieve open communication. As a result, at team gatherings information flows freely in all directions. The outcome is a quality product because members have put quality time into their efforts.

THE SOCIAL DYNAMICS: Stages of Team Building ©

It's important for team members to recognize that team building involves social dynamics. Whenever individuals are part of a group, an array of different behaviors should be expected. Group behaviors are largely contingent on the individual personalities of team members. It is tremendously helpful for the leader, in particular, to recognize the following stages. Doing so will allow the leader to determine the normalcy of individual staff behavior at each stage as well as create opportunities for team building at the next stage. The graphic below identifies the five stages of team building as follows:

Team building involves social dynamics.

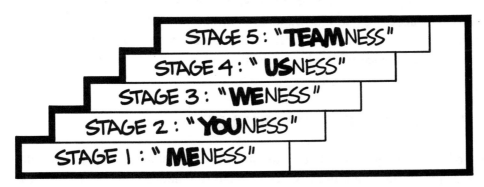

Another way of looking at the five stages of team building is to think of them as a process which helps individuals move from the egocentric stage of MEness, where individuals typically begin, to the more expansive stage of TEAMness. In the MEness stage, ego involvement is high and sharing is low. Individuals' willingness to take risks is also generally low. At this level, individuals are primarily concerned with their own basic needs: "What do they want from me?" and "Will I fit in?" Individuals often arrive with set agendas and competitive attitudes.

As security issues are dealt with and individuals perceive they are wanted and can contribute to the group, the YOUness stage develops. Here is the stage where individuals want to know one another's identity. A common question team members might ask themselves about another member is, "Who are you and how will you fit in?" Members are still working as individuals even though they are part of a team. Their actions are cautious. They are *searching* for answers to how they will work together and what the functions of team members will be. The team works as a collection of individuals, so effectiveness is still poor. The answers to these "you" questions propel individuals into the next stage of WEness.

For the first time, in the third stage, the team is able to work as a collective group of members. The "we" questions now dominate everyone's minds. Common issues that must be dealt with are:

*How will **we** work together?*
*How often will **we** work?*
*What will **we** work toward?*
*How will **we** contribute as individual team members?*

The fourth stage, that of USness, is a more committed stage. Team members probably have worked together for some time and feel comfortable with one another. As the team focuses on where they are headed, working toward a common purpose or direction, a sense of USness develops. They are no longer just a group of individuals, but they are a committed group supporting one another in the same goals and aspirations. Having a team mission certainly helps to keep the team focused and propelled toward the same target.

The final stage is the achievement of TEAMness or collegiality. At the highest level of team building, team members no longer perceive themselves as individuals but as a group that has shared successes and that wants to continue working together. Synergy, an energy of combined action, is the final product. A collective spirit has developed, and "working for the good of the team" is a high priority.

IMPORTANT FACTORS IN TEAM BUILDING

The final stage of team collegiality is one of the most difficult stages for a team to attain. Most teams never reach this stage, usually because the foundation in the previous team-building steps was not strong enough. To achieve the greatest success, keep in mind the following points about the team building process:

The building blocks in the process are sequential.

- **Sequential Steps.** The first and perhaps most important factor in team building is that the building blocks in the process are sequential. The acquisition of each step is based on laying a firm foundation by making sure the step directly preceding it is firmly in place. Skipping steps is counterproductive to the team-building process. It will be impossible for the team to achieve a true sense of team collegiality and commitment unless all the previous steps have been addressed. Each step helps to create a stronger foundation on which to build additional steps.

- **Deliberate Planning.** Effective teams rarely happen by chance; instead, they are deliberately planned. Team members recognize that their productivity will be increased by enhancing their team-building effectiveness. Their belief in the process intensifies their willingness to plan for a successful outcome.

- **Leadership Style.** The style of the leader can have a large impact on the effectiveness of the team. Teams that reach the highest level of team effectiveness are comprised of a group of individuals that have been empowered. What that signifies is that the leader or manager of the school site has released some of his or her power so that the members can share in their own decision-making. Leaders that are too authoritarian in their dealings with their staff are not conveying a sense of trust. It is often difficult for leaders, who in the past made most of the decisions, to share some of this responsibility with their staff. The process of achieving collegiality implies that the people affected by or involved in a decision have a voice in making it. In a school built on the premise of "shared leadership," the relationship between the administrator and staff is based on mutual trust, openness, and respect.

- **Team Personality Composition.** Without exception, every group is composed of a unique gathering of individuals. Each member not only has an individual personality different from any other in the group, but he or she also contributes to the group a different kind of role based on his or her strengths, talents, and style of personality. Some teams, just by the luck of the draw, are more balanced in terms of its members' various styles and personalities. For instance, there may be a more heterogeneous distribution of leaders and followers or isolaters and monopolizers so that personality types are more evenly dispersed, instead of a team of all isolaters and followers, or mostly all leaders and monopolizers. The best teams generally contain a balance of personality types. As a result, the team is able to capitalize on all the different but unique strengths of its members. It can be more difficult to work toward higher levels of team building if all members share the same personality type (for instance, all "power people" or all "isolaters" or all "compromisers"). The personality make-up of the team is an important factor for the leader to be aware of.

- **Frequency of Team Activities.** Clearly, teams that have the opportunity to work with one another on a frequent basis are going to develop a strong sense of collegiality more quickly than those that meet less frequently. It takes time for team members to feel comfortable enough with one another to be able not only to share personal beliefs but also to disagree amicably with other members. It takes time for members to build a sense of trust and recognize each member's unique strengths and talents. The only way teams can achieve synergy is by practicing their skills with one another.

- **Team Member Mobility.** Each time new members become part of the team, the team's dynamics change. New roles are added. Group dynamics also change when current members leave, transfer to a new site, or retire. If team mobility is especially high, added stress falls on the existing members because with each change it is necessary to begin again at the first step in the team-building process. Eliminating the process, regardless of how long existing members have remained together, leads to feelings of alienation on the part of the new member.

- **Realistic Expectations.** One of the largest deterrents to a sense of collegiality is the notion that we can achieve instant change. As a result, too often unrealistic timeframes are set for team building. When the team can't achieve the expectations that have been set, they perceive the missed goal as a team failure. In reality, the real cause of the failure was that the goal was unrealistic. It is important for the team to realize that institutional change generally takes *three to five years to create.* Some studies cite as many as seven years for change to fully take place. Helping the team recognize what research says about change helps everyone to keep in mind a more realistic perspective for goal acquisition.

Institutional change generally takes *three to five years to create.*

REACTIONS TO CHANGE

Creating change in the school system is rarely an objective, rational process. Strong emotional reaction to the change is always part of the process. Researchers studying the affective dimension of restructuring have uncovered fascinating findings about the emotional response of staff members. In the *1979 Annual Handbook for Group Facilitators*, University Associates, Don Kelly and Darryl Connor, identified an emotional cycle of change. The five stages in this cycle include:

Stages of Emotional Reaction to Change

Stage 1. Uninformed Optimism

Stage 2. Informed Pessimism

Stage 3. Hopeful Realism

Stage 4. Informed Optimism

Stage 5. A Sense of Rewarding Completion

Stage 1. Uninformed Optimism. This first stage of change is called the "honeymoon phase" because, in many cases, it is the easiest. Staff members know that change will be expected. The restructuring effort begins with energy and enthusiasm. It is often an "ideal phase" because participants aren't prepared for the difficulties that are bound to be encountered. It quickly is replaced by the second phase.

Stage 2. Informed Pessimism. Unexpected problems and difficulties are a typical part of any restructuring effort. Kelly and Connor warn that this stage can be a dangerous stage of the emotional cycle and morale frequently drops. Very often, the restructuring efforts are dropped because the staff cannot handle the tensions of the participants. In the majority of cases, the tension and pessimism begin with just a few of the participants. Their pessimism can quickly become a full-fledged catalyst so that their negative attitude spreads to all. If success in the project is going to prevail, it is necessary to go through the three remaining stages.

Stage 3. Hopeful Realism. Pessimism will begin to fade as some of the group's efforts succeed. This is why it is so important that the group not bend to the few resistant (and highly pessimistic) staff members. Small successes breed a larger feeling of hopefulness.

Stage 4. Informed Optimism. As successes in the group's efforts continue to build, confidence will be restored. The group begins to recognize that restructuring efforts are within reach. Group optimism prevails. The team is rejuvenated because they recognize they're "back on track."

Stage 5. A Sense of Rewarding Completion. Kelly and Connor describe this final stage as happening when those involved in the effort to change see the concrete results of their work. Here the group acquires the feeling of competence so essential in validating all the work that has transpired.

DEALING WITH RESISTANCE

One of the most stressful parts of change is the emotional resistance of some of its participants. Most people hate change since it "rocks the boat." It is important for the leader to recognize that individuals with low self-esteem are particularly difficult to deal with during this phase. Their risk-taking skills are typically quite low. Their personal security is being threatened during this phase due to their uncertainty of "what lies ahead for me." Change can be disturbing and frightening. Their world, as they know it, is being disrupted. It is critical that the staff be prepared for resistance which quite often can turn to hostility on the part of some of the staff.

Individuals with low self-esteem typically resist change.

Change is often a conflict-ridden process which frequently involves emotional upheaval. Staff members are continually being asked to deal with new techniques and restructuring efforts. The irony is that the staff has never been adequately prepared to deal with the change. The majority of the staff has never been trained in how to work together. Higher levels in team building are difficult to obtain without formal training in team-building skills, and yet, school site leaders are constantly being required to bring teams up to the highest stages without having the skills to facilitate the process. Tensions and emotions of concerned staff members can be open and volatile during restructuring. A major recommendation to any leader about to put his or her staff through the process of a major change is to first receive formal training in team building. It is often helpful to send a core team of staff members to receive specific training in such techniques as conflict resolution and problem-solving skills. Team leaders who have received such formal training can minimize major dissension among the group whenever problems and conflicts (which are the natural outcomes of the process) arise.

PREPARING FOR RESTRUCTURING

Restructuring is an energy and emotion draining experience. However, its successful outcome will benefit both staff and students. Being educated in the emotional stages that staff members will typically go through during the process of change is one way to prepare for the emotional roller coaster ride in the weeks ahead. The following points suggest other ideas school site leaders can incorporate during the restructuring process to help make the ride toward change easier:

- **Empathize with Staff Members.** It is always helpful to step back and consider what change will look like to resistant staff members. Predicting how individuals may react is possible by reflecting on what certain staff members may be concerned about and why. Severe emotional reactions to change can often be minimized if the leader first stops to empathize with the concerns of his or her staff.

- **Provide Lots of Advance Notice.** People hate to be told at the last minute about a change. They need the chance to prepare emotionally for the restructuring procedure. Thinking that you can postpone resistance by telling the staff at the last minute about the change is a mistake. Very often individuals will resent the change even more because they weren't given enough time to "think about it."

- **Map Out the Specifics.** Change is often disturbing to individuals because of the uncertainty it brings. They "don't know what will happen" and that element of insecurity is frightening. Uncertainty can be minimized by taking the time to tell everyone about all the specifics that are involved. The leader should prepare to give a presentation by thoroughly outlining all the parameters in the process of change. Whenever possible, provide a printed form listing what the process may involve.

Change is an emotional process.

- **Take It Slowly.** Change is an emotional process. Too much change too quickly generally leads to excessive stress. The timing in presenting the change to the staff is always critical. The rule is, "Only one change at a time." Too often the issue is compounded unnecessarily by introducing too many changes at a time. *Move slowly.*

- **Schedule Time to Communicate.** Deadlines place relentless pressures on staff members. Not enough time is available to just reflect and think about the restructuring. In most schools, schedules do not accommodate opportunities for discussion among staff members regarding the changes that are taking place. Many schools, recognizing the need for a dialogue, creatively alter the daily or weekly schedules to provide time for staff members to meet. This may mean starting classes five minutes earlier each day to allow two half days of release time every month. It could also involve rescheduling the lunch or recess programs to provide a twenty-minute time block for teachers to communicate. There are many creative approaches to scheduling that can provide the staff with the time they need to communicate.

- **Be Aware of Emotional Reactions to Change.** Any change will be met with an emotional reaction. Some staff members will react more strongly than others to the process and will openly and verbally resist the change. It is important that all staff members be prepared for such reactions. In the very beginning stages of the restructuring, staff members should be briefly in-serviced in the stages of emotional change.

- **Open Effective Communication Channels.** School buildings are notorious for not being conducive to communication. Schedules and classroom locations inhibit ongoing dialogues among staff members. However, ongoing communication is a critical element to successful restructuring. Somehow all staff members need to be continually kept abreast of ongoing changes and decisions. Some schools appoint one staff member as the "news reporter" who then publishes and distributes newsletters to staff members. Phone trees, centrally-located bulletin boards, weekly meetings or flyers are other techniques that can help in the communication process. One principal keeps a staff "sign-in" book on the secretary's counter. Each day the principal and staff members communicate school business and scheduling changes on a message page. Personal comments and ideas are also written down for all staff members to read. The book has become a personal message center that no staff member wants to miss; it has become a method for a large staff to keep in touch with one another.

- **Record Successes.** Beginning successes in the process of change are few and far between. Each success, when it happens, is a validation for staff members that "we're on the right track." Appoint one staff member to be the school "historian." A photo album or bulletin board should become a permanent fixture in the faculty room. Photographs, articles, quotes and interviews depicting successes in restructuring should be highly visual and constantly updated.

- **Enlist Support.** Staff members should constantly assess what they believe is needed to be successful in their restructuring attempts. Needs could include resources and supplies, or in-servicing by professionals who can provide information or training in an area the staff perceives as a "problem."

- **Schedule Time to Relax.** The process of restructuring can be emotionally and physically draining. Personal support systems for staff members can be helpful. Remember to provide opportunities for staff members to just have fun (no discussions about school allowed).

- **Provide Realistic Deadlines.** One of the greatest misnomers regarding the issue of change is that it will come quickly. One of the most important resources needed in restructuring is time. Unrealistic timeframes will create feelings of incompetence among the staff when the deadline is not met. It is better to set a longer deadline and then shorten it than to set a goal of rapid change only to have to continually lengthen the date. Staff members must be appraised that change is a slow, gradual process that always involves problems along the way that no one could have planned for.

- **Initiate Honest Dialogue.** Staff members generally hesitate to speak truthfully about their fears and concerns regarding the process of change. Too often they hold their fears inside and perceive themselves as being "all alone…no one else is feeling like I am." Before change can be successfully initiated at the site, participants must have the opportunity to engage in an honest dialogue with one another. The best and most healthy place to begin is with sessions where everyone has the opportunity to share their concerns about the process.

Participants must have the opportunity to engage in an honest dialogue with one another.

The facilitator in the process must be a fair-minded individual who has credibility among the group's members. An opener for dialogues that many have found successful is a Round Robin session. Staff members sit around in a circle and each one has the opportunity to verbalize (or pass) their response to an open-ended sentence statement such as: "One concern I have to the change is…" or "One question I have about the process is…" A recorder can write down paraphrases of participants' ideas on a large flipchart. Recording the responses is helpful for two reasons: 1) participants begin to see that others in the group have similar concerns and fears, and 2) at the conclusion of the Round Robin session the concerns can become the framework for questions and answers. Generally, staff members do not verbalize these questions to the principal or other staff members. This is an opportunity for all staff members to share verbally their ideas, opinions, and concerns. If the leader is not careful, the same staff members dominate a staff meeting. More reticent members too often refrain from commenting. For effective team building to develop, all staff members need to be heard.

One dialogue session will not be enough. The dialogue must be both formal and informal. It should transpire formally in the faculty meeting and informally in the faculty lounge. Small group as well as large group communication sessions should be arranged. Staff members must have the opportunity to really hear one another's views. Working together in a spirit of collegiality can never take place unless the group trusts one another and understands where each person is coming from.

IMPLEMENTATION DIP

Dr. Michael Fullan from the University of Toronto has explored in detail the emotional impact the restructuring process has on staff members' work performance. In his book, *The Meaning of Educational Change,* Fullan details his discovery of a phenomenon called the "implementation dip." Having an awareness of this phenomenon can be enormously helpful for school leaders as well as staff members as they deal with restructuring. Fullan explains that in the initial phase of change people basically agree to implement the new policy. As the changes are implemented, he noted, staff members undergo a *decline in their work performance or work quality.* Fullan emphasizes that this phase is quite normal. Problems among the staff can intensify because the decline can be quite humiliating and frustrating to the individuals. There are, understandably, feelings of awkwardness and guilt. Fullan points out, though, that the decline in skills is only *temporary.* Once the "dip" has been reached, behavior usually reorganizes at a higher level than before and the restructuring process becomes successful.

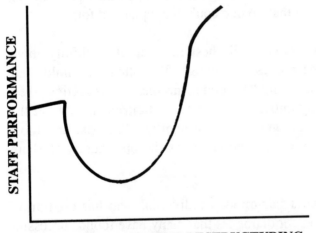

TIME PERIOD DURING RESTRUCTURING

STEP 1. INDIVIDUAL SECURITY: *The Getting Acquainted or Searching Stage*

Each of the five steps to team building addresses a critical element of esteem enhancement. The process begins with the Searching Stage in which each member is really a separate entity from the other staff members. No team characteristics have formed because each individual is still at the MEness level. Sharing of ideas and opinions during the Security step is rare. The members have not yet built a sense of trust toward one another. They don't feel safe sharing and opening up to others. Ego involvement is high. Members are cautious and concerned.

SIX CRITICAL WANTS

In general, each person has six basic *wants* that revolve around the individual's search for answers to the question, "How will I fit into my new environment?" It is important for the staff and leader to address the questions that most apply to them personally. Though there may be other questions the new team member would like to know the answers to, the "basic six" questions below generally are the key issues the new member has of his/her new staff and school beyond the issue of "salary":

> • **What is the school like?**
> • **Will I be wanted?**
> • **Who will I be with?**
> • **What do you want from me?**
> • **Will I be successful?**
> • **How will I be treated?**

• *What is the school like?*

What is the economic population of the school like?

What does my classroom look like?

What kind of facilities are available at the school?

How large is the school's student population?

What will be the size of my class?

Is there a faculty lounge?

What do teachers do for lunch?

What is the daily schedule?

What is the yearly schedule?

Are there any special traditions or events that are held?

What are the native languages of the students?

What are the cultures of the students?

What is the parent population like?

What kinds of materials and resources are available?

Does the school have any particular program emphasis?

What are the school's rules?

- *Will I be wanted?*

  Are the teachers receptive to having a new staff member?

  Who will I be replacing?

  Will my teaching strengths be recognized?

  Will I have the opportunity to share my ideas and opinions?

  Is there any resistance to my being a member of the team?

  Do the teachers on my grade level work as a team?

- *Who will I be with?*

  How many other teachers will I be with?

  How social is this group?

  Are there staff activities away from the school?

  If there are staff activities away from the school, am I expected to go?

  How many other teachers are on the same grade level I am?

  Is this a sharing group of teachers?

  What are the belief structures of my grade-level colleagues?

  How long have the other teachers been a part of the school?

  What are the past experiences of the other teachers at this grade level?

The new team member also has some questions that apply directly to the leader of the school site (or grade level). These questions might include:

- *What do you want from me?*

  What expectations do you have of me?

  What specific programs will I be teaching?

  What hours am I expected to be here?

  Will I be responsible for duties such as playground, lunch, or bus duty? If so, how often?

  Is any sign-in required?

  What are the policies for absences and arranging substitutes?

  Will I be allowed to attend in-service training of my choice?

  Will I be responsible for turning in weekly lesson plans?

How often will there be teacher meetings?

What expectations do you have of me outside of the classroom?

Am I responsible for helping with any school events outside my own classroom?

- *Will I be successful?*

How will I be evaluated?

How often will you be observing my room?

Will you let me know what you are looking for before you come in the room?

How much of my evaluation will be determined by test scores?

How will I know if I am successful?

Is there a particular curriculum that I should be familiar with?

- *How will I be treated?*

What is your communication style?

Can I count on you to back me up during a parental conflict?

If I have a problem, how should I approach you?

When are you available?

Are you approachable?

Are all your decisions final or do I have some kind of say?

In case of a discipline problem with a student, what kind of back-up can I expect from you?

ADDRESSING THE "WILL I BE WANTED" ISSUE (SEB 218-228)

These are some basic safety needs that must be addressed before team building can begin. Probably the first and most critical need of a new staff member is to feel that he or she is "wanted" by the new staff. This feeling of being wanted can be built by planning opportunities for new members to feel as though they have been "invited" to be part of the group. There are dozens of ways to extend invitations. Here are a few suggested "team invitationals" to help new members feel included:

The first and most critical need of a new staff member is to feel that he or she is "wanted" by the new staff.

1. **Welcoming Committee (SEB 218).** A group of staff members can serve as a Welcome Committee for each new member. The group personally visits the new member to extend an invitation of "welcome." The committee could at this time bring a "welcome gift" to the individual such as:

   - a basket of flowers
   - a large apple with a note card attached: "Welcome!"

- a staff directory or yearbook or handbook
- a card signed by all the "old staff members"
- a coupon for dinner or lunch to a local restaurant
- a basket of back-to-school goodies

2. **Buddy System (SEB 219).** Each new staff member could be paired with an "older staff member" serving in the role of "buddy." Ideally, the buddy mentor should be someone who works in the same grade level or position. The buddy personally visits the new member, perhaps inviting the individual to lunch. Here is when the new member can ask questions and address issues with someone who has the answers.

3. **Welcome Balloons or Flowers (SEB 220).** Many staff members welcome new members with a balloon or bouquet of flowers. Another idea is an "apple bouquet." Anything depicting the theme "welcome...we're glad you're here" is appreciated by the new member.

4. **Staff Card (SEB 221).** Purchase or create a large card with a caption such as "welcome to our team" on the front. Group or individual photos of all the staff members could appear on the outside. The inside of the card could have another caption such as "we're glad you'll be part of our team." Ask every available staff member to sign the card and present it to the new member.

5. **Welcome Basket (SEB 222).** Decorate a basket with colored cellophane paper and ribbon to serve as a "welcome basket." Attach a card to the outside of the basket with the names of all the staff members and a caption that reads "Welcome!" Fill the inside of the basket with simple goodies such as:

- a whistle
- a set of personalized business cards
- stickers
- "first day" supplies
- colored pencils or pens
- note pads
- rubber stamps
- teacher pencils
- a treat such as a candy bar or apple
- a school handbook

Any kind of items which signify the school could also be included such as:

- school pencils
- school notebooks
- school mascot
- bumper stickers
- school pennant
- school t-shirt
- school folder

6. **Parking Space (SEB 223).** Some staffs welcome a new member by marking a special parking space for that person to use for the first week of school. The space states the person's name and includes a sign stating "welcome," perhaps with the name of the individual's position.

7. **First-Week School Pack (SEB 224).** Create a packet of activities and items a new teacher might need during the first week of school. These could include: a lesson plan book, a whistle, an extra supply of band-aids, a school schedule, a school map, a directory of staff members' names and telephone numbers, a few school student "mingler" activities, colored teacher pencils, a "free yard duty" coupon (good for one time relief of a scheduled yard or bus duty if prearranged with the administrator), a set of stickers and student name tags.

8. **Welcome Door Sign (SEB 225).** Create a colorful large paper sign with the caption, "Welcome to our school!" Attach it to the individual's door. If possible, have all available staff members sign it.

9. **Name on the Marquee (SEB 226).** If the school has a marquee or front hall bulletin board, create a welcome sign for the new staff members, with their name, position, and a welcome caption, so that everyone in the community can read it.

10. **Invitation to a Luncheon or Breakfast (SEB 227).** Plan a luncheon, breakfast, brunch or dinner to welcome new staff members to the group. This gives everyone the opportunity to meet informally with one another.

11. **Staff Welcome Coupons (SEB 228).** To make a staff coupon book for a new staff member, duplicate the coupons on page 293 and distribute one to each current staff member. Only one cover coupon is needed per book. Ask staff members to voluntarily give something to the new staff member. Emphasize that the item should not be something they have to go out and purchase but should instead be something they already have. The best gifts are talents and energy. The staff members fill out the coupon below stating their "gift." The coupons are then stapled together inside the cover form and presented to the new staff member. "Gift" ideas include:

   - "I'll take your yard duty one time."
   - "I'll take your bus duty one time."
   - an extra pack of ditto paper
   - a lesson on astronomy
   - "I'll read to your class for 15 minutes."
   - the loan of a children's literature selection
   - a box of ditto masters
   - "I'll teach perspective drawing to your class."

SHARING INFORMATION ABOUT THE SCHOOL

It is often helpful for the leader and the school's existing team to sit down prior to the arrival of new staff members and think about the kinds of questions the newcomers may have. Esteem Builder Team members may wish to brainstorm the following question:

Pretend you're new to our staff. You have some natural concerns about coming to a brand new site. What kinds of questions do you have about our school, staff, and leader?

All thoughts should be recorded. At the end of the activity, the facilitator might ask the group: "How will we convey this information to our new members?" Such an activity not only helps the existing staff members empathize with the new members' possible feelings of insecurity on entering an established school site, but it also helps better prepare the team for the first steps of team building. The final outcome should be the development of a specific plan by the existing team for a more secure arrival of the new team. This activity lays the foundation for the first steps of team building, which is to create an environment that promotes a feeling of comfortableness for any new arrival. Such actions are certainly necessary since they are the preliminary steps in team building.

DISSEMINATING INFORMATION TO NEW TEAM MEMBERS (SEB 229-239)

There are many ways to convey information about the school, leader, and staff to new members. It is always best to create ways that are both manageable and fitted to your unique setting. A few suggestions follow:

- **Video Orientation (SEB 229).** If the school has videotaped school and classroom activities and events, the sections can be spliced together to create an orientation video. The video tape could either be presented to the new members to view at home or shown at a special faculty presentation.

- **Slide Presentation (SEB 230).** The video orientation could easily be adapted to a slide presentation of school activities. Ask any staff member who has taken slides throughout the year if they would be willing to share them for a one-time viewing. Many schools put together a slide show and play an inspirational song in the background. Songs such as "The Greatest Love of All" or "Wind Beneath My Wings" are especially appropriate. The school may wish to make extra slides so that the presentation may be used again with parents or other new staff members.

- **Photo Album (SEB 231).** Photographs of school and classroom events could be put in a school photo album. Many schools already have photo albums that are already available. A special gift for new staff members could be a small photo album containing a few selected pictures. Consider photos depicting special school events and traditions. Encourage staff members to add to it with photos of their own.

- **Scrapbook (SEB 232).** A scrapbook containing not only school-related photos but also news articles and news grams could be put together. An existing staff member could photocopy old newsletters and photos. A map of the school as well as the community could also be included. Many schools use the yearbook as a welcome gift to present to a new staff member and then (as with the photo album) encourage the individual to add personal momentos of school memories.

- **Yearbook (SEB 233).** Many schools publish a yearbook. If the school already has a yearbook, consider presenting new team members with their own personal copies. Signatures as well as written comments from staff members could also be included.

- **Bus Ride (SEB 234).** If the new members are unfamiliar with the community, a narrated tour can be very valuable. Not only will it help them become familiar with the street names, restaurants, and local businesses but it will also provide them with a firsthand understanding of the socioeconomic makeup of the families in the school's neighborhood.

- **School Tours.** Not only will new members want to find out about the community, but they will want to know more about their own school. Here are two possibilities for introducing these newcomers to their new workplace:

    1. *School Narrated Tour (SEB 235).* Pair new members with "old" staff members. The group of pairs take a guided tour of the school campus. The tour guide should make a complete list of all the places new members may want to be aware of...everything from the obvious, such as the individual's classroom, the office, faculty room, and ditto machine, to the less obvious (but equally important): the refrigerator, phone, and first-aid supplies.

    2. *School Checklist (SEB 236).* Another idea is to ask current staff members to create a checklist of all the items that would be on a narrated tour. This activity is similar to a scavenger hunt and generally works best if there is more than one new staff member involved. Give the checklist to a pair (or trio) of new staff members. Ideally, another pair of new members is working at the same time to try and find all the items on the list. The first group to find the items (and tell an old staff member their correct location) wins.

- **Staff Names.** One of the factors that creates insecurity for new staff members is not knowing the names of their colleagues. The staff can alleviate this anxiety by conveying such information to newcomers. Keep in mind that a picture of each staff member accompanied by his/her name and grade level is always appreciated more than a list of names. Pictures enable us recall names much more easily. Here are three possibilities to consider:

SCHOOL CHECKLIST

Directions: You and a partner are to work together to try and find as many of the following items at this school site as you can. Check off each one as it is located. Good luck!

• cafeteria	• school phones
• faculty room	• faculty restrooms
• student restrooms	• copy machine
• textbook rooms	• library
• playground	• playground equipment
• nurse's room	• principal's office
• extra band-aids	• phone directory of all students
• fire extinguishers	• custodian's room
• extra pencils	• movie equipment
• overhead projectors	• staff boxes
• yard duty schedule	• coffee mugs
• your classroom	• another teacher/same grade

---

1. *School and Staff Map (SEB 237).* Create a map of the school site that depicts the location of each classroom. Next, collect small photographs of each staff member (classified as well as certificated). The photos may need to be reduced on a copying machine. Only a picture of the individual's head is needed. The photo need not be any larger than one square inch. Glue the photo of each staff member next to his/her classroom or office. Under the picture type each member's name and position. Hand the map to new staff members. Note: The map can be enlarged on a copier to become a wonderful organizer on a hall bulletin board. Or enlarge the photos to a size appropriate for a large bulletin board and create the same map with all staff members' names and positions. Consider using the map as a first-week-of-school bulletin board to help not only staff members but also parents and students become acquainted with every one at the school site.

2. *Staff Directory (SEB 238).* Type a list of all staff members' names. Next to each name paste a small photo of the individual. Include also their position and office or classroom number. Duplicate a copy for each new staff member and place it in a colorful paper cover.

3. *Staff Yearbook (SEB 239).* The Staff Directory can be expanded into a Staff Yearbook. Provide all staff members with a copy of the SEB 239 Staff Yearbook form on page 294. Ask them to complete the information and turn in the form to a designated individual. The yearbook is created by gluing a photograph of each staff member in the space specified on the form. Duplicate the completed forms so that each new staff member has a copy of everyone's form. Alphabetize the pages by the staff member's last name. Create a table of contents in the front of the book which lists each staff member's name, grade level, and the page number in the yearbook where information on the individual can be found. A cover can be created by gluing a picture of the school on the front with cardstock-weight paper. Staple or bind the completed yearbook together and present a copy to each new staff member. Keep additional copies in the office for the unexpected arrival of another new staff member.

MOVING FROM "ME" TO "YOU"

When safety needs and security issues have been met, individual members can begin to look at the next step: YOUness. In the second stage of team building, staff members begin to discover the individual identities of their colleagues. They begin to look more closely at one another; they are ready to know more than just "what grade level" another person teaches. They want to know the personal side of each participant on the team. Common questions might include:

1. *Family Issues:* Are you married? Do you have children? How long have you been married? Is there a significant other in your life?

2. *Education Issues:* Where did you go to school? What was your major? What degrees do you have?

3. *Teaching Issues:* What is your favorite grade level? What is your favorite subject? How long have you been teaching?

SCHOOL CULTURE BANNERS   SEB 240

Purpose: To define the school's culture; to plan ways of disseminating information on this culture to new staff members.

Materials: A large piece of chart paper; colored marking pens, crayons, pencils and a 12" x 18" piece of white construction paper cut into the shape of a sports pennant for each team.

Procedure: Coming into a school site where an existing staff has operated for many years raises numerous questions for the individuals who are entering. The staff, students, and parents at the school have shared in certain traditions and events. Thus, it could be said that the site has a "defined culture" which makes it unique. An important job for the older staff is to convey to new team members all the factors that have created the school's culture. The School Culture Banner activity is one method to help old as well as new members define the culture.

Begin the task by asking existing staff members to brainstorm the specific traits which make the school unique. Explain that these traits may be related to, for example: school spirit, special annual events, traditions that have been passed on, mission statements or beliefs, special school programs or curriculum. One individual serving in the role of "recorder" writes down the events on a large piece of chart paper. Emphasize that no evaluations or put-downs of ideas are allowed. The following questions can be posed if brainstorming comes to a standstill:

- *Do we have a school mascot ... colors ... slogan ... song ... motto?*
- *What is our school mission statement?*
- *What makes us unique as a school?*
- *What special curriculum do we emphasize?*
- *What events do we hold annually?*
- *Do we have any special traditions?*
- *What is unique about our students ... staff ... community?*

Once a list has been created, the group's task is to figure out the best way to disseminate this information on the school's special traits to new team members. One way is to create School Culture Banners. Ask the large group to quickly divide into smaller groups of no more than six. Provide each team with colored marking pens, crayons, and pencils and a 12" x 18" piece of white construction paper cut into the shape of a sports pennant. Explain that each group's task is now to create a pennant depicting the factors that make the school a unique culture. Tell the group they may use words, pictures, or symbols to depict the images. Suggest that each banner has the school name and school colors.

Provide the group with a time frame (usually no more than fifteen minutes). Ask the groups to hang up their completed banners on a designated wall.

At the conclusion of the banner-making activity, ask each group to spend ten minutes discussing one critical question: "How will we convey the information we just drew on the banners to the new staff members?" Following the discussion, ask for volunteers from each group to share the ideas they generated. The final outcome of the discussion should be the development of a specific plan as to how the group will convey the information on school culture to new members. One idea is to print copies of the banners and staple them together as a "booklet," to be presented to new members. Another possibility is to leave the completed banners in a visible location such as the faculty room. As newcomers join the staff, established staff members could explain to them the information depicted on the banners.

STEP 2. INDIVIDUAL IDENTITY: *The Defining Stage*

Research points out that the first need of new members that the school site must address is the issue of security. A basic human need is to feel emotionally and physically safe in a new environment. Once the feeling of security is bridged, members begin to ask the next key questions: "Who will be with me?" and "How will I fit in?" The "who" and "how" questions center around the new members' desire to fit in and to know whether or not they have things in common with other team members. This is the Defining Stage. The members are trying to define the group membership by assessing who is in the group and how each individual can contribute as a team player. Thus, this stage involves developing individual identity. Members are finding out about one another's personal and professional sides as well as identifying or defining how they see themselves fitting into the group.

Identifying commonalities among team members can be addressed on two distinct levels: a) "things we have in common professionally and educationally" (the same in-service background, shared philosophy, knowledge of particular educational programs and curriculum, and b) "things we have in common personally" (the same hobbies and interests, age, geographic living location, children's ages, etc.). More often than not, these questions are not verbalized but remain unvoiced concerns.

STAFF ESTEEM BUILDERS

A few of the professional questions team members might have regarding other team members could include issues such as:

What are the educational backgrounds of my team members?

What are the subject/curriculum strengths of these individuals?

Will I be recognized for my unique strengths?

What type of in-services has the group previously had?

Will I fit into the group with my background?

Are these individuals receptive to new ideas? Can I risk sharing my ideas with this group?

What are the leadership styles of the group members? Are they listeners? monopolizers? compromisers? team players? isolaters?

Do individuals here share some of the same values and goals?

Are these individuals tolerant of differences?

Who will be the leader? the followers? the idea people? the knowledge base?

Which of these individuals have taught the same number of years as I have?

If I have a problem, who in this group can I turn to?

Who in this group will I feel most comfortable working and sharing ideas with?

The individuals with whom educators work frequently become the same persons with whom they socialize. After team members work together professionally for an extended period of time, they discover, in the process, that they also have numerous personal interests in common. Though team members do not have to socialize on a personal level to be effective as team members, the knowledge that commonalities are shared personally as well as professionally certainly contributes to a stronger sense of team cohesiveness. The questions team members frequently have about one another on a personal level might include:

Who on this team will I feel most comfortable with socializing?

Does anyone on this team live near me?

Can I trust these members to maintain confidentiality?

Does anyone on this team have children? Are their children about the same ages as my children?

Do members of this team enjoy being with one another?

Does anyone here share my same interest in…?

How often (if ever) do these individuals get together on a purely social level?

These personal and professional questions are offered merely as a starting place. Certainly, each individual has different kinds of questions that need answering. Perhaps the best starting place would be to ask members, "What professional and social questions would you like to ask the members of this team?" The team leader, in particular, needs to be aware of the questions and issues team members are concerned about. The leader can then address these issues in team discussions.

Each group is comprised of unique personalities. These personalities when joined together in teamwork will form the *team dynamics*. A shrewd leader can diagnose the team's individual members and predict group behaviors. Once the personalities, styles, and strengths of individual members are understood, the dynamics inherent within the group can be better understood.

Successful teams do not necessarily need "rapport" and "empathy." Those are characteristics generally involved in close friendships. In order to be effective, though, team members do need to have personal knowledge about one another. They certainly should know one another's strengths and interests. Knowing the other team members' personalities and leadership styles is also helpful. Peter Drucker describes this issue succinctly by stating, "Team members need not know each other well to perform as a team. But they do need to know each other's function and potential contribution."[1] This information helps the team delegate roles and recognize how each member can most successfully contribute to the team.

STAFF SELF-POSTERS   SEB 241

Purpose: To build staff identity and a sense of belonging; to increase awareness of individual staff member's uniquenesses and interests.

Materials: Poster board (or chart paper cut into 16" x 22" lengths) for each participant; glue or rubber cement; colored marking pens and crayons; magazines; photograph of each staff member (either a Polaroid snapshot taken at the school site, photograph from class pictures, or one from home). Baby pictures of photos of the individual's family can also be included.

Procedure: At a faculty meeting or staff gathering, staff members create a poster of themselves. Explain that any materials may be used to depict individuals' uniquenesses and interests. Each poster must somehow convey the following information:

- current photo (or baby photo);
- quote that fits their philosophy;
- magazine pictures that depict their interests;
- words/symbols that describe themselves; and
- photo of their family.

1. Drucker, Peter F. *Management*. New York: Harper & Row, 1985, 566.

Emphasize that all information should be on one side of the posters. When the posters are completed, they may be hung up in the faculty lounge. Staff members can also take time to explain the information on the poster. If different staff members are highlighted each week, the posters can be saved and hung in a central location for students to enjoy also.

PARTNER FOR SALE   SEB 242

Purpose: To provide the opportunity to identify unique attributes and characteristics about individual staff members.

Materials: A store-bought "For Sale" sign or handmade facsimile.

Procedure: Ask each member of the group to quickly choose a partner. Encourage everyone to choose someone they may not know well already. Explain that participants will have five minutes to interview their partner about their "life outside of school." The group may wish to brainstorm for a few minutes the kinds of questions they could ask their partner:

- Where did you grow up?
- Where have you lived prior to here?
- How many brothers or sisters do you have?
- Where did you go to school?
- Why did you decide to go into education?
- What are your favorite places to visit?
- What kinds of hobbies do you have?
- Are you married? If so, how did you meet your spouse?

If the group wishes, these questions could be written on the blackboard or chart paper. Explain to the group that after the five-minute interview, partners will switch roles so that the other partner assumes the role of the interviewer. Following the interview session, explain to the group that what was just done is not done often enough. Unfortunately, we may work together on a staff for days or months and often not know personal things about each other. Hold up the "For Sale" sign. Explain that the final part of the activity is for each person to take a few minutes and "sell" their partner to the rest of the group. Each participant is to introduce their partner to the group, telling a few things he or she has learned about the person that the rest of the group may not know. Continue the process until everyone has had a chance to be introduced by their partner.

HOBBY DAY   SEB 243

Purpose: To provide opportunities for staff members to find out about one another's interests and hobbies.

Materials: C1 Hobby Day Checklist (page 291), C2 My Interest (page 292), and if appropriate, C1/2 Hobby Day Award (page 293) from *Esteem Builders*.

Procedure: Explain that too often the staff's awareness of one another is limited to the roles they play at school. The Hobby Day Activity is a chance for staff members to share something about who they are outside of school. Assign participating staff members a particular Hobby Day for some time during the year. A few staff members will have the same Hobby Day. A different Hobby Day could be assigned each month. Post a calendar of assigned days in the faculty room. Reminders for the upcoming event could also be placed in boxes.

Distribute copies of the C1 Hobby Day Checklist and C2 My Interest forms to staff members. Explain that the forms are to be used merely as a guide for their Hobby Day exhibit. Explain that their students could use the forms for a similar classroom or school-wide event. Invite staff members to bring in samples, photographs, exhibits or anything else depicting their interests and to set up these items in the staff lounge or other central location. Emphasize that the hobby or interest could be anything: stamp collecting, knitting, sewing, traveling, fishing, coin collecting, quilting, reading, kids, etc. Exhibits could include any samples of the hobby and/or tools used in the hobby. Encourage staff members to also bring in directions of how another person may become involved in the hobby as well as books about the hobby they have found helpful.

TWO-MINUTE AUTOBIOGRAPHIES   SEB 244

Purpose: To increase the staff's awareness of the backgrounds and identities of their colleagues.

Materials: Timing device with a second hand.

Procedure: Ask participants to quickly form groups of four. Emphasize that there should be no more than four members in a group. Each member of the group will have two minutes to relate a short autobiography of their life. During this individual's recitation, no interruptions or questions from other team members are allowed. Explain that you (the facilitator) will keep track of time so that each person has two minutes of sharing. You will also tell the group when they are halfway through the assignment by calling out "one minute." At the end of the autobiography, all team members are to applaud their teammate. The activity then continues clockwise until everyone in the group has had a turn.

Ask each group to choose a "starter" (the first person to speak). Allow a few minutes of quiet time during which all group members are to think through their life and practice what they will say. At the completion of the group autobiography, allow a few minutes for team members to ask questions or respond to each other's autobiographical information.

Note: This activity can be invaluable in increasing awareness of other colleagues' individual identities. By keeping a list of the names of each team's members, you can repeat the activity at future staff gatherings but form groups comprised of entirely different members.

WHO AM I?   SEB 245

Purpose: To help staff members learn about themselves and each other.

Materials: SEB 245 Guess Who? questionnaire (page 295); a picture of each staff member; bulletin board.

Procedure: Start this activity at the beginning of the school year and continue until all staff members have had a turn. Distribute questionnaires to staff members and encourage them to complete the forms and then return them to a designated staff member or location. Also, ask them to attach a photograph of themselves to the forms. Explain that the questionnaires will be placed on a bulletin board to highlight different staff members.

Make a bulletin board featuring one or two staff members each week; display information from the questionnaires and pictures. Display the board in the staff lounge or other central location. To vary the activity, a caption such as "Guess Who?" could be written at the top of the board. Leave the staff members' names and pictures off of the bulletin board until Friday of each week. Inexpensive door prizes could be given to staff members who guess the name of the person in the picture. Be prepared with extra prizes just in case a number of people guess correctly. *Idea suggested by the Stockton Unified Self-Esteem Committee.*

LARGE NAME TAGS   SEB 246

Purpose: To provide the opportunity for staff members to find out personal information concerning one another.

Materials: Large tagboard or cardstock-weight piece of paper cut into a 12" square or circle and 24" piece of yarn for each participant; ample supply of hole punchers, magazines, glue, scissors and marking pens.

Procedure: At a faculty meeting, give each participant a 12" piece of cardstock-weight paper cut in a square or circle. Ask participants to now create a "name tag" based on their own identity using magazine pictures, words, or symbols. Tags must contain the following information: name, passions, dreams/goals, birthplace and photo (optional). Finished products could be laminated. Punch two holes near the top of each tag and string a 24" piece of yarn through the holes. Tie the yarn at the end. Staff members are to wear their tags during the first faculty meetings of the semester. They could also wear them during the first week of school so that students could find out something about the personal side of their teachers.

SNOWBALL   SEB 247

Purpose: To enhance staff members' awareness of one another's personal interests; to create the opportunity for staff members to interact with individuals they might not have previously.

Materials: Thin white paper cut into an 18" circle, and pen or pencil for each participant. Scissors, blackboard, or chart paper (chalk or marking pen) for the facilitator to write questions.

Procedure: Prior to the activity, the facilitator cuts a 12" white paper circle for each participant. Using a large black marking pen, draw an X through the circle. Write the numbers 1, 2, 3, and 4 in the circle...a different number for each space.

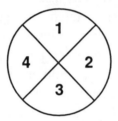

At a staff gathering held in a large room, ask participants to form a large circle around the perimeter of the room. Distribute paper circles to participants so that *every other* person in the circle receives a paper. Ask only the persons who received paper to print their name on the back (the side with the X in the middle of the circle is the front). Then ask participants to crumple their paper up "like a snowball." Tell them to now turn their backs toward the circle and toss their "snowball" into the circle. The participants who *did not receive a paper* are now to run in and grab a snowball, open it up, and determine whose name is written in the middle of the paper. That is the individual they pair up with. Tell the "newly-formed" pairs to retreat to some place in the room for ten minutes. Hand the partner who does not have a snowball a piece of construction paper. During that ten minutes, individuals are to interview one another about the following four areas in the other person's life.

1 = Childhood
2 = Adolescence
3 = College
4 = Adulthood

Any questions may be asked in one of these four areas (i.e. for childhood, "Where did you grow up?" or "How many brothers or sisters do you have?" or "What did your home look like?"). The interviewee may pass on any question(s) he or she chooses. The interviewer writes down any information he/she would like to remember about certain periods of their partner's life in the space marked with the corresponding number. At the end of five minutes, the pair switches roles so that the other partner is now the interviewer. The partner should now be given a paper circle snowball to complete as the other member of the pair did. The same interview task takes place. *Allow more time for the activity if needed.*

At the completion of the time, choose a follow-up activity appropriate to the size of the group.

For larger groups (over 25): Ask each pair to quickly find another pair in the room. Individuals must now introduce their partner to the other pair using the "filled-in snowball" as a guide.

For smaller groups: Individuals may introduce their partner to the larger group by stating one or two new items they discovered concerning the individual.

For follow up: Keep the completed snowballs and hang them up in the faculty lounge.

STEP 3. TEAM AFFILIATION: *Team Identity and Bonding Stage*

The third stage in team building is the development of team affiliation. Instead of feeling as though "I am an individual member of a team," members of a group that have achieved a sense of team affiliation feel that "I am a member of a team." They have gained a sense of security in the group, and they recognize how they can contribute as individuals. Individual identity is "secured" so to speak, which enables individuals to change their role description to "contributing team members."

Perhaps the easiest way to describe the difference in the team dynamics from Step 1 and 2 to the acquisition of Step 3 is to recognize that the behaviors of team members have changed from "individual contributions" to "collective contributions." The chart below shows the kinds of statements team members in the different stages might say:

INDIVIDUAL IDENTITY (STAGES 1 & 2)	TEAM IDENTITY (STAGE 3)
"I AM DOING IT!" "I BELIEVE IN THE MISSION." "I'M ON MY OWN." "I WILL TRY IT." "I DID IT!"	"WE ARE DOING IT!" "WE BELIEVE IN OUR MISSION." "WE'RE IN THIS TOGETHER." "WE WILL TRY IT." "WE DID IT."
FINAL OUTPUT: INDIVIUDALS WORKING INDEPENDENTLY TOWARDS MUTUAL GOALS.	FINAL OUTPUT: MEMBERS WORKING COHESIVELY TOWARDS THE MUTUAL GOALS.

In the Team Identity Stage of Step 3, social support toward one another is evident. The leader can sense the increased interaction among team members. Bonding as a team is apparent. The members feel affiliated with one another and, therefore, are more committed to working as a unit to achieve their mutual goals.

Creating a bond between staff members is not an easy task. Interpersonal dynamics among team members plays a large role in determining how long it takes to acquire this third step. The team leader plays a critical role in facilitating a feeling of team support. There are many factors that might deter the forming of staff cohesiveness. It is wise for the leader to carefully observe team behaviors that might connote team dissension. The leader should always keep an ear open to listen if members are frequently voicing comments such as the following:

My ideas won't make any difference. Like always, they'll just choose what they want.

It's just easier to stay in my room and do my own work. Working with others on this staff is just a big hassle.

No one ever shares ideas around here.

Why should I share with my grade-level members? They'll just take credit for my idea.

I'd rather eat lunch in my own room. The conversation in the faculty room is always so negative.

Everybody always does their own thing around here.

We can never agree on anything. Our meetings just end up in a big fight.

Nobody listens to anyone here.

Why should I bother? There's always the same two people that end up taking over and deciding their ideas are best.

These kinds of comments are clear "trouble signals." Negative, competing environments in which people don't feel their ideas and opinions count are counterproductive to the acquisition of Step 3. The leader must be aware that these issues are evident. Putting them off to the side, with hopes that "they'll go away" is no solution. In order for team affiliation to form, team members must experience one another's support. The sense of belonging is critical to the acquisition of a strong team.

WAYS TO ENHANCE TEAM AFFILIATION (SEB 248-251)

- **Downplaying Individual Recognition (SEB 248).** David and Roger Johnson in their research on cooperative schools explain that there are three ways interactions within each school may be structured. These include: 1. competitively (at such a site, individuals are competing to see who is "best"); 2. individualistically (in these schools, staff members work independently from other members); and 3. cooperatively (in these sites, individuals work together to attain mutual goals). The Johnsons stress that the interaction pattern which dominates the school environment will have "profound and widespread impact on school effectiveness." The Johnsons further state:

"The extensive research comparing the relative efficacy of cooperative, competitive, and individualistic efforts clearly indicates that cooperation among staff members produces great productivity, achievement, and motivation; more positive, caring, and committed relationships; greater acceptance and appreciation of differences; greater social support and assistance; higher self-esteem and psychological well-being; and great mastery of important social skills such as leadership, trust, communication and conflict skills. The amount of research and the consistency of the findings provide ample verification of the power of working together to get the job done."[2]

Competition among staff members is deadly. At this stage, it is counterproductive to the acquisition of team identity to place recognition on individual staff members. It is strongly recommended that any recognition of efforts and achievements at this stage be confined to acknowledgment of "team efforts." There are numerous ways this can be done:

- **Team Acknowledgment (SEB 249).** At a public gathering, such as a faculty meeting, acknowledge the efforts of the team by stating praise in the plural tense instead of the singular. "I want to acknowledge the tremendous efforts the eighth-grade science team has made on the textbook adoption. Would the five of you who are on the team please stand up so we can give you a round of applause?" Team praise means including the names of *all* team members in the acknowledgment.

- **Bulletin Board Acclaim (SEB 250).** Is there a bulletin board located in an area where all staff members can have access to it? If so, periodically place a note on the board acknowledging team efforts: "I just wanted to let you know how much I appreciate the energy all of you as a staff have put into the development of the school mission statement. Thanks!" or "The last faculty meeting was very productive largely because of the way each grade-level team pulled together. It's a pleasure working with you." If the school doesn't have such a space, consider tacking up a large piece of posterboard to use for the same objective.

- **Team Support Grams (SEB 251).** The key to the effectiveness of team acknowledgment is to remember to *do it consistently.* Usually, our intentions are better than our actions. We think about doing it much more often than actually giving the praise. To remind team members of the importance of providing team praise, duplicate a plentiful supply of the Team Support Gram (page 296). Place the grams in convenient locations so they are readily accessible to staff members. Encourage individuals to take a few minutes to fill out the form and present it to colleagues who are demonstrating team support and cohesiveness. Adults feel such messages are trite unless they are being acknowledged for actions that are earned and deserved. The earned aspect should be emphasized to the group.

CREATING OPPORTUNITIES TO WORK TOGETHER (SEB 252-257)

Helping teams move from the Getting Acquainted and Individual Identity Stages to the Team Affiliation Stage takes energy and planning. The more opportunities team members have to work together as a group, the greater the likelihood that team affiliation will be

---

2. Johnson, David W. & Roger T. Johnson. *Leading the Cooperative School.* Circle Pines, MN: Interaction Books, 1989, 1 & 7.

the outcome. There are numerous ways to create opportunities for teams to function as a group. The following ideas are offered:

- **Faculty Meeting Rotation (SEB 252).** To help individual team members gain an awareness of one another's teaching styles and strengths, consider "floating" the faculty meetings. Instead of always meeting in one central location, such as the library or the faculty room, rotate meetings so they are held in one another's classrooms. If staff size is too large, then consider rotating grade or subject level meetings. Such a practice helps staff members discover one another's personal styles and interests that are visually discernible in their classroom.

- **Retreats (SEB 253).** If at all possible, try holding a few faculty gatherings away from the building. Some faculties are able to hold a retreat over a weekend in an informal setting away from school. Most faculties consider the retreat an opportunity to really find out about one another. Since the time period together is extended, members have a chance to open up to each other and share ideas. Preferably, retreats are held on weekends so that the team has an adequate opportunity to be with one another and develop a greater sense of belonging. If getting away for an extended period of time is not possible, a retreat can be held for a shorter period, perhaps a day or an afternoon and an evening.

- **Switch Day (SEB 254).** One day of the school year is designated as Switch Day. During the day, every staff member switches job roles with another staff member. An upper grade teacher, for instance, would switch roles with a lower grade teacher. A custodian might switch jobs with a cafeteria worker. The principal might teach the kindergarten classroom. Ellen Stantus, principal of Davis County School in Salt Lake City, Utah, held a Switch Day at her school site. Stantus pointed out the value of the activity by stating, "Everybody decided at the end of the day that everyone's job has some positives and some negatives. Switch Day gave everyone the chance to 'walk in another's shoes.'"

- **Grade-Level Sharing (SEB 255).** To help staff members find out about one another's teaching styles, consider setting up grade-level sharing sessions. At each faculty meeting, teachers from a different grade level or subject area share for five minutes on "what we are teaching" or "what is working for us." Allow only one presentation per meeting until all staff members have had a chance to take part in the sharing.

- **Shared Treat Days (SEB 256).** The sad but true fact is that at most school sites the daily schedule is not conducive to allowing staff members to interact with one another. Usually, the school is too large for students to have lunch or recess at the same time, so the staff must take their breaks at different times. Many principals, recognizing that existing schedules can be detrimental to team building, make an effort to do some creative scheduling. Sometimes this means taking five minutes off of a lunch break each day so that there are a few extra minutes once or twice a month for faculty gatherings with all staff members present. Creative scheduling involves a lot of energy and brainstorming. Most schools find there are usually solutions to even the bleakest situations. Setting up a task force to look into ways to allow more full-member faculty gatherings may be well worth the effort.

- **Grade or Subject Level-Gatherings (SEB 257).** In order to function effectively as a team, members need to have the opportunity to work together. There are many ways to arrange team gatherings. Keep in mind that not all of these gatherings need necessarily be arranged around formal agendas. Consider possibilities for grade or subject-level gatherings such as:

- a breakfast before school on Fridays;

- a "wellness" walk after school;

- a coffee clutch at first break once a week;

- Treat Day every Friday with team members rotating the treats;

- a lunch once a month away from school (extend the lunch session by at least ten minutes with some creative scheduling).

Each team should develop their own plan for gatherings. For greater commitment, consider writing the plan down and turning it into a leader who will keep the team accountable.

ROUND ROBIN BELIEF STATEMENTS   SEB 258

Purpose: To provide staff members with the opportunity to find out one another's beliefs.

Materials: Chalkboard, flipchart, or butcher paper to write belief statements.

Procedure: When staff members are new to a building site or the staff has never had the opportunity to find out what the beliefs of their fellow staff members are, the creation of individual belief statements are often helpful. The belief statement should always be written so the views of each colleague are as precise as possible. Each staff member takes a moment to respond to the statement: "In order for schools to be most effective, I believe..." Sharing between partners in which each staff member verbally describes how he or she would respond to the statement often can precede the written idea. The activity may also be done in Round Robin style in which each staff member responds moving clockwise around a circle of colleagues. It is best to keep the group size to around ten. Belief statements could also include:

- I believe the most valuable thing our school can offer students is _____.

- I believe the most important thing we need to change in our school in order to be more effective is _____.

- I believe my greatest strength as an educator is _____.

- I believe the one thing our school should focus upon this year to offer students the best education is _____.

STAFF MEMBER SURVEYS   SEB 259

Purpose: To provide every staff member with an opportunity to voice his/her opinion.

Materials: Copies of surveys (one per staff member).

Procedure: Individuals low in security generally feel too threatened to speak out in front of a group. Nevertheless, they must be given the opportunity to voice their ideas and concerns if team cohesiveness is to transpire. A safer way to allow low risk-takers to be heard is to ask everyone to voice their concerns in writing. An anonymous response is acceptable. While the written response is by no means the preferable way to achieve a dialogue, it may be in some cases the safest "first step." A simple survey sent out to each staff member might read: "As you know, we are in the process of change. We need your ideas and concerns to help this process become successful. Please take a moment to list any questions, suggestions, or ideas you might have regarding the restructuring. You do not have to sign it, but please do turn it into the staff box. Thank you!"

"HOT DOT" SURVEYS   SEB 260

Purpose: To encourage team building through open communication. To allow each team member to hear where each other team member is coming from regarding critical issues. To quickly and easily determine one another's opinions.

Materials:

- "hot dots," stars or labels that are pre-glued (one label per participant).
- one long piece of butcher paper (about 18" x 80" or more in length).
- thick-tipped marking pen.
- masking tape or pins to hang up the butcher paper.

Procedure:

1. Identify an issue that the staff has been addressing or will be addressing in upcoming discussions. Ideally, the issue should be one that the staff wishes to find out the opinions of others.

2. Write the issue as an open-ended statement or question at the top of a long piece of butcher paper. Only one statement should be used at a time. The statement should be one in which the responses can be expressed on a continuum, either in a numerical value or in a range of opinions, from "strongly support" to "strongly do not support."

For example:

How many different schools have you worked in?
+10   9   8   7   6   5   4   3   2   1-

How do you feel about the new reading series?
Strongly support +10   9   8   7   6   5   4   3   2   1- Strongly do not support

---

An open-ended statement that could be used to begin creating a team identity might be:

> *The number of different schools you've taught in...*

Other questions requiring a numerical response include:

> *The number of different grade levels you've taught...*

> *How many different staff get-togethers do you think we should have during the year?*

> *How many different states have you lived in?*

Hot Dot Surveys are also an excellent tool to determine how the staff feels on important educational issues. They can be used as a quick clarification device to find out where staff members stand on a variety of professional questions. The following open-ended statements are suggested as survey questions to probe staff opinions regarding issues related to restructuring:

> *How strongly do you support the proposed school mission statement?*

> *How safe do you perceive our school campus to be?*

> *How important do you feel staff cohesion is toward the creation of an effective school environment?*

> *How well do you feel you understand the restructuring proposal that has been offered?*

> *How many in-services do you feel you need in the new state science curriculum?*

> *How important do you think team building with your staff is to an effective school?*

> *How important do you think a student's self-esteem is to their achievement and behavior?*

3. Create a continuum on the butcher paper appropriate to the question. Line off the continuum so there is a space designated for each number. Write the question across the top of the paper. Provide a "hot dot" sticker to each participant. Now ask each staff member to respond to the question by placing their sticker on the butcher paper next to the number that best matches their opinion.

How important do you think staff team building is to an effective school?
Strongly support +10   9   8   7   6   5   4   3   2   1- Strongly do not support

---

STAFF MEETING WHIPS   SEB 261

Purpose: To provide opportunities for staff members to find out about each other.

Materials: None needed; a stop watch is desirable.

Procedure: A "whip" is the name of an activity in which everyone quickly shares their response to a preset question or open-ended sentence stem. Generally, one person facilitates the activity by quickly pointing to people either randomly or in succession. A whip activity is a great way to begin or end a meeting. It could also be used as an energizer during a meeting. It need not be timely...but if a limit is desired, one person could act as a timekeeper so that the activity does not extend the preset time. One of the greatest advantages of the whip is that participants find out about each other in a very short time span.

The facilitator first decides on the "whip" question or sentence stem for the meeting. The same whip is used for the duration of the meeting so that everyone responds to the same sentence stem. This may be written on a blackboard or chart paper. Tell the group the question or sentence stem and encourage them to quickly think about their response. Remind participants that everyone who chooses to will quickly respond to the question or sentence stem. If participants are sitting in a circle, no facilitation is needed. A designated "first person" begins and then the circle moves either clockwise or counterclockwise with each person quickly filling in their response. If the seating arrangements are more random, explain that you will quickly point to people. Finally, remind participants that no interruptions or questions are allowed during the set "whip" time. At the end of the activity time could be provided for participants to ask other staff members to elaborate on their responses if desired.

Whip questions:

- One thing I'm looking forward to trying this week is _____.
- One thing I'm looking forward to doing this weekend is _____.
- One thing that worked well for me this week was _____.
- This week I wish I'd _____.
- I'm really happy that _____.
- I wish _____.
- If I'd only known years ago _____.
- A fun thing that happened this week was _____.
- One thing our grade level is working on _____.
- One thing we tried this week that was successful _____.

STAFF ESTEEM BUILDERS

- One thing I noticed about another staff member this week was _____.

- This week my kids are studying _____.

- A change I saw in a student this week was _____.

- One thing that was effective this week was _____.

- I can maximize the learning time in my classroom by _____.

- The last book I read to my class was _____.

- A great read-aloud is _____.

- One thing I hope to see happen this year is _____.

- The best science lesson I ever taught was _____.

- One thing I would like to change about this school is _____.

- One thing I would do differently next year is _____.

- One successful classroom management technique I use is _____.

- One way to improve the P.E. program is _____.

- One thing I can help other staff members with is _____.

- One successful activity I found is _____.

- The cafeteria would be a better place if _____.

- Happiness at my school is _____.

- If I wasn't a teacher I'd be _____.

- One resource all teachers should know about is _____.

- The thing I love about yard duty is _____.

- A funny thing that happened this week was _____.

- The best thing about this week was _____.

- I'm seeing progress with _____.

- A person I really wanted to thank but couldn't was _____.

- A special thing that happened to me was _____.

- Today I'm looking forward to _____.

- Tonight I'm looking forward to _____.

- Something I just did I'd like you to know about is _____.

- One thing I'm doing at home that's fun is _____.

- Did you know _____?

- One thing I'm trying is _____.

- I'm looking forward to _____.

- Does anybody have _____?

- Something I'd like to learn about is _____.

- I'm really proud of _____.

- Something I'd like to brag about is _____.

- I made a difference by _____.

- I wish we _____.

- A great movie, book, or place to go is _____.

- I just want to share that _____.

- I'm feeling really _____.

- To relax these days I _____.

- I'm sure glad I _____.

STEP 4: TEAM MISSION: *The Commitment Stage*

The fourth stage of team building is where the effectiveness of working as a group becomes evident. The team has already formed a solid feeling of security and trust with one another. They are well acquainted with one another's interests and capabilities. The group has defined how each team player will contribute to the "game." At this point, the team has usually had frequent opportunities to work together. As a result, they've bonded with one another. The first three steps have helped to generate a feeling of mutual support toward one another. They are, in reality, foundational steps on which the higher levels of productivity can evolve. Commitment as a team is the product of the fourth step. This sense of "we're working together and committed to one another" is a powerful factor in team effectiveness. The group fully understands their team purpose and they believe in this mission. Their energy as a team is more focused because they know what they're working toward.

It is important for the leader and team members to keep in mind that commitment is difficult to achieve until each member fully understands the viewpoint of the other members. One of the reasons why team commitment is able to gel at this level is because team members know, by now, not only the personality styles and personal interests of one another, but also the beliefs of their fellow colleagues. They've taken the time to recognize the other members' educational strengths and talents. They've also taken the time to listen and accept each other's point of views regarding the educational issues their team is addressing.

Perhaps the greatest barrier to teams being able to reach the stage of commitment is dissension in the group. Typically, dissension begins to fester because there is a breakdown in communication. More often than not, the breakdown is due to a problem that arises in the group, and instead of dealing with ways to solve the issue, the problem is pushed aside. The team commitment that had been building begins to unravel. Open communication at this level is critical. Unless the communication network flows openly up and down as well as sideways, the outcome is dissension among the group.

In almost every case, the dissension in the team could have been minimized before conflict set in. What is needed for that team to survive is specific training in techniques to handle problems that commonly arise in any team: communication difficulties, dissension and conflict among members, and problem solving. In the last few years the restructuring processes in education have put more and more to do on the shoulders of staff members. The concept of "shared decision-making" has been stressed in dozens of schools across North America and in staff membership ad hoc committees. Teachers are now being asked to play integral roles in hiring and setting budgets. These new responsibilities far exceed the typical decisions teachers made a few decades ago, such as placing orders for classroom materials and choosing a literature series for a certain grade level. The reality is that very few districts have taken the necessary steps to ensure team effectiveness in decision-making duties, let alone teach individuals the skills conducive to successful team building.

Research clearly indicates that effective team-building programs which create team collegiality require systematic training in team-building principles. Rarely are teams able to take part in complex decision-making and communication skills without such training. Frequent opportunities to practice team-building skills must be provided in order for individuals to process the skills. It is equally critical that the skills be continually modeled by the leader. Only then can the most effective team building take place.

There are many ways to facilitate open communication as a team. The fourth step in team building is to reach a level of group commitment. Specific techniques are provided in the following section which will enhance the team's ability to work effectively as a unit. These activities provide tools for handling dissension amicably and for dealing with problems as they arise. Finally, strategies are suggested to enable team members to clarify one another's belief statements. If commitment is the desired outcome of step four, then problem solving, open communication, and clarification of each individual's belief statements must be ongoing techniques to facilitate the team-building process.

TEAM VISION

Research indicates that organizations that are clearly focused on a common goal accomplish much more than groups that have only individual goals. A mission is what helps teams know where they are headed and gives them a clear purpose and direction for their efforts. The vision clarifies the mission and goals of the school. Much of the productivity and effectiveness of an organization will be contingent on the extent staff members are willing to work as a cohesive unit toward the achievement of the school's goals.

A team mission begins with a dream or vision of "What we could and should be about." The vision could be the answer to a global question such as, "What is effective education?" or an inquiry concerning the site such as, "What is the most effective school?" The vision generally begins on a personal level, when each individual reflects upon issues that directly apply to him or her: "The most effective teacher is…" or "Grade-level teams that are most effective look like…" Effective teams provide opportunities for individual members to convey their personal beliefs and dreams to one another. The following activities are designed to encourage team members to communicate their personal visions to one another and thus enhance the team's progress toward a shared mission.

BELIEF LADDER   SEB 262

Materials: SEB 262 Belief Ladder (page 297); pencil or pen for each team member.

Procedure: Explain to the group that the purpose of the activity is to help individuals clarify their personal beliefs about conditions that create effective schools and then to communicate these beliefs to one another. Ask participants, working independently, to think about how they would respond to the following sentence stem: *"I believe the most effective and ideal schools for students have these characteristics..."* Explain that individuals are to write down the conditions they believe characterize effective schools on the rungs of the Belief Ladder appearing on the form. Stress that there are no right or wrong answers and that, ideally, they should try to write the conditions in the order of their importance (#1 being the most important and #5 being the least important).

At the end of five minutes, or whenever participants have completed the task, ask the large group to quickly form into smaller teams of two (but no more than three). Explain that for the second part of the task partners are to communicate their beliefs to one another. Each pair is to decide who will talk first. Emphasize that debating ideas is not part of the process. Members are to listen to one another's personal beliefs. Allow five to ten minutes for participants to share what they have written on their Belief Ladders.

Finally, ask team members to combine the contents of their individual ladders to form a new ladder based on the shared beliefs of each pair. "Do you and your partner have any shared beliefs? If so, please see if you can create a new belief ladder based on the beliefs you have in common." Emphasize that consensus of beliefs is not the desired outcome. The important element during this phase is to determine if partners have any beliefs in common.

If time permits, allow partners to share with the group any commonalities they discovered. If the group size is over thirty, you may wish to have each pair join with another pair to share their new Belief Ladders as a foursome.

BELIEF INTERVIEWS   SEB 263

Purpose: The purpose of this activity is to provide team members with the opportunity to listen to one another's belief statements. During this activity, they will also have the chance to interview one another in-depth about their individual dreams and visions. This activity is particularly good to use when all staff members are gathered at a meeting.

Materials: None needed; a watch with a second hand is desirable.

Procedure: Ask the large group to quickly form into teams of three or "triads." Ask each triad to decide who in their threesome will be the "interviewee." The other two members of the trio will become "interviewers." Explain that during the activity the interviewers will ask the interviewee questions regarding important issues. In the interest of time, the facilitator will generally decide ahead of time what issue will be examined. This question generally deals with a key personal belief or a belief that will impact the group at large. Possibilities for discussion include:

- *What is your definition of self-esteem?*
- *What role do you think educators should have in the formation of their students' self-esteem?*
- *What is an effective school?*
- *What is an effective teacher?*
- *What characteristics do you think teachers need in order to best enhance student self-esteem?*
- *What skills do students need for the 21st century?*
- *What competencies should high-school students have at graduation?*
- *What should be our primary goal at this school site?*

Explain to the group that they have fifteen minutes to conduct the interview. Emphasize that interviewers are to ask questions but may not take issue with the interviewees' opinion. No debate is permitted. Tell the group that the goal is for the two interviewers to clarify in their own minds what the beliefs of the interviewee are regarding the issue. (*Note:* The trio may decide to change the rules and allow each member in the group the opportunity to be interviewed.) If time permits, ask interviewers to quickly explain to the large group the main beliefs of their interviewee.

COMMITMENT: THE VISION BECOMES THE TEAM MISSION

Team commitment naturally develops whenever staff members adopt a shared vision as their own. The shared vision binds team members together. Once the staff has agreed upon a mission statement, though, this by no means implies that team work toward commitment is completed. A common mistake is for team-building practices to slide downward after the team mission has finally been determined. The team falsely assumes that "our work is through...we made a decision and so we no longer need to work together as frequently." Nothing could be further from the truth. It is essential that the staff continue to communicate with one another about that vision and how they can best work together to see it become a reality.

KEEPING THE VISION VISUAL   SEB 264

Purpose: To reinforce the school's mission.

Materials: Possibilities are endless; a few are suggested below.

Procedure: Once the vision has become the group mission, it is critical to keep the mission visual. The simple but true principle about any guiding premise is: "The more you see it, the more you remember it!" Organizations have used this premise for years when they take their mission statement and create a national campaign around it. Billboards, stationery, magazine advertisements and television sound bites are some of the avenues for reinforcing the same statement. If this statement is said often enough, not only does the public *remember* the message but they also begin to *believe* it. Any organization can easily accomplish the same campaign. The technique is simple: *formulate your mission into a short statement and print it over and over in any context that is appropriate*. Here are a few suggestions:

- the school letterhead
- the school newsletter
- any staff release
- bumper stickers for cars
- visors or hats
- bookmarks
- book covers
- student folders
- lesson plan book covers
- hallway bulletin boards
- school banners or flags
- t-shirts

ONGOING STAFF RESPONSES   SEB 265

Purpose: To encourage ongoing communication among staff members.

Materials: A long piece of butcher paper (36" x 100"+); thick marking pen.

Procedure: Communication among staff members regarding the mission statement should be ongoing. What commonly happens during restructuring is that individuals begin the process by welcoming the change with energy and commitment. Then unexpected problems typically arise, and the energy and commitment that first characterized the group's efforts begin to wane. If communication is not ongoing, the result can be disillusionment among staff members toward the mission and, in too many cases, the end of the restructuring process.

Communication regarding the mission must be a continual process. One of the easiest ways to provide the opportunity for ongoing communication is to tape a piece of butcher paper to the wall of a faculty meeting area. Use a marking pen to print the mission statement at the top of the paper. Beneath the statement print the question: *"How is it going for you? Ideas…questions…concerns…we need to hear from you."* Staff members are then free to use the remaining space to write their feelings and thoughts regarding the mission. Keep the paper up for an extended period of time and don't be discouraged if no one answers at first. You're providing the opportunity for individuals to express their concerns and beliefs. Keeping the mission statement visual often enhances staff commitment and stimulates discussion among the group.

DEALING WITH PROBLEMS AND CONFLICTS

Problems are a normal element of social dynamics. Whenever a group of individuals with different ideas and personalities work together, dissension can result. Either the group learns to deal amicably with the problem or it fails to handle the problem constructively, in which case the situation can escalate to such an extent that the team is permanently impaired. Teaching the group how to deal with problems is critical in order to build an effective team. Unfortunately, problem-solving techniques are seldom specifically taught to a group. As a result, the group never reaches the higher stages of team building because the problems among individual members have escalated. Taking an active approach to solving problems is extremely important if the group project is to be successful. The facilitator must plan how to teach team members problem-solving methods so that they can deal with issues as they arise.

The following section contains specific problem-solving techniques that should be taught to teams on an ongoing basis. It is strongly suggested that the facilitator model each method to the team and then have the team role play the problem-solving technique. Later on, when difficulties arise, team members will then know how to deal constructively with the problems as well as buffer the dissension that could develop. (Additional activities and suggestions for enhancing problem solving can be found on page 110 of this manual.)

TRIADS   SEB 266

Purpose: Triads is a problem-solving technique used to enhance staff communication skills and diffuse dissension and conflict. It is so helpful in working toward solutions that the activity has been explained in both the staff-esteem (page 130) and team-building sections.

Materials: A stopwatch.

Procedure:

1. Divide the large group into teams of threes (triads). Ask each group to quickly "letter off" (A-B-C, A-B-C, etc.) until every team member is either an A, B, or C.

2. Next, assign roles to each team member. Instruct the group that during the task assignment the person designated as A will assume the role of the Case Presenter; B will be the Time Keeper, and C will be the Recorder. Now explain the specific duty of each role to the group. Write each duty as it is described on a flipchart or blackboard for participants to refer to for any needed clarification.

A = Case Presenter: Presents a "case" by telling the triad his/her interpretation of the problem. Emphasize that the case should be presented with specific details. "This is the problem and this is how I see it..." Emphasize that the case presenter should stick to the facts, since there is only a short amount of time to explain the problem to the group. Whenever possible, emotions and names of individuals should be eliminated from the description. Explain that emotions and names often escalate the issue.

B = Time Keeper: Keeps track of time by letting the group know the beginning and ending times for each person. The Time Keeper should also be an Encourager, who encourages the Case Presenter during the presentation.

C = Recorder: Listens for key ideas and facts from the presentation.

3. Set a specific timeframe for each member's task. Explain that the total time for each task will be ten minutes. *Note:* This is merely a suggested timeframe. The times could be reduced or expanded depending upon the length of time available. The facilitator will help the group stay on task by informing members of the timeframes after each section. On a flipchart or blackboard, write the timeframes agreed upon by the group:

3 Minutes: Present the Case
3 Minutes: Brainstorm Solutions
4 Minutes: Formulate the Plan

a) The Case Presenter chooses a problem or issue that directly concerns him/her. It should be an issue the individual cannot solve and would like to receive help from the group. The problem could be team oriented or one that impacts the individual in his/her work at the school. The Case Presenter describes the problem for three minutes to the other triad members. A few problems conducive to the Triad Problem Solving method are:

- "No one on this team listens to me."
- "One of my students never completes his assignments."
- "A parent is sending rumors about me to other parents."
- "Staff members are late coming to faculty meetings."
- "One team member never wants to share ideas or materials."
- "One of my students is so negative to other students."

The Time Keeper encourages the Case Presenter to stick to the facts and present the case. The Time Keeper also keeps the team on track by telling them when three minutes is over. The Recorder writes down key facts during the presentation.

b) The team now brainstorms solutions to the problem for three minutes. The Recorder writes down all ideas. The Time Keeper emphasizes to the team the brainstorming rules: "All ideas count" and "No judgments are allowed." The Time Keeper should discourage the team from debating any idea. This timeframe is designed to generate a number of ways to solve the problem.

c) Finally, the Recorder reads over the list of ideas the group generated. The team now begins to form a solution to the Case Presenter's problem. At the end of four minutes, the team will have developed a specific solution for the Case Presenter.

4. If time permits, roles and duties are now rotated. A becomes B, B becomes C, and C becomes A. A new case is presented using the same timeframe, and a solution is reached using the same procedure. Drawing a diagram on a blackboard or flipchart of the rotation sequence (see below) helps the group to see the rotation pattern.

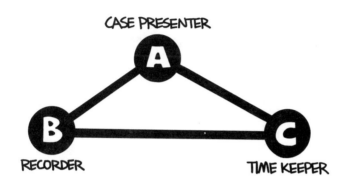

CAROUSEL   SEB 267

Purpose: To provide staff members with opportunities for problem solving.

Materials: 8 large-tipped marking pens; 8 to 16 sheets of large newsprint chart paper (24" x 36"); masking tape or pens.

Procedure:

1. Begin by brainstorming with the staff specific problems that are rendering their team-building efforts less effective. Problems should be ones staff members are personally facing. Write the problems on a large chart. Examples of problems that commonly impede team building include:

   • cliques
   • not sharing
   • the attitude that "the other place is greener"
   • nobody listens
   • too much to do and not enough time
   • people not treated equally
   • disagreements
   • resistance and unwillingness to change

2. The large group chooses eight problems. The majority vote wins. *Note:* Ideally, there should be four to six people in a group. Adapt the number of problems to fit the size of your staff.

3. The presenter now writes each problem at the top of a separate piece of chart paper and numbers each one consecutively from one to eight. (No less than six problems should be placed on the walls to ensure a variety of choices.)

4. Hang the charts in consecutive order around the room.

5. Ask the staff to count off in order from one to eight so that each person has a number.

6. Ask everyone to locate the chart that corresponds to their number and to stand near it.

7. Each group now chooses a recorder for their team. The recorder is instructed to print all ideas legibly on the chart.

8. The presenter explains the rules to the teams and serves as time keeper. Say, "The recorder will read the problem to your group. You then have three minutes to think of as many ways as you can to solve the problem. The recorder will print all ideas on the chart. Remember that all ideas count and should be recorded. No idea should be judged. Finally, do not discuss the ideas or mention any specific names of staff members as you problem shoot. Go!"

9. At the end of three minutes, each team rotates to the next consecutive numbered problem. Number 8 goes to number 1. The same process is repeated until each team has gone to all eight of the problems. If time constraints are an issue, reduce the time for brainstorming to two minutes for the last three or four problems.

10. The final task is for each team to go back to the problem they began with. The recorder now quickly rereads the problem and all the solutions the other teams have created. At the end of about three minutes, each team chooses one solution they think is the best way to solve the problem.

11. The presenter now quickly reads each problem and each team's chosen solution.

SOLUTION/NO COMMENT   SEB 268

Purpose: To provide staff members with the opportunity to learn problem-solving techniques.

Materials: Ten 3" x 5" index cards and a pen or pencil per participant.

Procedure:

1. The facilitator identifies an issue that is generating difficulty for the group as a whole. Not every team member may consider the issue to be a problem but it should be one that many of the participants have voiced concerns about. The facilitator may wish to informally survey individuals prior to the group meeting. A survey could be a simple request such as, "At the next meeting we will be discussing school-related problems that are impacting us. Please take the time to identify one school-related problem that concerns you. Write it down and turn it into the facilitator's box. Thank you!" Such issues could include:

   - involving parents in esteem building
   - building team collegiality (dynamics of team members)
   - improving school communication
   - restructuring
   - implementing the mission statement
   - improving student behavior
   - implementing the in-service topic

2. Ask the large group to quickly form into teams of four (quads) but no more than five. Ideally, teams should be sitting face to face around a table. Ask each group to choose a Task Director for the table.

3. Distribute about ten 3" x 5" index cards to each participant. Place about ten extra cards in the middle of the table. Each person will also need a pen or pencil for the activity.

4. Identify the problem/issue to the group. Explain that the group has five minutes to work "alone." During the five minutes individuals are to write down one situation in which the issue has created problems for them (either now or in the past). Emphasize that a different problem should be written on each card. Participants are to complete as many cards as they can in five minutes.

5. At the end of five minutes, all completed cards are handed to the Task Director. The cards are shuffled and placed face down in the middle of the table.

6. The person to the right of the Task Director begins the activity by turning over the first card. The card is then read aloud. Moving clockwise from the Task Director, each participant now indicates whether he/she has a "Solution" or "No Comment" to make. Emphasize that any solution is appropriate. Continue reading aloud the problems and discussing solutions for fifteen minutes.

GOAL SHOOTING   SEB 269

Purpose: To help team members generate solutions to problems that affect them as a group.

Materials:

- SEB 269 Goal Shooting Worksheet (page 298).
- Sample Goal Shooting Worksheet (page 299).
- Pen or pencil for each participant.
- Flipchart and pen, or blackboard and chalk for the presenter.
- 3" x 5" card for each quad.

Procedure:

1. Ask the group to quickly form into teams of four (quads) and no more than six.

2. Provide each quad with a 3" x 5" card and pen or pencil.

3. Ask participants to reflect upon a problem/issue they consider an impediment to restructuring. Allow teams to discuss these problems for five minutes. At the end of five minutes, ask teams to write down one problem on a 3" x 5" card. Explain that this issue is now their discussion topic.

    It is often helpful to give the group examples of problems/issues. The facilitator could write the example on a large flipchart prior to the activity. For instance, if the group is dealing with the restructuring needed to enhance self-esteem, topics could include:

    - Staff members feel appreciated and recognized by other staff members.
    - All staff is committed to enhancing student self-esteem.
    - Staff members feel a strong sense of belonging with one another.
    - Staff readily sees the need for a self-esteem program.
    - Staff members interact positively with one another and with students.
    - Staff can readily identify students with low self-esteem (or "at risk").
    - The school displays a climate of warmth and caring.
    - There is evidence of high staff morale.

4. Distribute a Goal Shooting Worksheet to each team. Explain that the "goal topic" (the issue they have chosen to discuss) should be written in the space provided on the sheet. A "Sample Goal Shooting Worksheet" may also be distributed at this time so quads can see a completed form.

5. Tell the group they have three minutes to brainstorm all "challenges" that could impede the implementation of this goal. "Challenges" should be written on the form. If team members prefer, they may choose a recorder to write all the challenges on a large piece of chart paper for easier visibility.

6. The group now has ten minutes to brainstorm solutions to the challenges. These are to be listed in the space on the worksheet called "Task 2." Emphasize that debating and evaluating of ideas are not allowed during this timeframe.

7. At the completion of the brainstorming session the presenter may choose one of the following options depending on time:

a. Each team chooses one of the solutions they generated and designs a specific plan for implementation. Allow twenty minutes minimum. Explain that the plan should be specific enough so that who, what, when, where and how are all covered in the plan.

b. Each team could take their solutions and "pass them" to another quad. If time permits (five minutes) each quad may quickly explain their problem and solutions to the other team. Each quad now takes ten minutes to read the other team's challenges and solutions and add other ideas for solutions to the form.

c. In smaller groups (less than twenty), quads could quickly share their ideas and solutions to the group as a whole.

STEP 5. TEAM COLLEGIALITY: *The Competence and Synergy Stage*

The fifth and final step in team building is when team collegiality is fully developed. In this stage, not only does the team work collaboratively as a unit, but all team members feel a full commitment toward one another. Team productivity and energy is at their highest point when team collegiality becomes a reality. Since the members' goal is collaboration, competitiveness is greatly reduced. When there is team collegiality, educators' support for one another is finally maximized.

Arriving at this highest level has been a gradual, evolving process of learning to trust one another. As individuals developed this trust, communication became more and more open. Together, they experienced successes as well as failures. In particular, each achievement accomplished as a team refueled the group's energy and encouraged them to work even harder. Gradually, support for one another reached a deeper and more personal level until a true sense of caring about each member of the team became a natural way of dealing with one another.

Anyone visiting a team that has achieved true collegiality can almost feel the synergy that has developed among its members. Some of the elements of collegiality can easily be seen. Communication is open and members in this team trust one another enough to freely verbalize concerns and problems. A climate of risk-taking has been deliberately fostered. Individuals feel comfortable voicing differences of opinions because they recognize they don't always have to be in agreement. They know, too, that their ideas will be accepted. If an individual is facing a problem, the group generally works together to try and solve that person's dilemma.

Another indication that collegiality has been achieved is when teachers walk freely in and out of one another's classrooms. Team members openly share ideas, materials, and resources. They freely acknowledge one another's unique strengths and talents, and they capitalize upon individual assets, knowing that such a practice will produce the greatest benefits for the school's learning environment. Perhaps the element of collegiality a visitor finds most striking is the practice team members commonly have of celebrating one another's successes. The group feels genuinely excited not only when the team achieves a goal but also when an individual succeeds. The environment is filled with adults who genuinely want to be there and enjoy being with one another. The best way to describe a team at stage five is by citing the comment those who have been a member of such a group frequently verbalize: "This is the kind of place I always dreamed I would work at...and now I am."

COMMITMENT SUSTAINERS   SEB 270

Purpose: Good teamwork obviously requires practice. Achieving a sense of team collegiality by no means ensures that the group will remain at such a high level. Much of the productivity of a school or team is contingent on the commitment of staff members to staying at such a high level to achieve their goals. "Commitment Sustainers" is a quick activity to help members recognize the need to work on an ongoing basis, not only as individuals but also as a team, to sustain the level they have achieved.

Materials: A 3" x 5" card and pen/pencil for each participant; flipchart and marking pen or blackboard and chalk for the facilitator.

Procedure: The facilitator chooses an open-ended sentence stem, such as one of those below, that is appropriate to the group's current needs.

What do I need to sustain my motivation?

What does the team I am a part of need in order to stay focused on our goals?

If I wanted to increase my enthusiasm for our team building efforts I would...

In order to enhance my/our self-esteem I/we could...

In order to sustain my/our excitement about this issue I/we need to...

It's easiest to sustain my/our motivation when...

To keep my/our energy level high I/we need...

Write the sentence stem on the flipchart or blackboard and then explain the task to the group. Explain that the sentence stem is designed to help the team or individual members reflect upon their behaviors and needs for personal motivation. Distribute a 3" x 5" card to each member and tell participants to copy the sentence stem on one side of the card. On the other side of the card, ask team members to answer the question based on their personal needs. Allow three minutes for the activity or until all members have completed the task. Finally, ask members to quickly choose a partner. Participants are to explain their answer to their partner. Explain that the partner may ask questions if he or she wishes. Allow six minutes for this activity. Provide a few minutes for the large group to discuss ideas generated by the sentence stem. This sharing of ideas as a group is particularly important since motivation needs that participants have in common may become apparent during the discussion. If this is the case, the group needs to seriously address how these needs can best be met.

TEAM COMMITMENT   SEB 271

Purpose: To reflect upon the meaning of team commitment; to provide an opportunity to strengthen team commitment.

Materials: SEB 271 Team Commitment (page 300); pen/pencil for each participant.

Procedure: Distribute a copy of the SEB 271 Team Commitment worksheet to each participant. Ask team members to reflect upon all the accomplishments the group has achieved. Emphasize the energy, work, and effort that went into such a process. Mention also that what has been achieved as a group required a high level of "team commitment" that many teams are never able to achieve.

Ask participants to quickly reflect upon two questions: *"What does commitment as a team mean to you?"* and *"What will you personally do to maintain this commitment?"* Then instruct participants to write their responses on the forms. Allow five minutes or until all participants have completed the task. Finally, ask participants to form a team of three (triads) and no more than four. Each person in the group is given time to verbalize their written responses to the group. Allow a few minutes for the group as a whole to discuss ideas generated in the triads.

TEAM CELEBRATION POSTERS   SEB 272

Purpose: One of the conditions that has helped the team achieve the stage of team cohesiveness is the sharing of team successes. Generally, this team has experienced the accomplishment of a set goal. Each success helped to refuel their commitment toward the team's goal as well as toward each other. Successes are too often minimized when, instead, they should be celebrated. Team celebration is one way to help the team focus on their accomplishments.

Materials (per team of four):
• Marking pens and crayons.
• 1 piece of plain poster board (18" x 24").
• 1-2 pieces of newsprint chart paper (18" x 24 ").
• Stickers, borders, and precut letters (optional).

Procedure:

1. Instruct the group to form teams of four (quads) and no more than five. Ask each team to choose a "recorder" for their team.

2. Explain to the group that they have made great accomplishments as a team. Emphasize that too often these team successes are overlooked, even though a great deal of time and energy went into achieving them. Ask quads to spend five minutes brainstorming all the accomplishments and successes the team has achieved. Emphasize that successes may be large as well as small-scale but each success is a step toward an important team achievement. The recorder writes down all ideas on the newsprint chart paper.

3. At the end of five minutes, ask the group to step back and look at their achievements that are now depicted visually on the newsprint. Teams could hold their pages up for other members to read. Explain that the ideas on the chart paper will now be used for the second part of the task. Instruct quads to now create a poster depicting the successes and accomplishments the team has achieved. Emphasize there is no right way to design the poster. Successes may be described using words, pictures, cut-outs, symbols, or even actual photographs. Allow the group at least twenty minutes to complete the posters.

4. Give each quad the opportunity to share their finished products with the group as a whole. Hang all posters in the faculty room or other location.

WELCOME

PRESENTED TO: _____

WE'RE DELIGHTED YOU'VE BECOME A PART OF OUR STAFF. HERE ARE A FEW COUPONS THAT YOU MAY FEEL FREE TO REDEEM FROM THEIR CREATORS AT ANY TIME!

THIS COUPON IS GOOD FOR _____

_____

YOU MAY REDEEM THIS COUPON IN ROOM _____

PRESENTED BY _____ WECOME!

WELCOME ABOARD

FROM _____ DATE _____

WE'RE GLAD YOU JOINED US!
REMEMBER, IF YOU EVER NEED ANYTHING, JUST ASK!

Esteem Builders' Complete Program
Jalmar Press, Rolling Hills Estates, CA

STAFF YEARBOOK

NAME: _____

POSITION: _____

OFFICE OR ROOM NO.: _____

PHONE NUMBER: _____

ADDRESS: _____

_____

_____

SIGNIFICANT OTHER: _____

HOBBIES AND INTERESTS: _____

_____

_____

_____

STATE BORN IN: _____

CHILDREN: _____

_____

_____

AN AREA I COULD HELP YOU IN IS: _____

_____

_____

Esteem Builders' Complete Program
Jalmar Press, Rolling Hills Estates, CA

GUESS WHO

Place of birth: _____

Number of siblings: _____

These are my favorite:

    Subject to teach: _____

    Television show: _____

    Movie: _____

    Place to visit: _____

    Sport: _____

    Book: _____

    Color: _____

    Ice cream: _____

    Movie Star: _____

    Song: _____

Finish each sentence:

    I love to: _____

    _____

    I have never: _____

    _____

    I would like to visit: _____

    _____

    One thing you may not know about me is: _____

    _____

    Something I'd really like to do in my life is: _____

    _____

    On the weekends I love to: _____

    _____

    My favorite pastime or hobby is: _____

    _____

Esteem Builders' Complete Program
Jalmar Press, Rolling Hills Estates, CA

TEAM SUPPORT GRAM

PRESENTED TO:

FROM:

BECAUSE:

THANK YOU! IT'S A PLEASURE WORKING WITH YOU!

Esteem Builders' Complete Program
Jalmar Press, Rolling Hills Estates, CA

BELIEF LADDER

"I BELIEVE THE MOST EFFECTIVE 'IDEAL' SCHOOLS FOR STUDENTS HAVE THESE CHARACTERISTICS..."

Esteem Builders' Complete Program
Jalmar Press, Rolling Hills Estates, CA

GOAL SHOOTING WORKSHEET

Team:

Goal Topic

Task 1: List challenges that could impede implementation of this goal. (1 minute)

_____

_____

_____

_____

_____

_____

_____

_____

_____

_____

_____

_____

TASK 2: Based on your list from above, brainstorm a solution for implementation at your site.

_____

_____

_____

_____

_____

_____

_____

_____

_____

_____

_____

_____

_____

Esteem Builders' Complete Program
Jalmar Press, Rolling Hills Estates, CA

GOAL SHOOTING WORKSHEET

Team: *Speckled Robins from Glen Cove*

Goal Topic

#4 Staff readily sees the need for a self-esteem program

Task 1: List challenges that could impede implementation of this goal. (1 minute)

- *Don't see as valuable--too time consuming.*

- *Just adopted literature-based series... how do we tie together?*

- *Biggest complaint..when are we going to do that?*

- *Some teachers are concerned we give in too easy to kids...they'll be spoiled by it.*

- *Don't see the need for it.*

- *Don't recognize that self-esteem can improve behavior and academics.*

TASK 2: Based on your list from above, brainstorm a solution for implementation at your site.

- *Have short faculty presentations about self-esteem.*
- *Plan a teacher in-service day on self-esteem.*
- *Visit other schools in area with self-esteem program.*
- *Interview school in area with self-esteem program.*
- *Find research articles, run off and distribute. Show validity.*
- *Do a faculty survey...how many see the need?*
- *Start discussion groups...*
- *Bring in professors in self-esteem.*
- *Purchase research-based materials.*
- *Quantify need for self-esteem to academics...what's our test scores now?... Absenteeism... behavior problems...*

Esteem Builders' Complete Program
Jalmar Press, Rolling Hills Estates, CA

TEAM COMMITMENT

What does commitment as a team mean to you?

_____
_____
_____
_____
_____
_____
_____
_____
_____
_____
_____
_____
_____

What will you personally do to maintain this commitment?

_____
_____
_____
_____
_____
_____
_____
_____
_____
_____
_____
_____
_____
_____

Signed _____ **Date:** _____

Esteem Builders' Complete Program
Jalmar Press, Rolling Hills Estates, CA

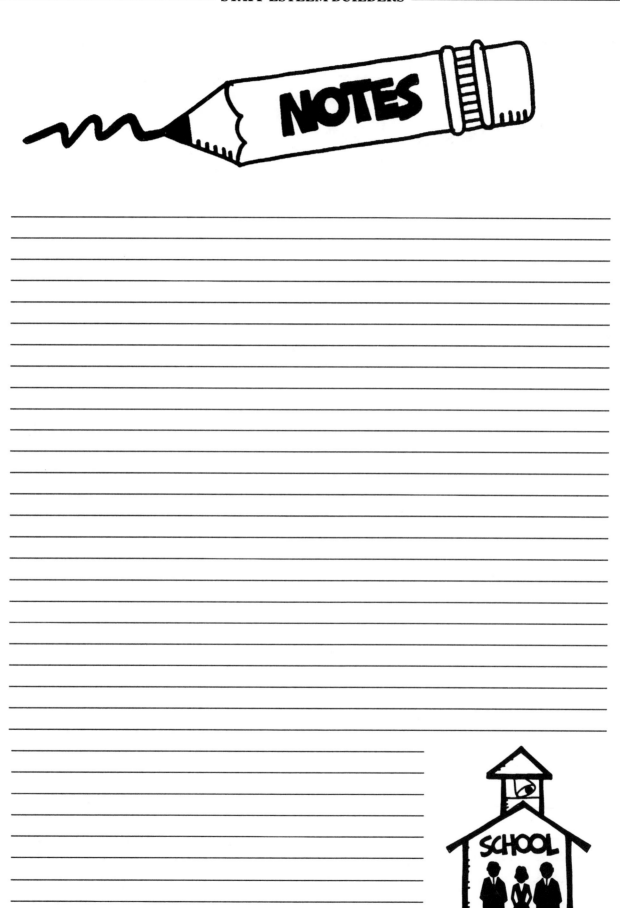

Conclusion

"All of us who make motion pictures are teachers—teaching with very loud voices. But we will never be able to match the power of the teacher who is able to whisper in a student's ear."
—GEORGE LUCAS

Recently, I conducted self-esteem trainings in Nebraska and at the conclusion of the training, the staff development coordinator drove me to the airport. In the middle of the trip I happened to notice a flock of geese flying over a cornfield headed for Canada. The classic V formation that geese fly in has always intrigued me. My driver explained to me why they stay in that V. Engineers have studied the geese's flying formation for years and discovered that there is a powerful rationale to this composition. The V formation gives the whole flock a seventy-one percent greater flying range than if they were to fly alone. Each bird, by flapping its wings, creates an uplift for all the birds behind it; thus, the flight is made easier since they travel on one another's thrust. One goose assumes the role of leader and flies out in front while the remainder of the flock fan out to create the wider part of the V. The geese behind the leader honk in unison as if encouraging the lead goose to continue the flight. Whenever the leader becomes too tired, the bird rotates back to the end of the V and a new goose assumes the lead position. Scientists have observed another remarkable fact about the geese: if one member of the flock is injured or sick, two geese will drop out of the formation to fly with the injured bird. They remain with the goose until the bird is either able to fly again or dies. Then the geese launch out in a small V formation of their own to catch up with the original flock.

The lessons we learn from the geese are invaluable and applicable to any organization. Whenever individuals combine their efforts, talents, and intelligence, the group becomes far more productive than if each member were to fly off in separate directions.

It is an indisputable fact that educators working together to touch students have the potential to make positive differences in their young lives. Of course, the reverse to this equation is also a potential outcome—the impact could quite possibly be negative. Whether the path they take is positive or negative lies within the teachers themselves.

Let's take the positive route for a moment and look at the tremendous possibilities in a classroom to make esteem-enhancing differences for students. Each day a student walks into a classroom, the teacher has the chance to help that child see himself/herself as a more capable human being. Each day presents one more opportunity for that educator to model critical life skills such as making decisions, handling mistakes, solving problems, and relating well to others, skills that might otherwise never be demonstrated to the child. Each day the teacher has the potential to help a student grasp a learning concept that could quite possibly develop into a professional goal. On some days, he/she might turn rain into rainbows for a child by helping him/her see the more joyous aspects of life. On many days, the teacher could create a haven in that classroom for the student to spend a few hours of emotional safety away from the personal traumas at home. And on a few special days, the teacher has a moment to make a major difference by helping a student recognize a strength or skill he/she may never have known before. These life-touching moments, when multiplied many times over in thousands of classrooms across the country, confirm that educators do have an enormous impact on the lives of their students, far more than any one person can imagine.

Teachers need to recognize their potential power as door openers to students' lives. All too often their world revolves around yard-duty schedules, jammed ditto machines, and irate parents. Such tasks are a far cry from what drew them to their chosen profession. In *Profile of Teachers in the U.S.—1990*, published by the National Center for Education Information, about three fourths of those surveyed cited as the primary reason for becoming teachers "a desire to work with young people."[1] No other reason came close to touching this one.

There is probably no more critical profession today than teaching. Educators could be, quite simply, the hope for the future of today's youth. The emotional support structures that used to nurture the esteem of youth are dying. Consider the changes that have occurred in just the last twenty years in the family structure. One out of every two American marriages ends in divorce. Increased economic pressures have led to many mothers hanging up their aprons and heading for the workplace. Neighborhood blocks in which families not only knew one another but held monthly barbecues are rapidly disappearing.

The society as a whole is rapidly undergoing change. The United States is now the most mobile society in the world. Each person moves an average of twelve times in a lifetime. The movie and record industry have many parents concerned about the kinds of messages and values being sent to their children. Violence has become for many children a way of life. *Omni Magazine* in its September 1992 issue reported that every day twenty-three American teenagers are killed by firearms. So many young people are carrying weapons to school now that a growing number of high schools across the country have students walk through a metal detector each morning before entering their classrooms. There is a greater need than ever before for increasing populations of alienated youth to connect with caring role models. While society appears to be rapidly depleting the availability of appropriate models for students, the school still offers an abundance of them—they're called *teachers*.

A look at a few statistics that impact today's youth adds validity to the truth that teachers have the potential for an enormous impact on the lives of their students:

---

1. Feistritzer, Emily. *Profile of Teachers in the U.S. — 1990*. Washington D.C.: The National Center for Education Information, 1990.

News item: The yearly American dropout rate is now twenty-nine percent. As many as sixty percent of high school students drop out of some inner-city schools (*Forbes*, July 1990).

News item: Close to 80,000 children were arrested for drug abuse or possession; another 160,000 were arrested for drinking or drunk driving (Children's Defense Fund, 1990).

News item: The chance a teenage boy will commit suicide is one in ten. The chance a teenage girl will commit suicide is one in five (*Omni Magazine*, September 1992).

News item: The homicide rate has doubled among ten- to fourteen-year-olds during the past twenty years. Homicide is now the leading cause of death among blacks fifteen to nineteen years old (American Medical Association survey on America's adolescents, 1991).

News item: Every sixty-seven seconds an American teenager has a baby (Children's Defense Fund, 1990).

News item: Compared with their parents' generation, today's six- to fourteen-year-olds are twice as likely to be murdered and three times as likely to commit suicide before they reach their eighteenth birthday (National Center for Health Statistics, 1990).

Yes, statistics are grim, and nothing can erase the destructiveness that has impacted youth in the past. Teachers, though, can make miracles happen. Consider these news bulletins that verify a teacher's impact and potential:

News item: A favorite teacher can become an important model of identification for a resilient child whose own home is beset by family conflict or dissolution such as in a divorce.[2]

News item: The largest and longest study on resilience in children found that one out of three grew into competent young adults. The key for all those who did succeed was that they had the opportunity to establish a close bond, a basic trusting relationship, with an adult, and in a large number of cases it was a teacher.[3]

News item: A comprehensive review of research identified the reason most frequently cited for why students drop out of school. "Disaffected students claim nobody cares for them. They perceive that there are no school officials, neighbors, parents, or other significant people in their lives who care about them leaving school."[4]

---

2. Wallerstein, J.S. and J.B. Kelly. *Surviving the Breakup: How Children and Parents Cope with Divorce*. New York, NY: Basic Books, 1980.

3. Werner, Emmy E. "High Risk Children in Young Adulthood: A Longitudinal Study from Birth to 32 Years." *American Journal of Orthopsychiatry*, vol. 59, no. 1, January 1989.

4. Hendrick, Dean Irving and David Hough, project directors. *Early School Leaving in America*. Study conducted by the California Educational Research Cooperative, University of California, Riverside.

News item: A study found that the teacher-student relationship is the most important aspect of effective prevention programs. Hospitable and welcoming teachers can make a great impact on troubled students by establishing quality relationships with their students.[5]

Perhaps the greatest tragedy is that no one has taken the time to let educators know what differences they can make. Teachers can help a student grasp onto one small spark of interest that could produce an explosion of possibilities in the future. They can find a speck of talent in a student hidden behind veils of self-doubt that could help him/her soar toward a new path of self-belief. The greatest hope for youth cannot be packaged or created on a ditto form. The greatest hope is already in the classroom—a caring teacher. The fundamental reform most needed in our schools is to empower the individuals who have the most direct line to the students—the teachers. School environments must be created that not only nurture the self-esteem of students but also the perceptions of the staff. Teachers need to know that they do make differences, and that their energy and countless hours are valuable and appreciated. As one educational analysis succinctly stated, "The change that is needed is rooted in the everyday lives of the teachers who are making learning come alive and spirits soar. In their classrooms is where our children's future is being shaped."[6] This book is a first step toward making the staff esteem-building process come alive so the goal of more empowered educators can become a reality.

5. Jones, Randall M., Kathleen Kline, Sue A. Habkirk, and Amos Sales. "Teacher Characteristics and Competencies Related to Substance Abuse Prevention." *Journal of Drug Education*, vol. 23, no. 3, 1990.

6. Seymour, Daniel and Terry Seymour. *America's Best Classrooms: How Award-Winning Teachers are Shaping Our Children's Future.* Princeton, NJ: Peterson's Guides, 1992.

RESOURCES FOR ENHANCING STAFF SELF-ESTEEM

The following publications are excellent sources to learn more about staff esteem building. While this list is a very small bibliography compared to all the books published on the subject, these are some of the most useful.

Bethel, Sheila Murray. *Making a Difference; 12 Qualities That Make You a Leader.* New York: Berkeley Books, 1990. Bethel believes there are twelve qualities all effective leaders possess in common.

Blanchard, Kenneth and Spencer Johnson. *The One Minute Manager.* New York: William Morrow & Company, Inc. 1982. Short, to-the-point, best-selling manual that describes essential leadership techniques.

Brown, W. Steven. *13 Fatal Errors Managers Make and How You Can Avoid Them.* New York: Berkeley Books, 1987. An excellent guide for managers detailing how to recognize problems with your employees and avoid them before they happen.

Covey, Stephen. *The Seven Habits of Highly Effective People: Powerful Lessons in Personal Change.* New York: Simon & Schuster, 1989. A step-by step approach for solving personal and professional problems.

Gordon, Thomas. *Leader Effectiveness Training: L.E.T.* New York: Bantam Books, 1980. An invaluable leadership manual with techniques for solving problems and enhancing communication skills.

Hickman, Craig R. and Michael A. Silva. *Creating Excellence: Managing Corporate Culture, Strategy, and Change in the New Age.* New York: New American Library, 1984. A no-nonsense resource book of management strategies.

Josefowitz, Natasha. *You're the Boss: A Guide to Managing People with Understanding and Effectiveness.* New York: Warner Books, 1985. Packed with tips, information, examples, and insights on the way different types of people think, act, and react toward one another.

Maslow, A.H. *Toward a Psychology of Being.* New York: Van Nostrand Reinhold, 1968. This is a classic that can never be outdated. It clearly spells out the needs individuals must have before the higher level needs or self-actualization can be obtained.

Peters, Tom and Nancy A. Austin. *Passion for Excellence: The Leadership Difference.* New York: Warner Books, 1985. The best-seller and sequel to *In Search of Excellence.*

Purkey, William Watson, and John M. Novak. *Inviting School Success: A Self-Concept Approach to Teaching and Learning*. Belmont, CA: Wadsworth, 1984. An invaluable manual for self-esteem building within all school settings.

Reasoner, Robert. *Building Self-Esteem: Administrator's Guide*. Palo Alto, CA: Consulting Psychologists Press, 1982. This small manual is an invaluable guide for the administrator. It is designed to accompany Reasoner's program: *Building Self-Esteem: A Comprehensive Program*. The program builds self-esteem using the same five esteem components as covered in *Esteem Builders*, and is quite compatible as a companion volume.

Roberts, Wess. *Leadership Secrets of Attila the Hun*. New York: Warner Books, 1987. Packed full of successful leadership insights in a short, highly-readable manual.

Simon, Sidney. *Negative Criticism And What To Do About It*. Hadley, MA: Values Associates, 1978. Presents invaluable concepts on handling criticism in a highly readable and simple format.

Zale, Dale. *Enhancing Self-Esteem: A Guide for School Administrators*. Sacramento, CA: Association of California School Administrators, 1991. A fifty-page manual designed exclusively for administrators in their quest to enhance the self-esteem of their staff, students, and selves.

Ziglar, Zig. *Top Performance: How to Develop Excellence in Yourself & Others*. New York: Berkeley Books, 1986. Specific techniques to enhance management style.

ADDITIONAL RESOURCES FOR ADMINISTRATORS

Beane, James and Richard Lipka. *Self-Concept, Self-Esteem and the Curriculum*. New York: Teachers College Press, 1984.

Bouge, E. *The Enemies of Leadership: Lessons for Leaders in Education*. Bloomington, IN: Phi Delta Kappa, 1985.

Brandt, R. "On Teacher Empowerment: A Conversation with Ann Lieberman," *Educational Leadership,* vol. 46, no. 8, 1989.

Briggs, L.D. "High Morale Descriptors: Promoting a Professional Environment." *The Clearing House: For the Contemporary Educator in Middle and Secondary Schools,* March 1986.

Brodinsky, B. "Teacher Morale: What Builds It, What Kills It." *Instructor,* vol. 40, no. 93, 1984, 36-38.

Buonamici, G.C. "Building Staff Morale: A Positive Approach. *American Secondary Education,* vol. 12, 1983, 9-10.

Burford, C. "Humor of Principals and Its Impact on Teachers and the School." *The Journal of Educational Administration,* vol. 25, no. 1, 1987.

Cook, D.H. "Teacher Morale: Symptoms, Diagnosis, and Prescription." *The Clearing House,* vol. 52, 1979, 355-358.

Ellenburg, F.C. "Factors Affecting Teacher Morale." *NASSP Bulletin,* vol. 56, 1972, 37-45.

Garmston, R. "Empowering Teachers: Some Practical Steps." *Thrust for Educational Leadership,* vol. 18, no. 2, 1988.

Grossnickle, D.R. "Teacher Burnout: Will Talking About It Help?" *The Clearing House,* vol. 54, 1980, 17-18.

Hersey, P. and K. Blanchard. *Management of Organizational Behavior: Utilizing Human Resources.* Englewood Cliffs, NJ: Prentice Hall, Inc. 1982.

Magoon, R.A. and S.W. Linkous. "The Principal and Effective Staff Morale." *NASSP Bulletin,* vol. 63, 1979, 20-28.

Miller, W.C. "Staff Morale, School Climate, and Educational Productivity." *Educational Leadership,* vol. 388, 1981, 483-486.

Sergiovanni, T. "Leadership and Excellence in Schooling." *Educational Leadership.,* February 1984.

Washington, R. and H.F. Watson. "Positive Teacher Morale—The Principal's Responsibility." *NASSP Bulletin,* vol. 60, 1976., 4-6.

RESOURCES TO ENHANCE PERSONAL SELF-ESTEEM

Branden, Nathaniel. *Honoring the Self: The Psychology of Confidence and Respect.* New York: Bantam Books, 1985. This author is a pioneer in self-esteem development and his books are classics in the field.

Branden, Nathaniel. *How To Raise Your Self-Esteem.* New York: Bantam Books, 1987. This shorter volume offers a step-by-step guide to strengthening self-esteem. Simple, straightforward techniques are offered.

Branden, Nathaniel. *Psychology of Self-Esteem.* Los Angeles: Bantam Books, Ash Publishing Co., 1969.

Essig, Don M. *Personal Excellence for Key People*. Eugene, OR: Don Essig & Associates. A one-of-a-kind-manual especially written for "key people"—secretaries, food service and custodial maintenance workers, all support staff in organizations. The workbook format teaches eight keys to achieving personal and work excellence.

Gibbs, Jeanne. *Tribes: A Process for Social Development and Cooperative Learning*. Santa Rosa, CA: Center Source Publications, 1987. An invaluable guide for any esteem builder. Dozens of group activities are provided that can easily be adapted for adults.

Helmstetter, Shad. *What To Say When You Talk to Your Self*. New York: Simon and Schuster, Inc. 1986.

Johnson, Spenser and Constance Johnson. *The One Minute Teacher: How to Teach Others to Teach Themselves*. New York: William Morrow and Co., 1986. An easy-to-use source describing the teaching principles of effective praising, goal-setting, and recovery.

Pike, Graham and David Selby. *Global Teacher, Global Learner*. London: Hotter and Stoughton, 1988. A definitive handbook for teachers exploring the theory and practice of global education. An extensive range of practical activities are provided for use in primary and secondary classrooms. A special section is also devoted to "teacher education."

Robbins, Anthony. *Unlimited Power.* New York: Fawcett Columbine, 1986.

Seligman, Martin. *Learned Optimism*. New York: Alfred A. Knopf, 1991. Scientific evidence supports the notion that optimism is vitally important in overcoming defeat, promoting achievement, and maintaining or improving health. The author offers a program of specific exercises to help break the habit of pessimism and learn the habit of optimism.

Semigran, Candace. *One-Minute Self-Esteem: Caring For Yourself and Others*. New York: Bantam Books, 1990. Exercises to enhance self-esteem.

Youngs, Bettie B. *Enhancing Educator's Self-Esteem: Criteria #1*. Rolling Hills, CA: Jalmar Press, 1992. Offers educators valuable advice on how they can keep their own self-esteem strong.

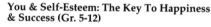

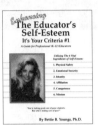

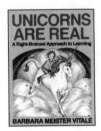